Sabine Bauer-Amin, Leonardo Schiocchet, Maria Six-Hohenbalken (eds.)
Embodied Violence and Agency in Refugee Regimes

I0092962

## Editorial

In times of increasingly impactful climate crises and ceaseless violent conflicts, new dynamics of forced migrations evolve every day. National policies are not the sole defining drivers of these dynamics, and scholars have to acknowledge international and transnational networks, relationships and sets of obligations that shape the realities independently of nation states' responses. The complexity of the matter has spread academic and public debates far and wide, ranging across issues of identity, social belonging, law, rights and duties, ethics and morality, heritage, economic and development models, religion and culture, war and peace and a myriad of other imperative topics. Few other general contemporary social processes have prompted as much debate as forced migration has today. This series aims to transit between topics, disciplines, modes of engagement with reality, theoretical proclivities, and different social scenarios and case studies pertaining to the realm of forced migration. Transcript's Forced Migration Studies Series publishes monographs and edited volumes on forced migration worldwide, engaging with theoretical-methodological developments whilst also examining concrete case studies. It is multidisciplinary and focuses hprimarily on the contemporary world.

The series is edited by Leonardo Schiocchet and Maria Six-Hohenbalken.

**Sabine Bauer-Amin** is a social anthropologist, research associate at the Austrian Academy of Sciences Institute for Social Anthropology as well as member of ROR-N. Previously, she has worked on the Middle East with a special focus on youth and issues of identity/alterity. Her current research focus lays on the situation of refugees from Iraq and Syria in Austria and beyond.

**Leonardo Schiocchet** has a PhD in anthropology (Boston University, 2011) and a Habilitation in social and cultural anthropology (University of Vienna, 2022). He is a researcher at the Institute for Social Anthropology (ISA) at the Austrian Academy of Sciences (ÖAW), a member of the Refugee Outreach & Research Network (ROR-n), and principal investigator of the FWF project »The Austro-Arab Encounter«. Since 2005, his work has focused on social belonging processes among Arab forced migrants.

**Maria Six-Hohenbalken** (Dr.) is deputy director of the Institute for Social Anthropology at the Austrian Academy of Sciences, and a lecturer in the Department for Social and Cultural Anthropology at Universität Wien. Her fields of interest include political violence, migration, refuge, memory studies, transnationalism and diaspora studies, and historical anthropology.

Sabine Bauer-Amin, Leonardo Schiocchet, Maria Six-Hohenbalken (eds.)

# Embodied Violence and Agency in Refugee Regimes

Anthropological Perspectives

[transcript]

ÖAW ÖSTERREICHISCHE
AKADEMIE DER
WISSENSCHAFTEN

iSa Institute for
Social Anthropology

**Bibliographic information published by the Deutsche Nationalbibliothek**
The Deutsche Nationalbibliothek lists this publication in the Deutsche National-
bibliografie; detailed bibliographic data are available in the Internet at http://
dnb.d-nb.de

© 2022 transcript Verlag, Bielefeld

Cover layout: Maria Arndt, Bielefeld
Cover illustration: Iman Hussein, original available at: www.iman-hussein.com
Copy-editing and proofreading by Thomas Gobbitt

Print-ISBN 978-3-8376-5802-6
PDF-ISBN 978-3-8394-5802-0
https://doi.org/10.14361/9783839458020
ISSN of series: 2751-1545
eISSN of series: 2751-1553

# Contents

## PART 3: Ambiguity and (Un)settlement in Agency

*To Gabriele Rasuly-Paleczek*
*in recognition of her invaluable contribution to the anthropology of forced migration.*

# Acknowledgements

The editors would like to thank several institutions and persons involved in the production of this edited volume: the *Institute for Social Anthropology* at the *Austrian Academy of Sciences* (AAS), which as our host institution financed this publication; the *Department for Social and Cultural Anthropology* of the *University of Vienna* and especially Gabriele Rasuly-Paleczek, who organized a panel at VANDA from which many of the publications here originate; the interdisciplinary exchange with colleagues from the *Refugee Outreach and Research Network* (ROR-n), which allowed fruitful discussion; and the *Innovation Funds* of the Austrian Academy of Sciences, which financed the project *Loslassen – Durchstehen – Ankommen* (Leaving – Persevering – Arriving) a collaboration in between the Institute of Urban and Regional Research and the Institute of Social Anthropology, resulting in the fundamental research that, in turn, provided the impetus for this publication.

# Introduction: Embodied Violence and Agency in Refugee Regimes

*Sabine Bauer-Amin, Leonardo Schiocchet, Maria Six-Hohenbalken*

In forced migration studies, "the refugee regime" is very often expressed in the singular, due to the influence of policy-oriented and humanitarian intervention-oriented approaches, and thus of academic disciplines such as demography, international relations and law. This usage implicitly entails the terms "global/international" and "legal", which in turn means that "the regime" has been analysed as a complex but single institution, or as a multi-level structure (Betts 2010; Kleist 2018). This implies, in turn, that "the refugee regime" has been studied against differing empirical contexts but is portrayed as a structure beyond them. The singular also means that "the regime" has often been approached at the cost of much of its internal subjectivity, let alone its complexity. However, actual situations of flight and the intrinsically interwoven multipolar regulations and restrictions on human (im)mobility suggest that "the refugee regime" is constituted "around contested and competing notions of sovereignty and belonging" (Kleist 2018, 169). It is in fact a much more complex meshwork of social relations and political principles, but also moral imperatives, dispositions, and experiences replete with affect. Through this lens, it becomes indispensable to understand which forces shape forced migration (im)mobility and the instruments and mechanisms designed to identify and engage with it, and how these instruments and mechanisms relate to each other contextually and to forced migrants.

This book engages with these broad questions through critical anthropological inquiry and carefully contextualized ethnographic case studies from Latin America to Europe and East Asia. It draws on the emerging literature on "regime complexity", referring to "the ways in which two or more institutions intersect in terms of their scope and purpose" (Betts 2010, 20, 35), and offers a more nuanced approach to: the study of what we prefer to call forced migrants and "refugee regimes" (in plural); the complex agency of diverse social actors in their engagement with each other; and how violence is often engendered by the very mechanisms created to protect forced migrants, and at times is even invertedly embodied by forced migrants and sympathizers themselves.

*

According to Gil Loescher (1994), "the refugee regime" had five main phases up until the 1990s, having developed as it confronted challenges to its authority: 1. the interwar period: marked by the absence of a general definition of who is a refugee, and by decentralized and limited policies; 2. the immediate post-Second World War era: marked by the emergence of the first general legal international instruments to regulate refuge; 3. the period of expansion into the "Third World" (late 1950s'-1970s): characterized by a switch to most refugees being located in camps in the Global South rather than in Europe; 4. the 1980s: marked by the superpowers' involvement in proxy wars and conflicts mainly in Africa, Asia and Latin America; 5. the post-Cold War era: marked by internal displacements and repatriations in situations of civil conflict.

It all started in 1921, when Global North governments established the High Commissioner for Refugees within the League of Nations, as the first multilateral coordinating instrument for refugees, with a mandate over Russian and later Greek, Turkish, Bulgarian and Armenian refugees. The idea was to reduce tension between nation states by actually addressing what these states saw as "the problem of refugees". In the 1930s, the major European powers agreed to extend this mandate to refugees from the former Russian and Ottoman empires, and later to those fleeing from Germany and Austria. This, however, did not constitute "an effective regime". Only specific groups were designated as refugees, and the mandate of the High Commissioner was deliberately narrow, restricted to providing only minimal protection (Loescher 1994, 353-354).

In the aftermath of the Second World War[1], international efforts to resolve the refugee crisis initially followed the interwar pattern of temporary measures to curb specific contextual situations. But such efforts proved to be highly ineffective in their responses, even to the Shoah, which was the main

---

[1] Before that, in 1943, the Big Four created the United Nations Relief and Rehabilitation Agency (UNRRA) with the aim of managing the repatriation of displaced people under Allied control. However, the UNRRA was not a refugee organization (Loescher 1994, 355), and was short-lived.

focus of such efforts (Loescher 1994, 355). It was then that the first international set of norms, rules, principles, and decision-making procedures – or what we call instruments (deliberate) or more broadly mechanisms (both deliberate and unintentional) – to regulate refugees emerged. To this day, these instruments are still the most established and long-standing mechanisms for governing human mobility (Betts 2010, 35). They are: the 1951 Convention on the Status of Refugees, defining who is a refugee and what are their rights; and the United Nations High Commissioner for Refugees (UNHCR), which had the mandate to ensure that nation states would comply with the 1951 Convention. Even though governments agreed to formulate these first set of rules and procedures in the early Cold War period (1949-1951)[2], they concomitantly limited "the regime's" responsibilities because they were "unwilling to commit themselves to indefinite financial costs and large resettlement programs" (Loescher 1994, 352).

When the flux of Eastern European refugees waned in the late 1950s, international instruments to manage refugees turned to the Global South. The UNHCR was, and still is, a donor-funded institution, and besides the USA, some of its main donors were colonial powers during the Cold War. In other words, some of the same countries producing refugees were also funding international refugee instrument in a bid to manage problems they themselves had often created. Since there were no communist states funding or managing these instruments, Global North states increasingly turned to them for the good image they offered and for solutions. Thus, the international refugee scenario in the 1980s was characterized by refugees fleeing regional conflicts in Central America, Asia and Africa, living in refugee camps and depending on the UNHCR for care and protection. It was then that large numbers of these refugees started to seek asylum in the Global North, causing the world powers to backtrack on their commitment to fund, development and support the international instruments to manage the refugees which they had themselves created. With the end of the Cold War, the 1990s also brought great changes to how refugees were managed internationally. Most forced migration processes emerging in this era were marked by ethnicity and religion

---

2    At the same time, the United Nations Works and Relief Agency for Palestine Refugees in the Near East and the United Nations Korean Reconstruction Agency were created – and set apart from the UNHCR – to manage specific groups of refugees located in strategic conflict areas where the USA (which at that time was the main patron of "the refugee regime") was involved, such as the Middle East and Korea (Loescher 1994, 358).

and were triggered by conflicts which were deemed internal to nation states or regions, even while these "internal" conflicts most often have deep roots in colonial struggles and the world-wide imposition of the nation state model.[3]

As a result of nation-state interdependence and globalization, however, many more international instruments regulating human (im)mobility and social relations were created, such as those regulating travel, labour migration, human rights, humanitarianism, peace-building, development and security.[4] Many of these mechanisms intersect significantly, some complementing instruments regulating refugees and some contradicting them. Among these, travel instruments are perhaps those which intersect with refugee instruments the most (Betts 2010, 15; Kleist 2018), especially in what relates to regulations on spontaneous asylum-seekers. This makes it no longer possible to "speak of a compartmentalized refugee regime; rather, there is now a 'refugee regime complex'" (Betts 2010, 12), in which instruments regulating refugees intersect with other regulations. These intersections can overlap, exist in parallel or be "nested within one another", thereby shaping nation states' responses toward refugees (Betts 2010, 13).

In addition, since its inception and up to the present day, international regulations on refugees not only occur through the international normative institutional framework of asylum developed around the principle of non-refoulement, but also through bi-lateral and multi-lateral state-to-state negotiations that bypass international organizations, and are typically known as "burden-sharing" practices (Betts 2015; 2010, 18). These latter practices are characterized by weaker and decentralized, non-legally binding political frameworks, such as the recent agreements between the EU and Turkey and the EU and Tunisia to keep forced migrants away from European borders. In fact, the preamble to the 1951 Convention clearly states that the premise of the international instruments on refugees is international cooperation (Betts 2015). Furthermore, many countries of refugee departure and host countries do not abide by the 1951 Convention. And the period following the so-called Summer of Migration, when large numbers of asylum seekers reached Europe in 2015, was significantly marked by European and non-European countries' (largely successful) strategies to circumvent non-refoulement norms (Betts 2015). Acknowledging that instruments regulating the lives of

---

3    See, for example, (Schiocchet 2011).
4    More recently, some authors have been including the refugee regime within the migration regime (see for example Kleist 2018).

refugees have increasingly depended on bargain and lobby among nation states is not only to acknowledge the complexity of a singular refugee regime, but also the plurality of intersecting contextual refugee regimes.

As the above paragraph suggests, from the outset international refugee instruments have depended on cooperation between nation states, this cooperation being the sole binding factor for refugee regimes. Refugee regimes are thus characterized by low built-in international accountability, given that the UN or any other international institution does not mandate sanctions or other reactive measures in case of non-adherence to international norms. In other words, as the Palestinian case presented by Schiocchet shows, when states do not abide by international legal refugee instruments, they may simply not suffer any consequences. This, in turn, means that it is imperative to understand mechanisms of refugee regimes in practice and in context, beyond the legal and global character of international legal refugee instruments and their supposedly binding characteristics.

Therefore, this book takes Betts' insights as a departure point, but differs in that it acknowledges not only international/global legal regulations as part of the mechanisms regulating the movement and lives of refugees, but also: a) regional (Kleist 2018, 167), national, and local instruments; b) legal but also political (Kleist 2018, 167), military, social or moral mechanisms alongside legal instruments; c) these mechanisms' targeting of not only refugees and not all refugees in general, but of specific groups of forced migrants defined by legal status, race, ethnicity, religion, or political inclination. This frame further differs from Betts' "refugee regime complex" because it acknowledges that rather than a single global regime, complex in nature, but geared toward a common goal and seeking homogeneity, the multiplicity of forces shaping instruments regulating the lives of refugees cannot be said to have the same goals, do not operate necessarily in the same levels or global arenas, and do not necessarily aim for international recognition and legitimacy. As such, we prefer to group these mechanisms under the definition of multiple, intersecting "refugee regimes".

Kleist (2018) argues that the lack of consensus on who is a refugee is the foundation for "the refugee regime", because if there was a consensual definition, there might have been a "refugee agency" as an administrative body, rather than a contradictory at heart, multi-institutional "regime". Our definition of "regimes" above, however, is in line with a Foucauldian approach that recognizes not only a multiplicity of social actors informing a given social situation, and the complexity and multi-directionality of agency within institutions and between institutions and social and individual subjects, but also the largely embodied and not necessarily deliberate character of dispositions and practices which are regulated by regimes of knowledge, or what Michel Foucault called "biopower" (1979) and "biopolitics" (2007).

Furthermore, instruments and mechanisms of refugee regimes more broadly are not limited to governments, international organizations or even to non-governmental organizations and private institutions. To the extent that academic debates on refugees help to define who is a refugee and the "regimes of truth" around the topic, our Foucauldian approach entails that these debates are also, among other things, an instrument within refugee regimes. Constant reflection on academic practice is thus imperative.

Heath Cabot, for example, suggests that "The business of anthropology reinforces the European refugee regime, which makes border crossers into targets of policing, intervention, and study" (2019, 261). She follows David Szanton's (2004) remarks that the "explosion of area studies in the 1970s and 1980s" would be an example of "academic work's imbrication in apartheid-like logics, emerging in the Cold War finding that hierarchized sectors of the globe" (Cabot 2019, 262). And following James Ferguson's discussion of Lesotho's development of the "anti-politics machine," she contends that anthropologists have critiqued the "depoliticizing ethos of humanitarianism"; that is, how the "imperative to 'do good' occludes the exclusion and even violence embedded in humanitarian practice" (Cabot 2019, 262), while the anthropological practice is in itself part of the "business" of refugee regimes and the "rescue industry" but does not tend to portray itself as such. The "anthropology of displacement in Europe's doorsteps", in particular, has the propensity to chase crises, "assuming that 'refugee experience' need to be studied", and "heeding the call to 'do good' through scholarship in ways that deflect attention from anthropology's own politics of life", which for her entails "notions of relevance", or a hierarchization of "which people, things, situations, and places are worthy or deserving of study" (2019, 262-263).

In this book we acknowledge the importance of Cabot's arguments on "anthropology as a business" but complexify it in that we understand that notions of relevance are guided by "disciplinary tradition": the rules and norms by which, among other things, a topic is deemed important in a given discipline, which in turn conflates the "business" aspect she highlights and moral imperatives (what Cabot calls the imperative to 'do good'), within a disciplinary framework that is legitimated by regimes of knowledge. In other words, we assume that what Cabot calls the "anthropology of displacement in Europe's doorsteps" or elsewhere is not only or mainly a business, but also stems from, for example, the discipline-generated need to pay attention to what is happening in the contemporary world and the drive to build synchronic models (focused on the ethnographic present). And while we prefer to use different terms that are more in line with our theoretical approach, we agree with Cabot that we must remain self-critical, and avert from writing about fashionable objects primarily because they open up job and/or funding opportunities, or simply because they are fashionable. In this sense, the first part of this book is self-reflective about approaches that "claim to critique or challenge power relations" (Cabot 2019, 263) while the book at large maintains a critical position on refugee regimes largely by focusing on refugee experiences. Far from completely detaching scholarship from these regimes, or reifying one single realpolitik-driven "refugee regime", each chapter in this book highlights the complexity and contextuality of the forces involved in regulating the lives of refugees world-wide.

According to our perspective as presented above, multiple national and international refugee regimes govern the lives of forced migrants simultaneously and often opposingly. Inasmuch as refugee law and governmentality originally aimed to protect refugees, like any mechanism of inclusion/exclusion, they often engender the violence they sought to manage or dissipate. To understand the mechanisms of these regimes and the violence they engender, one must turn to two of its most fundamental components: humanitarianism and securitization, which if they may appear to be contradictory at first glance, are in fact often just two sides of the same coin.

Unpacking humanitarianism shows how it affects refugee regimes on several layers. Despite the two being closely tied historically,[5] humanitarianism

---

5    There have been various humanitarian answers to crises throughout various epochs and across geographical locations. One incident shaped the future development of organized humanitarianism which stands out in particular was the intervention of Swiss Henry Dunant who became a witness to the aftermath of the battle of Solferino in 1859. He organized a local response, mainly amongst women and girls, to take care of the injured and sick soldiers regardless of their side in the conflict under the idea of "tutti fratelli" (we are all brothers). This experience inspired him to create a neutral organization dedicated to the care of wounded soldiers and to publish his ideas in "Un souvenir de Solferino". This book led to the emergence of the International Committee of the Red Cross and to the Red Cross Movement. His main principles were the neutrality of this agency, which became the basis of the later Geneva Convention (first

has developed into various forms, ranging from military, political and economic interference to direct humanitarian intervention and aid. Humanitarian intervention, in its form based on humanitarian law, refers to the act of using military force within another state, for example when there are major violations of human rights.

Humanitarian aid, on the other hand, does not depend on a third legal body but instead on the willingness of a state to allow humanitarian agencies to become active on their grounds whether in response to a crisis or as developmental agents. These forms are often intertwined and are united by the shared principle of "alleviating human suffering". Humanitarian aid is usually executed by non-government organisations. Critical analysis shows, however, how tightly linked these two developments of humanitarianism – military intervention and aid – (still) are. Michel Agier, in a consideration of the policing force of humanitarian aid, describes how interlinked while legally separated, these two developments are, when he writes, "it follows on the heels of and smoothes over the damage wrought by military intervention" (2010, 29).

Following the example of the Red Cross movement in the 19<sup>th</sup> century, the humanitarian aid sector has grown immensely in recent years, leading to the emergence of a humanitarian industry, mainly, but not exclusively, comprising relief organisations funded and staffed by the Global North to execute their ideas of aid in the Global South. With the growth of the sector, a platform was needed to bring NGOs, the Red Cross Movement, as well as the UN and its subordinates together, which happened when the Global Humanitarian Platform was founded in 2006 (Agier 2010, 35). Other similar initiatives then followed. As a result, humanitarian agencies agreed on a number of principles that should lead their actions in the field. These are "humanity, neutrality, impartiality and independence" (OCHA 2012), albeit different agencies have adapted these to their own visions, lingo and profiles. Thus, Elizabeth Cullen Dunn (2012, 1), in her critical analysis of humanitarian aid, observes that "Humanitarianism thus presents itself as an apolitical regime of care, one concerned with not only keeping people from dying but making them live".

Despite the attempts to clarify its roles and meanings, humanitarianism has developed polysemically. Ilana Feldman (2012, 156) describes the many faces of today's humanitarianism, demonstrating, again, the many ways that

---

signed 1864). This shows the historically tight connection between humanitarianism and refugee regimes.

the concept serves as a major element within refugee regimes, as described above. Humanitarianism is, primarily, a form of legal framework based on documents like the Geneva convention. Yet it is also a discursive field, based on compassion and spurred through the circulation of images of human(s) suffering. It is also a practice, focusing mainly on the delivery of aid in emergencies. Moreover, the anthropological literature engaging with humanitarianism is in dialogue with Giorgio Agamben's notion of "bare life", which implies the production of "pure victims" and "pure helpers", as designated by relief projects (see Feldman 2012, 155). This same literature has also questioned the claims of impartiality and apolitical self-understanding of humanitarian agencies, and has instead understood them as the continuation of politics by other means (Barnett 2009 and Calhoun 2006). And, according to Agier, the reinterpretation of terms fundamentally influences the humanitarian discourse, thereby forcing its repoliticization: "[I]t is because these actions put into play conflicting interpretations of the available words—'refugee,' 'vulnerable,' 'aid,' 'UN,' and so on—and in this act, they repoliticize humanitarian discourse." (Agier 2010, 40).

Didier Fassin and Mariella Pandolfi (2010) also critically engage with the question of humanitarian aid, by examining the power disparities between self-entitled powerful states in the Global North and assessing how they bring or protect human rights and, through this, how they both undergird national sovereignty and involve themselves in local politics. These forms of self-entitlement are not historically unpreceded, which is why Agier also refers to humanitarianism as "the left hand of empire".

Feldman also criticizes the humanitarian agencies' principle of being supposedly impartial and apolitical, whilst, however, rendering political questions, such as the situation of Palestinians, as a question of service providers. Hence, she clearly points to "[t]he focus on how humanitarianism constrains and disables", which "has illuminated crucial dynamics of a field that is generally valorized as 'doing good,' but these constraints are not all that needs to be understood about humanitarian effects" (2012, 156).

Agier, himself a humanitarian working with MSF, tells us that "humanitarian intervention borders on policing. There is no care without control", which he attributes to humanitarians being caught in processes, "seemingly pragmatic, but far too powerful for humanist goodwill" (Agier 2011, 4). For him, the establishment of large-scale refugee camps throughout the 1980s to protect vulnerable populations, served to prepare a "political strategy and control technique that closes the gates of the 'World'" for all those inside (ibid.).

Agier underlines the ambiguity of such places where humanitarians both protect whilst also having the "power of life and death", as well as having power over the "transformation of individual lives, [and] of social and cultural models" (ibid, 5). In turn, this ambiguity reproduces dependance and power asymmetries, while all too often humanitarians are unable to fulfill their own principles of impartiality and, conversely, are implicitly tied to policing structures that limit many forms of autonomous agency. Agier (2011, 4), who sees himself as a "critical humanitarian", finds even stronger terms for the policing character of humanitarianism by referring to it as "totalitarianism" and "in secret solidarity with the police order" (...) "that embodies the Western world's desire to control" others.

Hence, Dunn includes inherent violence in her definition of humanitarianism: "Humanitarianism is thus presented as a regime of violence as well as care, seeking not just to keep people from dying but to make them live in particular ways as dominated political subjects." (Dunn 2012, 1). Yet, in her research on aid in Georgia, she also criticizes Agier, by questioning the reach of humanitarianism that would allow it to be referred to as "totalitarianism". In her research following the war between Russia and Georgia and the breakaway of South Ossetia in the late 2000s, she describes the interplay of "six UN agencies, ninety-two NGOs, and five government ministries" (2012, 3) in their attempt to support the 250,000 displaced ethnic Georgians, their rivalries, competitions and challenges, as well as the changing perspectives of the affected IDPs (internally displaced persons) on the impact of these agencies on their lives. Dunn points to the limitations in ambitions and impact that others, like Agier, have attributed to NGOs (Dunn 2012, 3). Rather than being fully structured and organized, she acknowledges the amount of guess work and rule of thumb under which relief agencies operate. She then introduces the concept of *adhocracy* as the leading principle of humanitarian aid, which is, in itself, based on the contradictions between multiple refugee regimes and embodies "a form of power that creates chaos and vulnerability as much as it creates order" (Dunn 2012, 3). Dunn rightly identifies refugees, more specifically the IDPS of Ossetia, in her research, not as beneficiaries of humanitarian aid but as part of the means of production for organizations to meet the requirements of their donors (2012, 15).

As such, agency becomes another key concept for understanding the mechanisms of embodied violence inherent in refugee regimes. The understanding of agency as being relational extends back to, at least, Michel Foucault's concept of "the order of things", which he developed very early in his career and constituted one of the basic pillars of his thought (see Foucault 1961; 1966). According to this paradigm, agency is never a quality that a social actor possesses, or does not possess, but rather is embedded in the relationships and dispositions between them (Scherr 2012). More recent authors such as Albert Scherr or Bettina Schmitt, for example, develop this paradigm in relation to an overt theory of agency. Relational agency theories do not proclaim humans as unlimited in their autonomous possibilities, nor do they understand them as being socially determined through structural forces (Schmitt 2019, 3). These theories promote an understanding of agency as a result of previous positionings within social networks, rather than as being a characteristic of a person, institution or thing. Schmitt, in particular, argues that research must on the one hand focus on the facilitation and/or prevention of agency as a result of the social processes of forced migration and, on the other hand, on the relationship between agency and vulnerabilty, in what she calls the "agency-vulnerability nexus" (ibid, 5). Through this rela-tional approach, agency, just as vulnerability, may be understood as the result of complex relationship networks, vulnerable life situations and life stages. Hence, many of the chapters in this volume exhibit a focus on positionings and their implications, which in turn allows for a multi-dimensional analysis.

Relational agency theorists Mustafa Emirbayer and Ann Mische (1998, 974) argue that agency must be understood through its relation to temporality. They unpack the concept into three main dimensions, which they name as "iterational, projective, and practical-evaluative" and attribute them to dif-ferent temporalities, "a chordal triad composed of three analytically distinct elements (oriented variously toward the past, future, and present)". The it-erational dimension of agency is oriented towards the past and focuses on routines, patterns, dispositions or perceptions (1998, 975). Projectivity is ori-ented towards future possibilities of reconstruction, innovations, intentions or plans (1998, 984). The last, present-centered dimension is the practical-evaluative dimension that is mainly focused on real-world circumstances and context (1998, 994). These three dimensions allow actors to reconstruct and transform their surroundings. Their interplay explains why some forms of agency are more oriented towards the past, present or future. While the scope for agency in the respective ad-hoc context of forced migration might appear limited and diminishing, this temporal understanding of agency orientation causes us to broaden the focus of our narratives. Based on this insight, agency is not just a possibility to act in the present situation, but can also focus on striving towards an alternative future or the re-creation of old lives and subjectivities, as will be shown in this volume. While all chapters engage agency, some contributions underline its projective dimension to reinterpret one's exile, future or life plans (Schiocchet). Other contributions focus on agency in its itineral expressions for recreating routines, roles or ideas of "home" (Bauer-Amin, Nygren et al.). Again others, take a stronger focus on the practical dimension of agency and the ad-hoc possibilities of expanding or limiting one's scope for action that arise in the process (Monsutti, Mokre, Tan).

Yet, it remains important to not neglect the context of forced migration. Current tendencies in researching agency, in particular in volatile fields, also warn against over-emphasizing human capacity to act, while ignoring their vulnerability. In particular, Andresen et al. (2015, 9) warn against a short-cut usage of relational agency theories that would cut out the dependence on enabling conditions for certain forms of agency. The term forced migration already underlines the often-limited scope and coerciveness of situations for those affected by them. Also, Mackenzie et al. urge us to use the concept critically when oppression, abuse or restrictive political and social environments shape the experience of self-efficiency, yet, as described above, they do not undermine it altogether (Mackenzie et al. 2007, 310).

Agency and vulnerability often overlap particularly in contexts of violence and war. The danger of portraying refugees only as "exemplary victims" (Malkki 1996, 384), can be circumvented by a focus on people as social actors (Essed et al. 2004, 2). By highlighting agency and, in the process, putting the experiences of people in the centre, one also avoids generalisations. Norman Long (2001, 49) defines agency as "both a certain knowledgeability, whereby experiences and desires are reflexively interpreted and internalised (consciously or otherwise), and the capability to command relevant skills, access to material and non-material resources and engage in particular organising practices". According to him, the three elements of "knowledge-ability, capability and social embeddedness" constitute agency in empirical terms and thus the possibilities to act or reflect upon an individual's situation. Following Long further, agency becomes a crucial point of departure for any actor-centred approach. This approach allows due respect to be paid to intersectional factors such as gender, age, education or social class, and thereby will "rehumanise" refugee regimes by showing how they are experienced and what their real-life consequences are (Essed et al. 2004, 2). These consequences, in turn, reflect the ambiguity of refugee regimes and the selectiveness of their mechanisms of inclusion and exclusion.

Refugees find ways to recover their agency even within these strict corsets of refugee regimes. They carve out possibilities and find ways to overcome their powerlessness and respond to the coerciveness and violence engendered within these regimes. Undoubtedly, some are pushed into defying the regulations (Harrell-Bond 1986; Lubkemann 2000). Others reclaim agency through social media and the abilities new technologies allow them; become founders of their own initiatives in their countries of residence; reconstitute their social identity (Malkki 1995; Wilson 1994); reinterpret their exile; contribute to new emerging cultures (e.g. Nordstrom 1997); or "creatively reformulate social relations and replot life strategies" (Lubkemann 2019, 216).

Similar to Essed et al.'s usage of the term "agency", we do not limit our focus to only the agency of forced migrants but also acknowledge the interconnectedness of their agency with the agency of bureaucrats, humanitarian workers, policy makers and other social actors (Essed et al. 2004, 2). As such, they are both the human face of refugee regimes, as well as their interpreters, implementers, executers and defiants.

People on the move are typically exposed to multiple national and international refugee regimes, and have to deal with liminalities, obligations, prescriptions, requirements, dependencies and subordinate integration. The entailments of these overlapping regimes and how refugees experience them are of particular concern within this volume. This edited volume therefore presents a multifaceted comparative approach, contrasting a range of national and international refugee regimes, and groups of refugees with multiple ethnic, social and religious backgrounds.

To sum up, the concept of humanitarianism was developed around the idea of a humanity common to all peoples, and the need to acknowledge and safeguard its values. This was endorsed in the principle of nonrefoulement (Gibney 2000, 690) and the Responsibility to Protect (R2P), which serves as a guideline for international actors to protect victims of international conflicts since 2005.

This stands in sharp contrast to the securitization policies for refugee regimes, which instead of protecting refugees, mainly protect borders and territories from people transgressing them. This tension materializes, for example, in the establishment of so-called safe zones in transit countries like Libya (Klepp 2010, 3-9), the Frontex mission in the Mediterranean (Klepp 2010) or Hot Spots in Lesbos. These policies encompass centralised accommodations during asylum procedures, temporary protection and the meticulously planned steps and regulations regarding the stay and deportation of forced migrants in countries executing "protection". These are all faces of securitization regimes which are aimed at controlling forced migrants and limiting their mobility and agency to and within countries of protection. Some chapters in this volume refer explicitly to the ambiguities of humanitarianism and securitization, while others make further forms of inherent violence and its effects in refugee regimes visible. In this edited volume, two relatively young and interdisciplinary anchored social anthropological research fields are connected: refugee studies – with a critical approach to humanitarianism – and the anthropology of violence. Both fields have hardly found space in anthropology before the 1980s (see Colson 2003; Chatty 2014; Nordstrom 2004; Schepper-Hughes and Bourgois 2004, Whitehead 2001).

Scientists engaged in the anthropology of violence have argued that studies of violence can never be reduced to evident structures and visible acts, but should instead attach importance to its various symbolic and psychological forms, as well as to forms of (re)presentation.[6] Thus, research on violence differs between direct and indirect, collective and individual, legitimate and illegitimate, concrete and structural, physical and psychological as well as manifest and symbolic violence. This conceptualisation encompasses the acts and consequences of intentional threat and force to harm the other (Lorion 2001, 16192). Social scientists brought in concepts like "markets of violence" (see Elwert 1999), brought their focus to violence on civilians in the shadows of wars (Nordstrom 2004), and elaborated on the continuum of violence in war and peace (Scheper-Hughes and Bourgois 2004).

The facticity of violence is just one pole of research, the other is centered around the subjectivism of experiencing violence and its long-term effects on the individual. These specifications and epistemological approaches must be taken into account when approaching embodied violence and its long-lasting effects in and for refugee regimes.

Göran Ajimer and Jon Abbink (2000) inaugurated the study of violence by integrating communicative, symbolic and ritual aspects into their ontological understanding. The closer focus on the "meaning" of violence on diverse social and individual levels is a hallmark of this approach. Violence is never without meaning or "senseless", but has a strong symbolic component (Schmidt and Schröder 2001) and can be seen as a "cultural performance" (Whitehead 2004).

---

6    "Violence entails inflicting emotional, psychological, sexual, physical and/or material damage. It involves the exercise of force or constraint perpetrated by individuals, on their own behalf or for a collective or state-sanctioned purpose" (Stanko 1996, 896).

Public violence studies have examined "organizational outcomes", results of "coordinated destructions" and, e.g., questions of "(fragmented) resistance" (Tilly 2001, 16206ff). We suggest that these questions could be better developed if they were detached from a territorial/space centred focus and were instead directed toward a more deterritorial or transnational understanding of refugee regimes.

To analyse violence on various structural, symbolic and cultural levels, the epistemological and methodological research focus of the anthropology of violence encompasses intersubjective levels as well as political components. Approaching the complexity of embodied violence in refugee regimes allows us to grasp the structural, physical, symbolic and psychological effects of violence in refugee regimes. Veena Das (2007) has convincingly shown how violent experiences, besides being witnessed and remembered, become part of ordinary life. Thus, to perceive the effects of violent experiences, scholarship needs to consider refugee regimes in historical depth.

Besides elaborating on the structural, psychological and other above-mentioned dimensions of the inherent violence in refugee regimes, it is necessary to consider its performativities[7], ranging from border-closing speeches, narratives of criminalisation, intended deterrent effects arising from the deportation of asylum seekers, and how these enforce the legal or epistemological categories discussed above. The sources and agents of such performativities can be seen as crucial mechanism of embodied violence, which not only encompass political discourses and practices, but also humanitarian ones.

These considerations also lead us to consider the epistemologically and methodologically relevant triangular approach to the study of violence, encompassing the victim, the perpetrator and the witness. In each specific empirical context, refugee regimes are characterized by often overlapping, mutually dependent and interacting triangles of violence. In other words, as with the role of INGOs and their relationship to powerful states, these positions become blurred.

Anthropological research on violence has focused on the diverse strategies of silencing and the denial of violent acts – mostly in the aftermath of events. The research interest extends from the rhetoric and logic of denial,

---

7    Performativity here refers to the power of language to change the world. Language not only describes the outer and inner world, but also works as a kind of social action. Performativity relates to the execution and ascertainment of what is expressed linguistically.

to questions of credibility of victims or witnesses, political rationalities, responsibilities and media manipulation. Various forms of denial are not only individual or group affairs, but also happen even on state levels (e.g. Robben 2012). Forms of implicatory denial can arise when violent acts are performed in a moral vacuum where perpetrators and performers are relieved of any responsibility (Cohen 2001). At first glance, this field might not look relevant to the study of refugee regimes, but the overlapping of anthropologies of forced migration and violence is evident in the long-lasting effects of embodied violence in refugee regimes. Here, again, the list of topics is long, for example, the selective process of granting asylum to some groups and not others, the denial of responsibility for care and provision, rhetoric about asylum-seekers, and so forth. In this regard, Bandura's outline of moral disengagement, which becomes manifest for example in moral justifications or in the displacement of responsibility, is also a constructive approach to employ in the study of strategies and effects of inherent violence in refugee regimes (Bandura 2002).

The denial of legally entitled asylum procedures, the experiences of push backs and that of limited residence permits over decades, among others, are forms of implicit denial of rights, an integral part of a fragmented social fabric, and reflects exposure to violence in various refugee regimes. Moreover, it is only in the last few years that some host countries have acknowledged the long-lasting effects of the violence experienced by asylum seekers in their countries of origin. The undecipherable interplay of experienced violence in asylum procedures, deportation or the constant threat of being deported, trauma specific treatment necessities, and questions of intergenerational transmission of extreme violence are still only incipient topics of research. And scrutinizing embodied violence in refugee regimes – short and long term – entails raising the question of its long-lasting effects.

Didier Fassin notes the contradiction in refugee regimes between compassion and repression (Fassin 2019, 5050), but these two sides are not mutually exclusive. Both protection and control in effect work towards channelling agency through mechanisms of either tutelage and victimisation or criminalisation. Even when states recognise the need to provide a "safe and protective environment" (Gibney 2000, 690) they often base this right on responsibilities for refugees and additional control mechanisms.

*

This volume consists of three sections, all of which acknowledge the strong interconnectedness of refugee regimes, violence and agency. The selection and arrangement of the chapters shows the diversity and arbitrariness of refugee regimes, given the overlapping national, inter-national and selective forces at stake. In doing so, the chapters reveal the inherent coercive violence present in all levels of refugee regimes: from the violence of displacement and expulsion, to the violence of stereotypification and exclusion in host countries, or essentialisation within academic knowledge production.

The violence of refugee regimes begins with conceptualising forced migration and displacement. This is not only done by politicians, legal experts or the media, but also by academic researchers themselves. By preferring one concept over the other, researchers shift the perceptions of their audiences, turn a blind eye to painful experiences encountered by the refugees, or add enforced categories on perceptions of the self. In the first section of this volume, Heidrun Friese, Alessandro Monsutti and Leonardo Schiocchet put the terms of engagement with refugee regimes and agency into perspective, as well as overlapping and intersecting approaches, such as border regimes or concepts of diaspora. Their chapters provide insight on how nation states, international actors, and scholars approach this topic.

Friese reminds us that the notion of "humanity" derives from the Latin "humare", meaning to bury someone. These roots are conspicuous in her chapter, for she analyses how border regimes in the Mediterranean combine humanitarianism with the surveillance of mobility and "necropolitics" (Mbembe 2003; 2019). These borders no longer serve to protect against other sovereign states and military incursions, but instead seclude nonstate transnational actors, thereby creating what she calls a "tragic border-regime" (Friese 2017a, b; 2019a). Such a regime, in turn, amounts for what Jacques Rancière (2014, 135) calls "the transformation of the democratic theatre into the humanitarian theatre", characterized by the exclusion of mobile people from the political realm. The naturalized order of nation-states, sovereignty and citizenship, marginalises illegalized people, aliens, residents and citizens and allocates unequal, asymmetric socio-cultural and political rights. Moreover, the overlap of humanitarian intervention and border management creates a "humanitarian border" (Walters, 2011), distinguishing between humans and the superfluous. Friese urges us to subvert this border to uphold a European moral and political order that rejects the logic of mobility as emergency and the erasure of the rights of "others". She reminds us that the substance for change is already there. For, beyond control, current borderlands are also shared spaces of civility and activism.

Monsutti departs from Thomas Faist's (2008) invitation to amalgamate scholarly traditions and "think outside existing boxes". He suggests that experiencing the "inequalscape" of a post-Cold War World – the most unequal in human history – should entail re-examining our conceptual framework of human mobility to reveal the human cost of existing dichotomous categories such as migration/forced migration. According to him, we must heed the moral fatigue of those arriving at Europe's doorsteps towards inequality. Mobility should be seen as a moral protest and a political act, a testimony to the immorality of global moral polity. Likewise, our conceptual toolkit must become a political act. Monsutti's "ethnographic wandering" among Afghans in Lesbos (Greece), Friuili (Italy) and Calais (France) illustrates his reasoning by appealing to the reader's own sense of morality.

Schiocchet closes this section by questioning to what extent speaking of a diaspora in cases such as the Palestinian, strongly marked by exile, captures the collective experience of the displaced. He concludes by suggesting that common Palestinian expressions of their situation point to a fundamental experiential dimension of displacement that must be brought to the centre of analysis. This in turn, suggests that the anthropology of (im)mobility must turn to the affective dimension of experience, beyond territorial displacement, if it is to understand forced migrants' relative space of agency within the refugee regimes imposed on them, including regimes of knowledge constructed or empowered by academics themselves. Moreover, beyond discussing the concept of exile, his chapter urges caution with regard to the poorly reflected academic usage of various staple concepts expressing human (im)mobility, such as diaspora, hybridization, and transnationalism.

In the second section, Maria Six-Hohenbalken, Yeo Seon Park, Sabine Bauer-Amin and Denise Tan analyse the complexity and arbitrariness of refugee regimes. By showing the effects, developments and porosity of these, they point to the violence exerted on forced migrants' lives. These chapters single out and discuss the inherent coercion present within processes of inclusion and exclusion, even when they are not perceived as such by governments, volunteers, and others.

Six-Hohenbalken unpacks the various concomitant refugee regimes affecting the fate of diverse groups of Iraqi refugees. Several refugee regimes had historically developed in Iraq and, hence, govern the lives of refugees of various ethnoreligious groups, creating multipolar forces and challenges for nation states, NGOs and the refugees themselves. Historical and recent political developments show ambiguities and ambivalences within Iraq as an emitting, transit and target country for refugees. Six-Hohenbalken also points to the transnationalisation of various communities due to the continuation of violence within Iraq, which influences individual actors, NGOs and policy makers. These different refugee systems create inclusion and exclusion based on previous historic developments, their interdependencies and multipolarities. Based on these complex interplays, she discusses whether and how these refugee regimes limit or enable refugees' agency. The chapter is based on empirical studies based in Iraq, Armenia, Austria and Germany, and focuses especially on the situation of Yezidis from Sinjar (Iraq), their situation as Internally Displaced People and as asylum seekers in Europe and beyond.

Where Six-Hohenbalken goes back to the 1930s in her analysis, Park takes us to a context of a relatively newly developing refugee regime based on the global aspirations of South Korea. She questions whether refugee status determination and the debate on integration should fall solely into the legal realm. By examining the discourses and policies surrounding refugees, she shows the development of the Korean refugee regime in relation to global and mainly European developments, as exemplified by the so-called "Yemeni incident", in 2018. However, she also considers refugee communities existing prior to the new Refugee Act, and to their inclusion into local society beyond legalisation. By doing so, she shows institutional gaps and porosity, as well as contradictions between historically developed local inclusion, and the new desire for managing Yemeni refugees according to global refugee regimes. Park suggests a more holistic approach towards refugee inclusion in Korea. In this way, the question of refugees does not remain in a divisive and political arena, but opens space for the public to imagine what it means to live in diversity and how we engage with global phenomena which are inseparable from our everyday life.

Bauer-Amin draws attention to the usage of the politically-discussed term "integration" in national refugee regimes and the exclusion mechanisms this usage produces by looking into the tendency of the Austrian state to fuse migration and refugee regimes, and into the consequences for those who are affected by it. She argues that this conflation causes a neoliberally induced devaluation of people who cannot find employment. While the current public debate on Austrian integration revolves around the fast acquisition of language and inclusion in the labour market, elderly refugees are often unable to fulfil these criteria, which leaves them with limited prospects and little room for improving their current situation in Austria. Within this refugee regime, forced migrants who cannot integrate quickly into the labour market, are excluded and marginalized. In addition, non-governmental or private humanitarian initiatives often focus on engaging young adults into civil society rather than focusing on the specific situations of the elderly. This leads to an exclusion and marginalization in particular of elderly refugees and causes the denial of their value for the community and as testimonies of a pre-war Syria.

Tan underlines the role of NGOs in refugee regimes through her ethnographic research in Izmir, and through comparison with two other recent case studies. International and local NGOs are central actors within the context of refugee regimes, as many states rely on their services for the implementation of national migration and integration policies. Departing from an understanding of civil society as inclusive of not only formal international and national NGOs, but also of informal networks (see Layton 2004), Tan points to the critical situation of formalized civil society in present-day Turkey. Many Turkish NGOs and initiatives were founded in recent years to work exclusively with refugees. On the one hand, the Turkish refugee regime is characterized by a constant tension created by the urgency within the host country to support refugees and set against the desire to control them. On the other hand, the focus on non-formalised civil society shows how refugees manage their new life situations without interference or support from official NGOs. By considering un-official forms of civil society, she highlights the role of self-organised refugee groups. Through this, she shows the porosity of civil society, which, in turn, allows refugees to recover their agency, create their own organisations and empower others.

The contributions in the third section discuss the contradictory discourses and mutually exclusive narratives at play in the humanitarian rhetoric. In this section, titled *Ambiguity and (Un)settlement in Agency*, Monika Mokre, Mirian Souza and Katarina G. Nygren, Sara Nyhlén and Rozalie E. Böge show how refugee regimes limit and shape refugee experiences of agency. They outline how the selectivity, volatility and ambiguity of refugee regimes is shaped by representational considerations, which in turn influence and shape public discourses and guide the expectations of NGOs, volunteers and practitioners towards refugees. This section therefore exposes and problematizes tensions between agency and refugee regimes by evoking and recapitulating refugees' own experiences of unsettlement.

Mokre critically analyses the application of the vulnerability concept when large numbers of refugees started to arrive in Austria from 2015 onwards, and the subsequent change to a discourse on threat and security measures. Mokre argues that this was not a swing from one political strategy to another, but rather that both discourses are complementary. Referring to a postcolonial concept of desubjectivation, she suggests that policies representing refugees as endangering and endangered are forms of biopolitics, and coining people as vulnerable, or fragile, without social and political rights, turns longing for agency and participation into a kind of threat. The chapter focuses on gender related differences, showing how young male refugees, predominantly of Afghan origin, are excluded from the re/presentation of vulnerable persons, and how their specific reasons for refuge are neglected. While vulnerability concepts were often exclusively applied to "womenandchildren" (Enloe 1993, 166), in discussing the young male's perspective, Mokre shows inherent conceptual ambiguities.

Mirian Alves de Souza's contribution also focuses on gender related topics and scrutinizes the ambiguous images of refugee women. She shows how organizations acting upon Syrian refugees in Brazil deploy divergent images of ideal behaviours. The expectations herein and the entanglement with cultural conceptions or perceptions of traditional versus modern, reverberate in the aid work of humanitarian agents, fostering or impeding refugee agency. Souza thus scrutinizes the expectations that NGO workers have with regard to their clients' agency and to serve their specific imagery. In devising agency, refugees have to muddle through various rhetoric, and to grapple with contradicting images and ideology-laden representations to engage with the host society. This affects almost all aspects of life - social, temporal or spatial.

Katharina Nygren, Sara Nyhlén and Rozalie Böge discuss how people whose prospects for a positive asylum application are rather poor, and whose possibility for residency might only be temporary, engage in finding space in an urban Swedish setting. Applying an innovative methodological approach based on visual anthropology, photo-elicitation and walk maps, these authors depict the place making practices of asylum applicants. Refugees' subjective engagements in (dis)connection with former and new environment in spatial-temporal strategies of home-making, shows the importance of referring to the past (belonging) and to the nature in the residence country.

This edited volume contributes towards a growing number of studies which bring the voices of refugees to the forefront and expose the violence inherent in refugee regimes. Using a qualitative approach and highlighting refugee agency, the contributors analyse the often-neglected social implications of (inter)national refugee regimes. The intrinsic violence of refugee regimes transcends national borders: it is international, national, society based, internalised, and embodied, and it urgently needs due attention by scholars.

## References

Agamben, Girgio. 1998. *Homo Sacer: Sovereign Power and Bare Life*, trans. Daniel Heller-Roazen. Stanford: Stanford University Press.

Agier, Michel. 2010. "Humanity as an identity and its political effects (a note on camps and humanitarian government)." *Humanity: An International Journal of Human Rights, Humanitarianism, and Development* 1, no.1: 29-45.

—. 2011. *Managing the undesirables: refugee camps and humanitarian government.* Cambridge: Polity Press.

Aijmer, Göran, and John Abbink, eds. 2000. *Meanings of Violence: A Cross Cultural Perspective.* Oxford: Berg.

Andresen, Sabine, Koch, Claus and Julia König. 2015 „Kinder in vulnerablen Konstellationen. Zur Einleitung." In *Vulnerable Kinder. Interdisziplinäre Annäherungen*, edited by Andresen, Sabine; Koch, Claus and Julia König, 7–19. Wiesbaden: Springer.

Bandura, Albert. 2002. "Selective Moral Disengagement in the Exercise of Moral Agency." *Journal of Moral Education* 31, no.2: 101–119.

Barnett, Michael. 2009. *The international humanitarian order.* London: Routledge.

Betts, Alexander. 2015. "The Normative Terrain of the Global Refugee Regime". *Ethics & International Affairs* 29, n.o.4: 363–375. https://ethicsandinternatio nalaffairs.org/2015/the-normative-terrain-of-the-global-refugee-regime /. Accessed on 06/29/2021.

—. 2010. "The Refugee Regime Complex". *Refugee Survey Quarterly* 29, no. 1: 12–37.

Cabot, Heath. 2019. "The business of anthropology and the European refugee regime". *American Ethnologist* 46, no. 3: 261–275.

Calhoun, Craig. 2006. "The Imperative to Reduce Suffering: Charity, Progress and Emergencies in the Field of Humanitarian Action." In *Humanitarianism in Question: Politics, Power, Ethics*, edited by Michael Barnett and Thomas Weiss, 73–98. Ithaca: Cornell University Press.

Chatty, Dawn. 2014. "Anthropology and Forced Migration." In *The Oxford Handbook of Refugee and Forced Migration Studies*, edited by Elena Fiddian-

Qasmiyeh, Gil Loescher, Katy Long, and Nando Sigona, 74 – 85. Oxford: Oxford University Press.

Colson, Elizabeth. 2003. "Forced Migration and the Anthropological Response." *Journal of Refugee Studies* 16, no. 1: 1–18.

Das, Veena. 2007. *Life and Words: Violence and the Descent into the Ordinary.* Berkeley, Calif.: University of California Press.

Dunn, Elizabeth Cullen. 2012. "The chaos of humanitarian aid: adhocracy in the Republic of Georgia." *Humanity: An International Journal of Human Rights, Humanitarianism, and Development* 3, no. 1: 1–23.

Elwert, Georg, ed. 1999. *Dynamics of violence: processes of escalation and de-escalation in violent group conflicts.* Berlin: Duncker & Humblot.

Emirbayer, Mustafa, and Ann Mische. 1998. "What is Agency?" In: *American Journal of Sociology* 4: 962–1023.

Essed, Philomena, Frerks, Georg, and Joke Schrijvers. 2004. "Introduction: Refugees, Agency and Social Transformation". In *Refugees and the Transformation of Societies: Agency, Policies, Ethics and Politics*, edited by Philomena Essed, Georg Frerks, and Joke Schrijvers, 1-16. New York/Oxford: Berghahn.

Faist, Thomas. 2008. "Migrants as Transnational Development Agents: An Inquiry into the Newest Round of the Migration–Development Nexus." *Population, Space and Place* 14: 21–42.

Fassin, Didier. 2019. "Refugees, Anthropology, and Law". In *The International Encyclopedia of Anthropology*, edited by Hillary Callan, 5050-5059. Oxford: Wiley & Sons.

Fassin, Didier, and Mariella Pandolfi. 2010. *Contemporary states of emergency. The politics of military and humanitarian interventions.* New York: Zone Books.

Feldman, Ilana. 2012. "The humanitarian condition: Palestinian refugees and the politics of living." *Humanity: An International Journal of Human Rights, Humanitarianism, and Development* 3, no. 2: 155172.

Foucault, Michel. 2007. *Security, Territory, Population: Lectures at the College de France 1977-1978.* Basingstoke: Palgrave.

—. 1979. *The History of Sexuality Volume 1: An Introduction.* London: Allen Lane.

—. 1966. *Les Mots et les choses. Une archéologie des sciences humaines.* Paris: Éditions Gallimard.

—. 1961. *Folie et Déraison: Histoire de la folie à l'âge classique.* Paris: Librairie Plon.

Friese, Heidrun. 2019. "Framing Mobility. Refugees and the Social Imagination. " In *Die lange Dauer der Flucht – Analysen aus Wisssenschaft und Praxis,* edited by Josef Kohlbacher and Maria Six-Hohenbalken, 45–62. Vienna: Austrian Academy of Sciences Press.

Friese, Heidrun. 2017a. *Flüchtlinge: Opfer – Bedrohung – Helden. Zur politischen Imagination des Fremden.* Bielefeld: transcript.

Friese, Heidrun. 2017b. "Representations of Gendered Mobility and the Tragic Border-Regime in the Mediterranean. In: Special Issue Women in the Mediterranean." *Journal of Balkan and Near Eastern Studies* 19, no.5:541–556.

Gibney, Matthew J. 2000. "Between Control and Humanitarianism: Temporary Protection in Contemporary Europe." *Georgetown Immigration Law Journal* 14, no. 3: 689–708.

Harrell-Bond, Barbara. 1986. *Imposing Aid: Emergency Assistance to Refugees.* Oxford: Oxford University Press.

Kleist, Olaf. 2018. "The Refugee Regime: Sovereignty, Belonging and the Political of Forced Migration". In *Was ist ein Migrationsregime? What Is a Migration Regime?*, edited by Andreas Pott, Christoph Rass, and Frank Wolff, 167-185. Wiesbaden: VS Springer.

Klepp, Silja. 2010. "A contested asylum system: The European Union between refugee protection and border control in the Mediterranean Sea," *European Journal of Migration and Law* 12, no.1: 1–21.

Layton, Robert. 2004. "Civil Society and Social Cohesion – A Reassessment." *Working papers/Max Planck Institute for Social Anthropology* 63.

Loescher, Gil. 1994. "The International Refugee Regime: Stretched to the Limit?" *Journal of International Affairs* 47, no. 2, Refugees and International Population Flows: 351–377.

Löwenstein, Heiko. 2017. „Identität als Scharnier zwischen Bewusstsein und Agency. Oder: Meads Sprachlosigkeit gegenüber geteilter Emotionalität." In *Netzwerke, Kultur und Agency. Problemlösungen in relationaler Methodologie und Sozialtheorie*, edited by Heiko Löwenstein and Mustafa Emirbayer, 210–224. Weinheim: Basel.

Long, Norman. 2001. *Development Sociology. Actor Perspectives.* London, New York: Routledge.

Lorion, Ray. P.. 2001. "Violence as a Problem of Health." In *International Encyclopedia of the Social & Behavioral Sciences* 24, edited by Neil J. Smelser and Paul Bates, 16192– 16196, Amsterdam: Elsevier.

Lubkeman, Stephen. 2019. "The Anthropology of Forced Migration in Africa". In *A Companion to the Anthropology of Africa*, edited by Roy Richard Grinker, Stephen C. Lubkemann, Christopher B. Steiner, and Euclides Gonçalves, 199-227. Oxford: Wiley & Sons.

Mackenzie, Catriona, McDowell, Christopher, and Eileen Pittaway. 2007. "Beyond 'Do No Harm': The Challenge of Constructing Ethical Relationships." *Refugee Research, Journal of Refugee Studies* 20, no. 2: 299–319.

Malkii, Liisa. 1995. "Refugees and Exile: From 'Refugee Studies' to the National Order of Things." *Annual Review of Anthropology* 24: 495–523.

Mbembe, Achille. 2003. "Necropolitics (tr. Libby Meintjes)." *Public Culture* 15, no. 1: 11–40.

Mbembe, Achille. 2019. *Necropolitics* (tr. Steven Corcoran). Durham/London: Duke (orig. *Politiques de l'inimitié*. Paris: La Dévouverte, 2016).

Nordstrom, Carolyn. 1997. *A Different Kind of War Story*. Philadelphia: University of Pennsylvania.

Nordstrom, Carolyn. 2004. *Shadows of war: violence, power, and international profiteering in the twenty-first century*. Berkeley: University of California Press.

Rancière, Jacques.2014. *Das Unvernehmen. Politik und Philosophie*. Frankfurt am Main: Suhrkamp.

Scheper-Hughes, Nancy, and Philippe Bourgois, eds.. 2003. *Violence in War and Peace. An Anthology*. Oxford: Blackwell Publishing.

Scherr, Albert. 2012. "Soziale Bedingungen von Agency." In *Agency. Qualitative Rekonstruktionen und gesellschaftstheoretische Bezüge von Handlungsmächtigkeit*, edited by Bethmann, Stephanie, Helfferich, Cornelia, Hoffmann, Heiko, and Debora Niermann, 99–121. Weinheim: Basel.

Schiocchet, Leonardo. 2011. "Far Middle East, Brave New World: The Building of the Middle East and the Arab Spring." *The Perspective of the World Review* 3, no.2. (English Edition). Brasilia/Brazil: IPEA: 37-80.

Schmidt, Bettina E., and Ingo Schröder, eds. 2001. *Anthropology of Violence and Conflict*. London: Routledge.

Schmitt, Caroline. 2019. "Agency und Vulnerabilität. Ein relationaler Zugang zu Lebenswelten geflüchteter Menschen. " *Soziale Arbeit. Zeitschrift für soziale und sozialverwandte Gebiete* 68, no. 8: 282–288.

Stanko, Elizabeth. A. 1996. "Violence." In *The Social Science Encyclopedia*, edited by Kuper, Adam and Jessica Kuper, 896–897. London: Routledge.

Szanton, David L. 2004. *The Politics of Knowledge: Area Studies and the Disciplines*. Berkeley: University of California Press.

Tilly, Charles. 2001. "Public Violence." In *International Encyclopedia of the Social & Behavioral Sciences*, edited by Smelser, Neil J. and Paul B. Baltes, 16206–16211, Amsterdam: Elsevier.

Walters, William. 2001. "Foucault and Frontiers: Notes on the Birth of the Humanitarian Border." In *Governmentality: Current Issues and Future Challenges*, edited by Ulrich Bröckling, Susanne Krasmann, and Thomas Lemke, 138–164. New York: Routledge, 2011.

Whitehead, Neil L., ed., 2004. *Violence*. Santa Fe, N.M.: School of American Research Press.

Wilson, Ken, and Jovito Nunes. 1994. "Repatriation to Mozambique: Refugee Initiative and Agency Planning in Milange District, 1988–1991. " In *When Refugees Go Home*, edited by Tim Allen and Hubert Morsink, 182-250. London: James Currey.

# PART 1: The Terms of Engagement

# European Border Regimes: Necropolitics, Humanitarianism and the Democratic Order

*Heidrun Friese*

## The Argument

> The new refugees were persecuted
> not because of what they had done
> or thought, but because of what they
> unchangeable were — born into the
> wrong kind of race or the wrong kind
> of class or drafted by the wrong kind of
> government.
> Hannah Arendt, The Origins of Totali-
> tarianism (2017, 385)

The Mediterranean became the "world's deadliest border", a lethal site where
the humanitarian system of aid and care intersects with "crimes of peace"
(Albahari 2015a), camps, illegal push-backs and deliberately letting racialized
people die. In 2020, migrant fatalities worldwide amounted to at least to 2.329
out of which 770 died in the Mediterranean.[1] The Search and Rescue mis-
sions (SAR) in the Mediterranean by NGOs are criminalized and obstructed,
whereas the Coast Guard of Italy and Malta cooperate with the corrupt 'coast
guard' of Libya in illegally pushing back migrant's boats to its shores. The *European Border and Coast Guard Agency* (Frontex) is reported to push back migrants

---

1   IOM notes 339 fatalities in Sub-Saharan Africa, 308 in North Africa, 97 in the Middle
    East, 51 Horn of Africa, 280 at the US-Mexican Border, 81 in the Caribbean (IOM, Missing
    Migrants, total of deaths recorded from January 1 to November 1, 2020: https://missin
    gmigrants.iom.int, 01.11.2020.

from Greece to Turkey, not least the appalling conditions and recurrent incidents in the Greek camp of Moria show that current European border policies fly in the face of law and Human Rights. Current European border-regimes are marked by paradoxes and tensions. These regard, firstly, the constitutive "democratic paradox" (Mouffe 2000), secondly, they entail the tensions between the Universal "Rights of Man" (Arendt 1949a, b) and the nation-state and connected to that, thirdly, the tensions of hospitality that situate mobile people between friend and foe.

Pointing to the genuine undemocratic moment that makes up the constitution of a *demos* entitled to self-rule and autonomous deliberation, transnational mobility challenges the democratic order. Democratic orders are based on inclusion and marked by exclusion, the division into those who are endowed with civic and political rights and those who are excluded; this demarcation is a key feature of sovereign power and the nation-state. Mobility and borders thus powerfully uncover the distinction between illegalized people, aliens, residents and citizens, a division that distributes unequal, asymmetric socio-cultural and political rights. At the same time, it challenges the naturalized order of nation-states, sovereignty and citizenship based on laws of origin, birth, autochthony and poses the urgent question who is the 'We' ('we, the people who rule ourselves') and the political actors of democratic practices.[2]

As Wendy Brown (2010) forcefully demonstrates, the walls and borders of our present times differ from those of the 20th century. No longer do they operate as fortresses against other sovereign states and military incursions, instead they are built against nonstate transnational actors – individuals, organizations, industries, movements, groups – and are not linked to the well-known Westphalian logics, the "Westphalian grammar" (Benhabib 2004).[3] We certainly do not live in a post-state, post-sovereign era. However, in globalized times the nation-state is losing its exclusivity with regard to the question of sovereignty. As part of the paradoxes of democracy – and hardly by chance – borders are re-affirmed, performed and symbolically upheld, creating and

---

2    This crucial question is even more evident in times of populism and nationalist-ethnic slogans such as 'We are the people' seeking to affirm naturalized citizenship.

3    Critically assessing 'classical' political theory, she disagrees with Michael Hardt's and Toni Negri's argument that the sovereignty of the nation-state has transformed into a global empire as well as she rejects Giorgio Agamben's view that sovereignty is to be coupled with bare life.

enacting the "tragic border-regime" (Friese 2017a, b, 2019a),[4] given that the "ultimate expression of sovereignty resides, to a large degree, in the power and the capacity to dictate who may live and who must die" (Mbembe 2003, 11).[5] The governance of current border-regimes – a configuration of different (non-)governmental actors and heterogenous, even contradictory practices, policies and representations – are tragic not only because it deliberately leaves mobile people to die in no-man's lands, the margins, the border of the democratic order, but because they reveal the paradoxical – if not the aporetic – foundations of the inclusive-exclusive democratic order and thus mark the political. At the same time, current border-regimes are marked by tensions between universal human rights and the particular political community, the tensions between "proxi humanitarianism" (De Lauri 2016, 3–4) and surveillance, policing, confinement. In such a way, the refugee regimes, its international institutions, actors, issues and policies intersect with border regimes – in complementary and/or contradictory ways – and it has been argued (Betts 2010, 12) that we can no longer "speak of a compartmentalized refugee regime" but rather, there is now a "refugee regime complex" that overlaps with the border regime in which "States engage in forms of institutionalized cooperation that have a direct and an indirect impact upon refugee protection."

Practices of doing the border reflect these tensions and enact the social imagination which produces the figures of mobile people as victim, enemy or hero (Friese 2017a, b, 2019a). Humanitarianism, humanitarian 'realism' foster (signifying) practices that fix mobile people in the deplorable, pitiful position of victims. The relation between (illegalized) mobility and victimhood negates political agency. Caught in the circularity – the victim cannot escape victimhood – mobile people cannot enter the sphere of the political. What is taking place is, as Rancière remarks, "the transformation of the democratic theatre

---

4    The notion takes up Cornelius Castoriadis' insights regarding tragedy (see Friese 2019a, 47–48).

5    Mbembe is interested in "those trajectories by which the state of exception and the relation of enmity have become the normative basis of the right to kill. In such instances, power (and not necessarily state power) continuously refers and appeals to exception, emergency, and a fictionalized notion of the enemy. It also labors to produce that same exception, emergency, and fictionalized enemy" (2003, 16). Drawing on Foucault's notion of biopower, he asks how its "mechanisms [...] are inscribed in the way all modern states function" given that "they can be seen as constitutive elements of state power in modernity" (2003, 17).

into the humanitarian theatre" (Rancière 2014, 135, transl. author), a transformation that leads to de-politization, the negation of the political and the exclusion of mobile people from the political realm. Whereas the humanitarian theatre re-produces the mythology of the victim and "humanitarian borders" (Walters 2011),[6] the performative dimension of walls, the border "spectacle" (De Genova 2013), the theatre of surveillance and policing, the "necropolitics" (Mbembe 2003, 2019) reiterate the imagination of the racialized stranger, the foreigner as foe who is to be kept out of the political community, an enemy who does not belong to humanity and can be made die or to be kept in a timeless *limbus*, a no-where of camps and precarious dumping sites.

These tensions have been addressed by concepts of "humanitarian reason", "humanitarian government" (Mavelli 2017; Walters 2011; Fassin 2007b, 2011, 2013) to "describe the simultaneous and conflicting deployment of humanitarianism and security in the government of 'precarious lives' such as refugees" (Mavelli 2017, 809).[7] Both can be considered as forms of biopolitical power and government which reduce human beings to naked life (Arendt 1949a, b; 2017; Agamben 1995).

This is precisely Hannah Arendt's objection against the "Rights of Man". Starting out from a brief and certainly not exhaustive discussion of Hannah Arendt's seminal analysis on the "Rights of Man" (Arendt 1949a, b; 2017), in a first step, the tension between universal human rights and its articulations in the nation-state will be addressed. As will be evidenced, current 'humanitarian' border regimes miss the political, namely the "right to have rights" (Arendt 2017, 390) and re-iterate the social imagination and the victim-foe distinction. Against this background, the European border-regimes, the multilocal borderwork in the Mediterranean and the tensions between humanitarianism on one side and surveillance, policing, the "necropolitics" (Mbembe 2003; 2019) on the other, will be sketched in order to demonstrate that these am-

---

6    Walters continues: "The emergence of the humanitarian border goes hand in hand with the move which has made state frontiers into privileged symbolic and regulatory instruments within strategies of migration control. It is part of a much wider trend that has been dubbed the "rebordering" of political and territorial space. The humanitarian border emerges once it becomes established that border crossing has become, for thousands of migrants seeking, for a variety of reasons, to access the territories of the global North, a matter of *life and death*. It crystallizes as a way of governing this novel and disturbing situation" (Walters 2011, 138, emphasis by Heidrun Friese).

7    For a comprehensive overview, see Benthall (2018); Redfield (2012).

bivalences and tensions not only mark undesired mobile people in particular but are inscribed into the liberal democratic order as well.

As will be argued, what is at stake is not only a *moral* question but a *political* one, what is at stake is a European political order that rejects the erasure of the rights of Others, its current necropolitics and the logic of mobility as emergency and exception.

## Universal Human Rights and the Nation-State

Against the background of a broader investigation of imperialism and the historical settings of the colonial racial order, the appalling cruelty to and plundering of Africa, the breakdown of the rule of law that characterizes the *Heart of Darkness*, Joseph Conrad's narration of the collapse of moral and civilizational standards, Hannah Arendt's famous analysis of the relations between nation-state, refugees and Human Rights focuses on the tensions between the "Rights of Man" (the "Declaration of the Rights of Man and the Citizen" in 1789 and the UN "Universal Declaration of Human Rights" in 1948) and its particular articulations in the sovereign nation-state: [8]

> The same essential rights were at once claimed as the inalienable heritage of all human being *and* as the specific heritage of specific nations; the same nation was at once declared to be subject to laws, which supposedly would flow from the Rights of Man *and* sovereign, that is, bound by no universal laws and acknowledging nothing superior to itself. The practical outcome of this contradiction was that from then on human rights were protected and enforced only as national rights (Arendt 2017, 301).

Such an argument critically scrutinizes the logic of sovereignty that underlies citizenship and allows for the denial of rights to those who are excluded and do not belong to the nation-state via citizenship. Furthermore, "the perplexities of the rights of man" (Arendt 2017, 380), the German version reads "Aporien der Menschenrechte" (1998, 601), originate in the reduction of refugees to

---

8    First published in 1949 (1949a, b) and later on as part of chapter 9 ("The Decline of the Nation-State and the End of the Rights of Man") in *The Origins of Totalitarianism* (2017 [1951]). See as well "We Refugees" (Arendt 1994) and "Nation-State and Democracy" (2006). For central contributions to current debates on human rights, see Balfour and Cadovabal (2004); Rathore and Cistelecan (2011).

the "abstract nakedness of being human" (2017, 392), the "abstract nakedness of being human was their greatest danger" (2017, 392) and, as Arendt insists, "the abstract nakedness of being human and nothing but human" (2017, 389). This indissoluble double-bind of the Rights of Man cuts through the political community. It establishes the divide, the inequality between the citizen who conducts a political, good life proper to man and those who are not entitled with civil and political rights and are nothing but naked life, mere life.[9] "Equality" as Arendt argues against natural law and

> in contrast to all that is involved in mere existence, is not given to us, but is the result of human organization insofar as it is guided by the principle of justice. We are not born equal; we become equal as members of a group on the strength of our decision to guarantee ourselves mutually equal rights (Arendt 2017, 394).

Equality is not simply given as natural, but is an outcome guided by justice, a decision, an enactment created in praxis, it is made in and through cooperation, negotiation, struggle, it becomes – in Rancière's version (2010) – through the enactment, the acting as political subjects who demand the rights that they are denied. I shall come back to this point in a moment.

> This new situation, in which 'humanity' has an effect assumed the role formerly ascribed to nature or history, would mean [...] that the right to have rights, or the right of every individual to belong to humanity, should be guaranteed by humanity itself (Arendt 2017, 390).

However, "it is by no means certain whether this is possible. For, contrary to best-intentioned humanitarian attempt [...] It should be understood that this idea transcends the present sphere of international law which still operates in terms of reciprocal agreements" (Arendt 2017, 390–91). Being enshrined in the order of the nation-state, human rights fail to be enforced (not even a cosmopolitan order that might ensure implementation and enforcement). The *aporia* resides in the rightlessness to belong to any political order:

> The calamity of the rightless is not that they are deprived of life [...] but that no longer belong to any community whatsoever. Their plight is not

---

9    See Agamben on *zoe* and *bios politikos*, "private life and political existence" (Agamben 1998, 187/209–10). For a detailed account of the concepts "bios, zoe, life" in Aristotle, Arendt, Agamben and Esposito, see as well Dubreil and Eagle (2006).

that they are not equal before the law, but that no law exists for them; not that they are oppressed but that nobody wants to oppress them. Only in the last stage of a rather lengthy process is their right to live threatened; only if they remain perfectly 'superfluous', if nobody can be found to 'claim' them, may their lives be in danger (Arendt 2017, 387).

The rightless superfluous "human waste" (Bauman 2007, 28) does not have a place in the world, be it even the negative place of oppression. "The right to have rights", the right to act, to speak and to be judged, is the right "to have a place in the world" and to belong to a political community (Arendt 2017, 388).[10] The right to have rights is a right to belong to the world, to the political community, that is: to bear political agency.[11] A political community that negates such a right to others, deprives itself, and ultimately it negates its being human (see Menke 2016), or, to put it another way, negating belonging to a political community and political participation, negates the human community present in the Other:[12]

if a human being loses his political status, he should, according to the implications of the inborn and inalienable rights of man, come under exactly the situation for which the declaration of such general rights provided. Actually, the opposite is the case. It seems that a man who is nothing but a

---

10    See Seyla Benhabib's reading and her analysis of the discursive structures of Arendt's chapter and the "right to have rights" (2004, 56–61). See especially Franziska Martinsen who argues that Human Rights should include rights of participation. As she notes, "the current exclusion of a huge number of human beings that are marked as 'refugees', 'stateless persons' or simply 'Others' is not just a moral but a political problem" (2019, 267, transl. mine).

11    In Balibar's reading, the right to have rights "refers to the continuous process in which a minimal recognition of the belonging of human beings to the 'common' sphere of existence". This "insurrectional element of democracy [...] predetermines every constitution of a democratic or republican state". It "requires the direct participation of the *demos*. [...] Arendt's argument clearly recognizes the importance of the egalitarian or insurrectional element constitutive of democratic citizenship, but there is more: what she displays is the dialectical relationship of this element and the politics of civility" (Balibar 2001, 18).

12    Balibar notes: "Humans simply are their rights. But – and here is the antinomic character – the same institutions that create rights, or better said, allow individuals to become human subjects by reciprocally granting rights to each other, also destroy these rights, and thus threaten the human" (Balibar 2007, 734).

man has lost the very qualities which *make it possible for other people to treat him as a fellow man* (Arendt 2017, 393, emphasis added).[13]

Jean-Francois Lyotard's reflection on *The Other's Rights* (1993) starts out with the question of the Other in Arendt's line, and he immediately notes: "to banish the stranger is to banish the community, and you banish yourself from the community thereby" (Lyotard 1993, 136).[14] Taking up Arendt's central point, namely the refugee's deprivation of having a place in world and being judged for action and opinion, Lyotard addresses the deprivation of the right to speak and to address citizens (the deprivation of the interlocutory right), the "wrong", the "harm" to being excluded from the "speech community" (1993, 143).

> The Latin *sacer* (sacred) expressed the ambivalence of the abject: human refuse excluded from the interests of the speech community, yet a sign, perhaps, in which the Other has left his mark and deserving respectful fear (Lyotard 1993, 145).

What comes into play is – as in Giorgio Agamben's account (1998) – the figure of the *homo sacer*, whose abject non-place resides in the refusal to welcome him, the Other as a legitimate interlocutor, the refusal of listening, its silence and incessant translation. What also comes into play is the determination to master the Other, to master irreducible otherness which, however, will always have been already present.

However, the invocation of the right to have rights establishes yet another *aporia*. How could those who have been excluded from a common world, who have no public voice, those who do not count and are objects of deprivation, "those excluded from politics possibly claim the right to have rights?" (Schaap 2011, 22). Discussing Arendt's understanding of the political, Jacques Rancière (2010) notes that the ontologization, the distinction between bare life (*zoe*) and *bios politicos* (2010, 64), i.e. the distinction between the private, the social and the life of the citizen, the political life proper to man, depoliticizes human rights. The crucial question is not who is the subject of human right, man or

---

13    As Arendt continues: "This is one of the reasons why it is far more difficult to destroy the legal personality of a criminal that is of a man who has taken upon himself the responsibility for an act whose consequences now determine his fate, than of a man who has been disallowed all common responsibilities" (Arendt 2017, 393).

14    See Benhabib's reading (2004) as well as Ingram's account (2008). For a reading of Marx and Arendt on human rights, see Hamacher (2014).

citizen because human rights are part of the political sphere and thus, part of dispute, litigation, negotiation, contestation and struggle:[15]

> Man and citizen do not designate collections of individuals. Man and citizen are political subjects and as such as are not definite collectivities, but surplus names that set out a question or a dispute (*litige*) about who is included in their count. Correspondingly, freedom and equality are not predicates belonging to definite subjects. Political predicates are open predicates: they open up a dispute about what they entail, whom they concern and in which cases (Rancière 2010, 68).

The question is not that of abstract rights of man versus effective rights of the citizen as in Arendt, but *dissensus*: "A dissensus is not a conflict of interests, opinions or values; it is a division inserted in 'common sense': a dispute over what is given and about the frame within which we see something as given". Dissensus therefore, is "the putting of two worlds in one and the same world. The question of the political subject is not caught between the void term of Man and the plenitude of the citizen with its actual rights. A political subject is a capacity for staging scenes of dissensus" (Rancière 2010, 69). Unwrapping Arendt's version – "human rights obfuscate the fact that it is only by virtue of our membership in a political community that we have any rights at all" (Schaap 2011, 34) – Rancière opens up a space of political subjectivation:

> The very difference between man and citizen is not a sign of disjunction, proving that rights are either void or tautological. It is the opening of an interval for political subjectivation. Political names are litigious names, whose extension and comprehension are uncertain, and which for that reason open up the space of a test or verification. Political subjects build such cases of verification (Rancière 2010, 69).

The right to have rights thus, is linked to the politics of rights and resides in the spaces opened up by action and subjectivity (see also Ingram 2008). Just as citizenship is not only formal, legal status but can be seen as a collective form of activity, an "active citizenship" (Isin 2009a), rights can be seen as an active space responding to their absence.

---

15    Rancière notes the traps, the vicious circle of Arendt's argument: "the Rights of Man are the rights of those who have not the rights that they have and have the rights that they have not" (2010, 67).

Furthermore, as Engin F. Isin (2009b) has argued, the rigid split between the rights of man and civil rights is no longer tenable. The split and the paradoxes between rights that humans possess for the sheer fact that they are humans and civic rights which are connected to citizenship (the first being 'human' the latter being connected to nation-states and governments) no longer holds. Since the historical period to which Arendt refers, these "two regimes have now converged through international covenants and charters of 'human' rights to the extent that it has become impossible to distinguish between 'human' and 'citizenship' rights" (Isin 2009b, 1).[16] Additionally, these rights are a "contested site of social and political struggle" which lead to complex and even contradictory interconnections between legal practices and institutions (Isin 2009b, 3). Paradoxically however, and as a consequence of such a convergence, these political sites are increasingly substituted by procedural, legal battles and specialized lawyers, the sovereignty of states is strengthened and thus, the "human rights regime makes it difficult to defend the rights of others" (Isin 2009b, 11).

Despite the historical developments of Human Rights, what is still at stake are the question of and the tensions inherent in current border regimes. The shift "from Man to Humanity and from Humanity to the Humanitarian" (Rancière 2010, 63) contains the tensions between humanitarianism and necropolitics, the distribution of "abject spaces" (Isin and Rygiel 2007) where 'emergencies' are created and proclaimed, rights are suspended and the state of exception is the rule on one hand and humanitarian governance is enacted on the other. The urgent question remains how these ambivalences and aporias affect not 'only' those who are marked as victims or enemies in particular, but how the democratic order is marked by these tensions in general.

---

16  The "convergence" of human and civil rights (which comprise the right to security) has developed through various Committees and international conventions such as the International Covenant on Civil and Political Rights (ICCPR) and the International Covenant on Economic, Social and Cultural Rights (ICESCR), the International Convention on the Elimination of all Forms of Racial Discrimination (CERD), the Convention on the Elimination of All Forms of Discrimination against Women (CEDAW), the Convention against Torture and other Cruel, Inhuman, or degrading Treatment or Punishment (CAT), the Convention on the Rights of the Child (CRC), the European Court of Human Rights (ECHR), as Isin remarks (2009b, 7).

## The European Border Regime: "Necropolitics" and Humanitarianism

The current border regime in the Mediterranean, its techniques of govern-mentality combine logics of security, control, surveillance, military interven-tions and policing and, to take up Michel Foucault's formulation, enact "the power to let die" (2001, 291, trans. author).[17] The strategic fervor of gaining total control and mastery enacts a "necropolitics" (Mbembe 2003, 2019) and unfolds an every-day, routinized "topography of cruelty" (Balibar 2001), a ge-ography of destruction, violence, suffering, death and camps.[18] Such biopo-litical necropolitics which name sovereign decision on death – "the power and the capacity to dictate who may live and who must die" (Mbembe 2019, 66) – is racialized. Race is the dividing line. At the borders, the racialized 'super-fluous', those who Zygmunt Bauman provocatively called the "human waste" (2007, 28) of the globalized, capitalist order, are left to die and the normaliza-tion of dissuasion, its inherent violence of measuring the utility or uselessness of humans to be discarded, is customized.[19] Push-backs to camps where tor-ture is the rule and forced "re-patriation" to an alleged "homeland" which – for good reasons and with the will to risk their lives – mobile people had fled, become an asset of the political agenda and European public opinion, eager to get rid of the unwanted.[20]

Mobility is seen through the prism of security, deterrence, confinement, camps, expulsion and lethal border practices – the triage of the fittest – have

---

17    These are of course, linked to current border policies and globalization, which "har-bors fundamental tensions between opening and barricading, fusion and partition, erasure and re-inscription. These tensions materialize as increasingly liberalized bor-ders, on the one hand, and the devotion of unprecedented funds, energies, and tech-nologies to border fortification, on the other." Tensions are worked out between "global networks and local nationalisms, virtual power and physical power, private appropria-tion and open sourcing, secrecy and transparency, territorialization and deterritorial-ization", the state and the nation (Brown 2010, 19).

18    The various aspects of border death have been addressed by contributions in Cuttita and Last (2020). The relation between biopower as power to promote life or preclude it to the point of death in the "defense of society" (Foucault 2003) has been widely discussed.

19    For a phenomenology of "violence and civility", see Balibar (2009).

20    The term "re-patriation" is of course part of the trinity of birth/natality, the State/nation and territory (Agamben 1996, 40) that characterizes the nation-state, fixes citizenship, belonging and is to be a founding category of *Heimat*. Kim Rygiel (2016) explores "the issue of 'dying to live'" and relates it to questions of biopolitics, citizenship and activism.

become (politically) acceptable, even if they are a blunt violation of human rights, international conventions, and the international law of the seas. These practices question the rule of law and contribute to the normalization of its non-application, the normalization of its suspension. In line with Arendt's and Agamben's analysis, they enact the ultimate sovereignty of the nation state and establish a border between those who are let die and those who ought not to let die and, again show the paradoxes of human rights and of liberal democracy. Current policies contribute to the expulsion of the rightless and – again in line with Arendt – to the destruction of the political ties by a political community. At the same time and iterating the tensions of hospitality, current border regimes couple the logics of hostility with those of reception, accommodation and welcome, it chains the figure of the (public) enemy (*hostes*) to that of the victim and 'humanitarian' reason and charity (Friese 2014, 47–64, 2017a).[21]

Current efforts to 'manage' undesired mobility merges aid and care with policing, control, technocratic-technological logics, managerial 'best-practice' fiction with 'humanitarian' impetus and legitimation. The border regime includes aid and relief organizations, public and private investment, the military industries into one framework. Humanitarian discourse, knowledge and practices of care have been integrated into the lethal regime, the framing and legitimization of border control and enforcement. At the borders a variety of non-governmental actors operating, following an explicit humanitarian agenda (such as SAR-missions)[22] creating an ambivalent space. The overlapping of humanitarian interventions and border management makes up what William Walters calls the "humanitarian border" (2011).[23] Such a complex configuration make "care functions" to become "a technology of border enforcement" and are "increasing the reach of the state to govern more bodies and more spaces" (Williams 2015, 11). At the same time, a hierarchy of victims with regard to their visibility is established. Due to dramatic, medialized (and

21    Jacques Derrida (2000a) addressed the tension in his remarks on hostipitality. The term addresses the tensions between welcoming, reception, acceptation, offering and their negation, hostility, a tension which is inherent in the Latin words *hospes/hostis* which relate friend and foe to hospitality.

22    For a detailed account of the "humanitarian fleet" in the Mediterranean, see Stierl (2018).

23    Walters scrutinizes "the materialization of the humanitarian border within particular forms of knowledge, and the constitutive role which politics plays in making and changing humanitarian borders" (Walters 2011, 139).

aestheticized) images of rescue, there are those who are highly visible and those who are left to a nameless, unseen death beyond Europe's borders in the Mediterranean."

The nascent border business, a sort of "Humanitarianism Limited" (De Lauri 2016,2) provides care, services and security infrastructure reaching from technology to personal and combines public affairs with private enterprise (Friese 2012). Combining what has be seen as "disaster capitalism" (Naomi Klein), the "humanitarian industrial complex" (Dadusc and Mudu 2020), "the humanitarian" is not "a set of ideas and ideologies, nor simply as the activity of certain nongovernmental actors and organizations" rather, it is "a complex domain possessing specific forms of governmental reason" (Walters 2011, 143).

"Humanitarian government" has most prominently been defined by Didier Fassin "as the administration of human collectivities in the name of a higher moral principle which sees the preservation of life and the alleviation of suffering as the highest value of action" (Fassin 2007b, 151).[24] The central question is, of course, how moral principles and orders, and the ethical are to be 'translated' into juridical orders and into democratic deliberation in nation states. Again, we are faced with the paradox of democracy. Ethical demands and the moral order might allow, if not recommend, that any person who wishes to be admitted as a fellow-citizen in any nation-state should be, whereas democratic deliberation of the particular political community might decide not to admit anyone as citizen and to insist on holding control of transnational mobility and admission to citizenship.[25]

The critique of humanitarianism and humanitarian government engages the victimization of subjects, the stabilization of current border regimes and the de-politicization of mobility.

> [The] focus of humanitarian action remains tied to a victim-centered approach as the core of a complex infrastructure of professionalized and institutionalized practices of aid. We know that humanitarian actions cannot be reduced to the relationship between giver and receiver, but we also know that there is a structural and inevitable correspondence between the

---

24    For an analysis of the biopolitical aspects of "politics of life" in humanitarianism and humanitarian intervention, see Fassin (2007a).

25    This paradox and the claim for open borders has been extensively discussed. See most prominently the contributions of Carens (1987), Cassee (2016), Bauböck (1994), Fine (2013).

figures of helpless victims and their humanitarian counterparts (De Lauri 2019, 149).[26]

Humanitarianism fixes the figure of the victim in time and space, it fixes the single event of a disaster, of a crisis in a timeless, ahistorical and permanent state of humanitarian 'emergencies' that need to be governed. In such a way, the humanitarian border produces its own crises which, however, are but the consequences of specific political decisions and policies that cause the humanitarian crisis in the first place. The governance of mobility, restrictive policies of mobility and regulations such as the Dublin regulation and their consequences produce the permanent state of emergency and humanitarian crisis:

> Humanitarianism creates new geographies with their specific limits, and through its 'humanitarization' of borders—that is, the process through which borders are redefined as spaces of humanitarian crisis and emergency—it has the consequence of obscuring crucial issues of ordinary politics and political action (De Lauri 2019, 150).

The humanitarization of border practices contributes

> to the discursive legitimation and spatial delocalization of exclusionary policies and practices. The conflation of human trafficking (the exploitation of human beings) and 'smuggling', i.e. the services to transport people who are deprived of rights of movement, who just don't have 'legal' access to mobility, is just one example of the 'humanitarization' of borders which is to legitimize policing and the 'war' against so-called traffickers (Friese 2014, 121–126; Webber 2017).

Moreover, humanitarianism contributes to a symbolically and legally subordinate inclusion of migrants in the European space" (Cuttita 2018, 783). In such an asymmetric situation, the victim is at best the passive receiver of aid and care – and in turn is requested to be grateful for the poisoned gift (Moulin 2012) – but is certainly not a political subject, an active fellow citizen allowed to participate and to take a "place in the world which makes opinions significant and actions effective" (Arendt 2017, 387–388). By negating such agency, by reducing the victimized to bare, naked life, humanitarianism enforces (even

---

26    See as well the contributions in De Lauri (2016). For a concise overview, see De Lauri (2020).

with the best intentions), the expulsion of the victims from belonging to a political order – that is, in the sense of Arendt, the right to have rights. In the same vein, the focus on pitiful, innocent victims to be taken care of or to be rescued by white heroes and saviors, obfuscates the historical und political circumstances and postcolonial structures that created the victims of current border regimes in the first place (Friese 2017a, 56–58; Danewid 2017).

As a consequence, "political change is anesthetized in favor of humanitarian goals" (De Lauri 2019, 150). The reduction of the political question of mobility to a 'humanitarian issue' or a permanent 'humanitarian crisis' certainly does not contribute to set a right of free movement on the political agenda and to strengthen the case for open borders, both of which are basically political and not humanitarian claims.

> Once a crisis is qualified in specific terms (that is, as a humanitarian crisis), it directly calls for a specific power to manage and administer it. In opposition to a historical narration that is 'disrupted and episodic' (Gramsci [...]), the humanitarization of borders in crisis is a universal salvific narrative that creates a constant nexus between human suffering and the need for humanitarian exceptionalism. This exceptionalism in managing borders translates into exaggerated security practices and consolidates the hierarchization of borders as something 'natural'—thus normalizing the political and social scrutiny of those who can and those who cannot cross a border (De Lauri 2019, 157).

Mobility challenges the democratic order and the nation state, caught in the paradoxes of democracy it certainly creates spaces of struggle. Whereas on one hand such spaces are generated by the figure of the victim, some strands of activism craft the figure of the hero and imagine mobile people as the autonomous avant-garde of resistance against the global neoliberal capitalist order.[27]

However, current borderlands are sites of activism and active citizenship from the "borders and margins" (Stierl 2016) that allow for shared spaces of civility and the belonging to a political community of citizens, a hospitable welcome of an Other and a political space advocating for less exclusionary politics of mobility and the right to have rights.[28] Therefore, we need to re-

---

27  See Papadopoulos and Tsianos, 2008 and Papadopoulos, Stephenson and Tsianos, 2008. For a critique, see Friese 2017a, 65–72.

28  For an account of negotiating the "right to have rights", see Coddington et al. (2012).

think "the relationship between mobility, rights and status that are so fundamental to concepts of modern citizenship", mobility and mobility rights to rearticulate new forms of citizen subjectivities" (Nyers and Rygiel 2012, 12).

> The Rights of Man become humanitarian rights, that is, the rights of those who cannot enact them, of victims whose rights are totally denied. Nevertheless these rights are not empty; political names and political places never become merely void. The void is always filled by somebody or something else; by becoming the rights of those who cannot enact the Rights of Man do not become null and void. If these rights are not 'truly' those of the victims, they can become the rights of others (Rancière 2010, 72).

What is at stake, is the opening of a political space that moves beyond the asymmetric categorizations of mobile people as victims, enemies or heroes in order to promote politics of hospitality and a "political project of equality" (De Lauri 2019, 160) that allows to enact a political space and multivocal subjectivities. Mobile people demand dignity, the right to mobility, equal treatment, a 'normal' good life with security. They "embody a quest for liberty, rather than for help. They demand rights, rather than permissions" (Albahari 2015b, 2) and ultimately: the right to have rights.[29] What is at stake, therefore, is a European space to come that rejects current necropolitics, the logic of emergency and crisis and the erasure of the rights of others. What is as stake is the objection against the a-political and alleged 'humanitarian' border regimes that enforce and re-iterate the social imagination and the victim-foe distinction.

In July 2020, the Italian public was faced with the photo of a drowned man from Eritrea whose body had been left in the waves of the Mediterranean for weeks (Ziniti 2020).[30] No one had cared to salvage his corpse. Once upon a time, to mourn and to bury the dead was considered to be a distinct human worth, virtue and excellence which separate humankind from the reign of nature and bare life. The notion of 'humanity' derives from 'humare', the Latin

---

29    This holds true especially for asylum-seekers. As Albahari notes "deterrence, intelligence, surveillance, anti-smuggling activities, border enforcement, and policing and readmission collaboration with Turkey, Libya, and Libya's African neighbors […], the right to seek asylum is being de facto transformed into a state-granted permission to seek asylum" (2018, 121).

30    The economy of attention needs even more shocking images. Such images which expose racialized bodies to public view and the consume of the horrendous border spectacle are part of current humanitarianism (Friese 2017a, 49–52).

verb for burying someone.[31] Posting ethics, right and justice against power and the order of the polis, Antigone's protest had been considered as a founding text of European self-understanding and the tensions between ethics, the Law and the laws of the polis.[32] The same tension holds for the absolute *Law* of hospitality – the Law to unconditionally host an Other and the *laws* of the political community which pervert the former, as Jacques Derrida (2000b) insistently remarks.[33]

Given the ongoing distinction between humans and superfluous, racialized 'human waste' to be left to die – and to be exposed as corpses – or to be amassed in the nowhere of camps, ethics and justice have become denigrating concepts, the target of hate or at best the naïve 'hyper-moral'. 'Moral terror' is set against political 'realism' and the alleged welfare of the 'We' of the nation. In such a vein, right and justice are expelled from the political, as well as ethics is separated from the political, however: the former engages the latter. In this sense, the drowned man is not a victim but a subject whose demand to hospitality, whose right to have rights have been negated. Again: "to banish the stranger is to banish the community, and you banish yourself from the community thereby" (Lyotard 1993:136). We live in dark times.

## References

Agamben, Giorgio. 1996. *Mezzi senza fine. Note sulla politica*. Torino: Boringhieri.

Agamben, Giorgio. 1998. *Homo Sacer: Sovereign Power and Bare Life* (tr. Daniel Heller Roazen). Stanford: Stanford University Press [orig]. *Homo sacer: Il potere sovrano e la nuda vita*. Torino: Einaudi, 1995.

Albahari, Maurizio. 2015a. *Crimes of Peace: Mediterranean Migrations at the World's Deadliest Border*. Philadelphia: University of Pennsylvania Press.

Albahari, Maurizio. 2015b. "Europe's Refugee Crisis." *Anthropology Today, No.* 31, 5: 1–2. ULR: https://doi.org/10.1111/1467-8322.12196.

Albahari, Maurizio. 2018. "From Right to Permission: Asylum, Mediterranean Migrations, and Europe's War on Smuggling." *Journal on Migration and Human Security* 6, no. 2: 121–130. DOI: 10.1177/2331502418767088.

---

31    I would like to thank Sabine Bauer-Amin for drawing my attention to this relation.

32    For a reading of Hegel's reading of Antigone, see Derrida (1990, 166–90).

33    The difference, the gap, the abyss between the absolute, unconditional Law of hospitality and the laws of the political community is marked by the capital/lower case.

Arendt, Hannah. 1949a. "Es gibt nur ein einziges Menschenrecht." *Die Wandlung* 4:754–770. (www.hannaharendt.net/index.php/han/article/viewFile /154/273, 10.01.2017). Engl. The rights of man; what are they? *Modern Review* 1949, summer: 24–37.

Arendt, Hannah. 1949b. "The Rights of Man; What are they?" *Modern Review* 1949, summer: 24–37.

Arendt, Hannah. 1994 [1942]. "We Refugees." In *Altogether Elsewhere. Writers on Exile*, edited by Marc Robinson, 110–119. Boston/London: Faber & Faber.

Arendt, Hannah. 1998. *Elemente und Ursprünge totaler Herrschaft. Antisemitismus, Imperialismus, totale Herrschaft* (6. Aufl.). München: Piper.

Arendt, Hannah. 2006 [1963]. Nationalstaat und Demokratie. *Hannah Arendt.Net. Zeitschrift für politisches Denken*, No. 1, 2 (http://www.hannaha rendt.net/index.php/han/article/view/94/154, 06.08.2018).

Arendt, Hannah. 2017 [1951]. *The Origins of Totalitarianism*. London: Penguin.

Balfour, Ian, and Eduardo Cadova, eds. 2004. Special Issue: And Justice for All? The Claims of Human Rights. *The South Atlantic Quarterly*, 103, no. 2/3.

Balibar, Étienne. 2001. "Outlines of a Topography of Cruelty: Citizenship and Civility in the Era of Global Violence." *Constellations* No. 8, 1: 15–29.

Balibar, Étienne. 2007. "(De)Constructing the Human as Human Institution: A Reflection on the Coherence of Hannah Arendt's Practical Philosophy." *Social Research* 74, no. 3: 727–38.

Balibar, Étienne. 2009. "Violence and Civility. On the Limits of Political Anthropology (tr. Stephanie Bundy)." *Differences. A Journal of Feminist Cultural Studies* 20, no. 2/3: 9–35. DOI: 10.1215/10407391-2009-002.

Bauböck, Rainer. 1994. *Transnational Citizenship: Membership and Rights in International Migration*. Aldershot: Edward Elgar.

Bauman, Zygmunt. 2007. *Liquid Times. Living in an Age of Uncertainty*. Cambridge: Polity.

Benhabib, Seyla. 2004. *The Rights of Others: Aliens, Residents and Citizens*. Cambridge: Cambridge University Press.

Benthall, Jonathan. 2018. "Humanitarianism as Ideology and Practice." In *The International Encyclopedia of Anthropology*, edited by Hillary Callan, London: John Wiley & Sons, DOI: 10.1002/9781118924396.wbiea2089. Available online: https://onlinelibrary.wiley.com/doi/full/10.1002/978111892439 6.wbiea2089 [accessed 10.12.2021].

Betts, Alexander. 2010. "The Refugee Regime Complex." *Refugee Survey Quarterly* 29, no. 1: 12–37. URL: https://doi.org/10.1093/rsq/hdq009.

Brown, Wendy. 2010. *Walled States, Waning Sovereignty*. New York: Zone Book.

Carens, Joseph H. 1987. "Aliens and Citizens: The Case for Open Borders." *Review of Politics* 49, no. 2: 251–273.

Cassee, Andreas. 2016. *Globale Bewegungsfreiheit. Ein philosophisches Plädoyer für offene Grenzen*. Berlin: Suhrkamp.

Castoriadis, Cornelius. 1997 [1983]. The Greek *Polis* and the Creation of Democracy. *The Castoriadis Reader* (trans. D. Ames Curtis), 267–289. Oxford: Blackwell Publishers.

Castoriadis, Cornelius. 1987. *The Imaginary Institution of Society*. Cambridge, MA: Polity.

Coddington, Kate, Catania, Tina R., Loyd, Jenna, Mitchell-Eaton, Emily, and Alison Mountz, Alison. 2012. "Embodied Possibilities, Sovereign Geographies and Island Detention. Negotiating the 'Right to Have Rights' on Guam, Lampedusa and Christmas Island." *Shima: The International Journal of Research into Island Cultures* 6, no. 2: 27–48.

Cuttitta, Paolo. 2018. "Delocalization, Humanitarianism and Human Rights: The Mediterranean Border Between Exclusion and Inclusion." *Antipode: A Radical Journal of Geography* 50, no. 3: 783–803. URL: https://doi.org/10.111 1/anti.12337.

Cuttita, Paolo, and Tamara Last, eds. 2020. *Border Deaths. Causes, Dynamics and Consequences of Migration-Related Mortality*. Amsterdam: Amsterdam University Press.

Dadusc, Deanna, and Pierpaolo Mudu. 2020. "Care without Control: The Humanitarian Industrial Complex and the Criminalisation of Solidarity (manuscript)." *Geopolitics*, URL: https://doi.org/10.1080/14650045.2020.17 49839.

Danewid, Ida. 2017. "White Innocence in the Black Mediterranean: Hospitality and the Erasure of History." *Third World Quarterly*, 38, no. 7: 1674–1689. DOI: http://dx.doi.org/10.1080/01436597.2017.1331123.

De Genova, Nicholas. 2013. "Spectacles of Migrant 'Illegality': The Scene of Exclusion, the Obscene of Inclusion." *Ethnic and Racial Studies* 36, no. 7: 1180–1198. DOI: 10.1080/01419870.2013.783710.

De Lauri, Antonio. 2019. "Humanitarianism and Borders. A Critique of the Humanitarian (B)order of Things." *Journal of Identity and Migration Studies* 13, no. 2: 148–166.

De Lauri, Antonio, editor. 2016. *Humanitarianism. Power, Ideology and Aid*. London/New York: I.B. Tauris.

De Lauri, Antonio, editor. 2020. *Humanitarianism. Keywords*. Leiden/Boston: Brill.

Derrida, Jacques. 1990. *Glas* (tr. John P. Leavey and Richard Rand). Lincoln/ London: University of Nebraska Press (orig. *Glas*. Paris: Galilée, 1974).

Derrida, Jacques. 2000a. "Hostipitality." *Angelaki. Journal of the Theoretical Humanities*, No. 5, 3: 3–18. DOI: https://doi.org/10.1080/09697250020034706

Derrida, Jacques. 2000b. "Of Hospitality. Anne Dufourmantelle Invites Jacques Derrida to Respond." (tr. Rachel Bowlby). Stanford: Stanford University Press.

Dubreuil, Laurent, and Clarissa Eagle Clarissa. 2006. "Leaving Politics: Bios, Zōē, Life." *Diacritics*, "Bios", Immunity, Life: The Thought of Roberto Esposito 36, no. 2: 83–98. URL: http://www.jstor.com/stable/20204128.

Fassin, Didier. 2007a. "Humanitarianism as a Politics of Life. " *Public Culture*, No. 19, 3: 499–520. DOI: 10.1215/08992363-2007-007.

Fassin, Didier. 2007b. Humanitarianism: A Nongovernmental Government." In *Nongovernmental Politics*, edited by Michel Feher, 149–160. New York: Zone Books.

Fassin, Didier. 2011. *Humanitarian Reason: A Moral History of the Present*. Berkeley: University of California Press.

Fassin, Didier. 2013. "The Predicament of Humanitarianism." *Qui Parle*, Special Issue: Human Rights between Past and Future 22, no. 1: 33–48.

Fine, Sarah. 2013. "The Ethics of Immigration: Self-Determination and the Right to Exclude." *Philosophy Compass* 8, no. 3: 254–268. DOI 10.1111/phc3.12019.

Foucault, Michel. 2001. *In Verteidigung der Gesellschaft. Vorlesungen am Collège de France (1975-76)* (tr. Michaela Ott). Frankfurt am Main: Suhrkamp [orig. *Il faut défendre la societé*, Paris: Seuil/Gallimard, 1996].

Foucault, Michel. 2002 [1984]. "Confronting Governments: Human Rights." In *Michel Foucault. Power. Essential Works of Foucault*, Vol. 3 (1954-1984), edited by James D. Faubion, 474–475. London: Penguin.

Foucault, Michel. 2003. *Society Must be Defended. Lecture Series at the Collège de France, 1975-76* (tr. D. Macey). New York: Picador.

Friese, Heidrun. 2012. "Border Economies. Lampedusa and the Nascent Migration Industry". *Shima: The International Journal of Research Into Island Cultures*, Special issue on detention islands (edited by Alison Mountz and Linda Briskman) 6, no. 2: 66–84.

Friese, Heidrun. 2017a. *Flüchtlinge: Opfer – Bedrohung – Helden. Zur politischen Imagination des Fremden*. Bielefeld: transcript.

Friese, Heidrun 2017b. "Representations of Gendered Mobility and the Tragic Border-Regime in the Mediterranean." Special Issue Women in the Mediterranean, *Journal of Balkan and Near Eastern Studies* 19, no. 5: 541–556. DOI 10 .1080/19448953.2017.1296260.

Friese, Heidrun. 2019a. "Framing Mobility. Refugees and the Social Imagination." In *Die lange Dauer der Flucht – Analysen aus Wisssenschaft und Praxis.* Edited by Josef Kohlbacher and Maria Six-Hohenbalken, 45–62. Wien: Verlag der österreichischen Akademie der Wissenschaften. DOI 10.1553/3520-3533.

Friese, Heidrun. 2019b. "Mobilität, Grenzen und das Paradox der Demokratie." In *Konfliktfeld Fluchtmigration. Historische und ethnographische Perspektiven,* edited by Reinhard Johler and Jan Lange, 83–103. Bielefeld: transcript

Hamacher, Werner. 2014. "On the Right to Have Rights: Human Rights; Marx and Arendt (tr. Ronald Mendoza-de Jesús)." *The New Centennial Review* (Law and Violence) 14, no. 2: 169–214.

Ingram, James D. 2008. "What is a 'Right to Have Rights'? Three Images of the Politics of Human Rights." *American Political Science Review* 102, no. 4: 401–416. URL: https://www.jstor.org/stable/27644535.

Isin, Engin F.. 2009a. "Citizenship in Flux: The Figure of the Activist Citizen." *Subjectivity,* 29: 367–88. DOI:10.1057/SUB.2009.25.

Isin, Engin F.. 2009b. "Two Regimes of Rights? ECPR Workshop. Practices of citizenship and the politics of (in)security. Lisbon, 14-17 April 2009." Published in *Citizenship and Security: the Constitution of Political Being,* edited by Xavier Guillaume and Jef Huysmans 2013. London: Routledge, 53–74. URL: https://doi.org/10.4324/9780203361931.

Isin, Engin F., and Kim Rygiel. 2007. "Abject Spaces: Frontiers, Zones, Camps." *The Logics of Biopower and the War on Terror: Living, Dying, Surviving,* edited by Elizabeth Dauphinee and Cristina Master, 181–203. Houndmills, Basingstoke: Palgrave. DOI: 10.1007/978-1-137-04379-5_9.

Lyotard, Jean François. 1993. "The Other's Rights." In *On Human Rights – The Oxford Amnesty Lectures,* edited by Stephen Shute and Susan Hurley, 135–147. New York: Basic Books.

Martinsen, Franziska. 2019. *Grenzen der Menschenrechte. Staatsbürgerschaft, Zugehörigkeit, Partizipation.* Bielefeld: transcript.

Mavelli, Luca. 2017. "Governing Populations Through the Humanitarian Government of Refugees: Biopolitical Care and Racism in the European Refugee Crisis." *Review of International Studies* 43, no. 5: 809–832. DOI:10.1017/S0260210517000110.

Mbembe, Achille. 2003. "Necropolitics. " (tr. Libby Meintjes). *Public Culture* 15, no. 1: 11–40.

Mbembe, Achille. 2019. *Necropolitics* (tr. Steven Corcoran). Durham/London: Duke (orig. *Politiques de l'inimitié*. Paris: La Dévouverte, 2016).

Menke, Christoph. 2016. "Zurück zu Hannah Arendt – die Flüchtlinge und die Krise der Menschenrechte. " *Merkur* 70 (volltext.merkur-zeitschrift.de, 26.12.2016).

Mouffe, Chantal. 2000. *The Democratic Paradox*. London/New York: Verso.

Moulin, Carolina. 2012. "Ungrateful Subjects? Refugee Protests and the Logic of Gratitude. " In *Citizenship, Migrant Activism and the Politics of Movement*, edited by Peter Nyers and Kim Rygiel, 54–72. London/New York: Routledge.

Nyers, Peter, and Kim Rygiel, eds.. 2012. *Citizenship, Migrant Activism and the Politics of Movement*. London/New York: Routledge.

Papadopoulos, Dimitris, and Vassilis Tsianos. 2008. "Die Autonomie der Migration. Die Tiere der undokumentierten Mobilität." *Translate* (http://translate.eipcp.net/strands/02/papadopoulostsianos-strands01 en?lid=papadopoulostsianos-strands01de, 22.08.2013)

Papadopoulos, Dimitris, Stephenson, Niamh, and Vassilis Tsianos. 2008. *Escape Routes. Control and Subversion in the 21th Century*. London/Ann Arbor: Pluto Press.

Rancière, Jacques 2010. "Who Is the Subject of the Rights of Man?" In *Dissensus*, edited and translated Steven Corcoran, 62–75. London/New York: Continuum.

Rancière, Jacques. 2014. *Das Unvernehmen. Politik und Philosophie*. Frankfurt am Main: Suhrkamp.

Rathore, Aakash Singh, and Alex Cistelecan, eds.. 2011. *Wronging Rights? Philosophical Challenges for Human Rights*. London: Routledge.

Redfield, Peter 2012. "Humanitarianism." In *A Companion to Moral Anthropology*, edited by Didier Fassin, 451–467. Chichester: John Wiley & Son,

Rygiel, Kim. 2016. "Dying to Live: Migrant Deaths and Citizenship Politics Along European Borders: Transgressions, Disruptions, and Mobilizations." *Citizenship Studies*, special issue The Contentious Politics of Refugee and Migrant Protest and Solidarity Movements: Remaking Citizenship from the Margins) 20, no. 5: 545–560. https://doi.org/10.1080/13621025. 2016.1182682.

Schaap, Andrew. 2011. "Enacting the Right to have Rights: Jacques Rancière's Critique of Hannah Arendt." *European Journal of Political Theory* 10, no. 1: 22–45. DOI: 10.1177/1474885110386004.

Stierl, Maurice. 2016. "A Sea of Struggle – Activist Border Interventions in the Mediterranean Sea." *Citizenship Studies*, special issue The Contentious Politics of Refugee and Migrant Protest and Solidarity Movements: Remaking Citizenship from the Margins 20, no. 5: 561–578. https://doi.org/10.1080/13621025.2016.1182683.

Stierl, Maurice. 2018. "A Fleet of Mediterranean Border Humanitarians." *Antipode: A Radical Journal of Geography* 50, no. 3: 704–724. URL: https://doi.org/10.1111/anti.12320.

Topac, Özgün E.. 2019. "Humanitarian and Human Rights Surveillance: The Challenge to Border Surveillance and Invisibility?" *Surveillance & Society* 17, no. 3/4: 382–404.

Walters, William. 2011. "Foucault and Frontiers: Notes on the Birth of the Humanitarian Border." In *Governmentality: Current Issues and Future Challenges*, edited by Ulrich Bröckling, Susanne Krasmann and Thomas Lemke, 138–164. New York: Routledge.

Webber, Frances. 2017. "The Legal Framework: When Law and Morality Collide." In *Humanitarianism: the Unacceptable Face of Solidarity*, edited by Liz Fekete and Frances Webber, 7–21. London: The Institute of Race Relations.

Williams, Jill M.. 2015. "From Humanitarian Exceptionalism to Contingent Care: Care and Enforcement at the Humanitarian Border." *Political Geography* 47: 11–20. URL: http://dx.doi.org/10.1016/j.polgeo.2015.01.001.

Ziniti, Alessandra. 2020. "Quell'uomo in mare che nessuno ha voluto salvare." *La Repubblica*, 16.07.2020, 10 (https://rep.repubblica.it/pwa/generale/2020/07/15/news/a_testa_sotto_-262048811/, 19.09.2020).

# Mobility as a Political Act[1]

*Alessandro Monsutti*

Thomas Faist builds on his past endeavour (see, for instance, Faist 2008) to consider the relevance of migration to reflect about today's world. He develops his argument on a series of paradoxes. While the world forms a "moral polity" where most sovereign nation-states subscribe to some shared fundamental principles of human rights, the existing international refugee regime is failing to fulfil its mandate in favour of people in search of protection. People labelled as refugees rely on their own strategies to cope with hardship (Monsutti 2008). The international organizational and political structure as we know it has proven unprepared to face a situation that remains quantitatively limited, if we consider that in 2015 – widely depicted as a year of unprecedented migration crisis – the number of people who applied for asylum in the European Union corresponded to approximately 0.25 per cent of the total population of the host countries. There is a discrepancy between formal rights and actual access to these rights. On the one hand, the countries with the highest number of refugees are not party to the 1951 Convention or the 1967 Protocol; on the other hand, the countries that have ratified international texts relating to refugees develop restrictive policies for granting a legal status of protection. Then, the liberal paradox – as labelled by James Hollifield – con-sists of a tension between national interests and the respects of universal rights. Finally, the welfare paradox expresses a tension between the social rights of citizens and the deregulation of the labour market progressively eroding the living conditions of the same people.

In such a situation, Thomas Faist asks how can we analyse the prominence that migration issues have acquired in European and North American political discourses and public perceptions? How can we understand and counter the

---

1   First published as: Monsutti, Alessandro. 2018. "Mobility as a political act", *Ethnic and Racial Studies*, 41:3, 448-455, DOI: 10.1080/01419870.2018.1388421.

current trend of rejection and exclusion towards migrants? If we consider the so-called European migration crisis of 2015, how can we explain that some of the better-off segments of the world's population feel threatened by a handful of asylum seekers? Ultimately, how can we make sense that the "feeling of being 'under siege' has become increasingly pervasive in the contemporary Western world"? (Hage 2016, 38).

One generation after the collapse of the Soviet Union, the wave of optimism that might have prevailed in the 1990s is now behind us. The uncertain future of the European Union, the strengthening across Western countries of right-wing and xenophobic movements reaffirming national sovereignty over any alternative forms of political organization, the incapacity of the United Nations and the international community to bring peace to places such as Syria, Iraq or Afghanistan are only symptoms that people are not mobilized anymore by grand narratives of progress and global peace. In that sense, we live in a post-post Cold War world.

Every January, Oxfam publishes a report on the world's economy. The respected nongovernmental organization documents year after year the growing inequality that characterizes our global world. Since 2015, the richest one per cent has owned more wealth than the rest of humanity. According to the most recent estimates, just eight individuals own the same wealth as the poorest half of the world (Oxfam 2017). The Panama Papers, leaked in 2015, converge in showing the massive concentration of financial resources in the hands of few people. According to the economist Gabriel Zucman, eight per cent of the world's wealth – corresponding to 7.6 trillion dollars – is held in accounts located in tax havens; the loss in global tax revenues can be estimated at 200 billion dollars per year (2015, 35, 47). Economic growth benefits the richest, while the rest of our world's society – especially the poorest but also the middle class – suffers. In spite of the wishful thinking of the Millennium Development Goals, our world is the most unequal ever in human history. And the disparities are becoming more and more visible at global but also national levels.

Besides the series of conflicts that are shaking the Middle East but also Africa, the current migration flows can be understood more broadly within this "inequalscape", to play with the categories proposed by Arjun Appadurai in the 1990s. In front of such ever increasing – and ever more rapidly increasing – inequalities, one may wonder how the balance of power inherited from the colonization and decolonization processes can be maintained for long. Shouldn't we assume that we are only witnessing the prelude of more massive population displacements? Shouldn't we expect that the major mi-gration waves have not really begun yet? Shouldn't we look for new utopia and drastically change our vision of humanity's future? If we limit our-selves to the field of migration, shouldn't we rethink a conceptual and policy frame-work (starting by questioning the distinction between economic migrant and forced migrant and recognizing that a rights-based approach to development and migration is incomplete) that has proven inadequate to understand and operate with what might retrospectively appear as a very modest movement of people?

Even if we should be wary of mainstream discourses according to which we are "in an era of unprecedented human mobility, with more people on the move now than at any other time in recorded history," as repeated by stake-holders such as William Lacy Swing (2013), Director General of the Interna-tional Organization for Migration (for a historical contextualization showing that the figures are far from being so clear, see Hoerder 2002 and McKeown 2004), it is difficult to disagree with Thomas Faist when he asserts the pro-found relevance of migration to think about the world in which we live. I consider here as a working hypothesis that mobility, beyond any dichotomy between voluntary and forced migration, must be situated in this global land-scape of exclusion, that mobility can be seen as a form of moral protest and a political act, or at least as an act with wide-ranging political dimensions and effects. In that sense, beyond any label, mobile people represent a testimony of the immorality of our global moral polity.

I illustrate this point with three vignettes from my ethnographic wander-ing among Afghans from the island of Lesbos, the port of entry in Europe for many of them, to Friuli, on the north-eastern border of Italy, and finally the (in)famous jungle of Calais, where many asylum seekers ended up in very pre-carious living conditions.

Wednesday 28 January 2015, I visit the Screening Centre run by the Greek authorities near Mytilene, the main town of the island of Lesbos. I am con-ducting a research commissioned by UNHCR on the protection situation of Afghan refugees and asylum-seekers in various European countries (Donini, Monsutti, and Scalettaris 2016). The local representative of the UN agency for refugees introduces me to the local police chief. This middle-aged man looks disenchanted but not unconcerned by the plight of the people landing on the shores of his country. He seems almost content to let me discover the dreary working conditions of his team and the absurdity of the situation. I pass the brand new Reception Centre financed by the European Union. It is not in use

... "No staff!" comments soberly my guide, "EU pays only for infra-structures, not salaries." I get access to the adjacent site where Iraqis, Afghans and others are packed behind barbed wire fences. I talk first to the young female physician who is in charge of the small team of Médecins du Monde running the dispensary. She joyfully proclaims: "At least, here they are safe!" I look around and find difficult to share her happy mood. I am then approached by a group of Iraqi Kurds. As I do not have access to their living quarters, they ask to borrow my smart phone to take some photo-graphs, insisting that I need to be aware of their accommodation conditions. They come back with a series of images that are just appalling: wrecked mat-tresses, bathroom sinks severed from the walls, blocked toilets and broken pipes ... As I am asking if there are any people from Afghanistan, two young men approach me. Dressed with training suits, a scarf tied around their necks, they are covered with mud, drenched and cold. At first coy, they do not stop talking once they get started. Reza and Mahdi are Hazaras originating from Central Afghanistan, where I spent time in the past, but they grew up in Iran. They crossed the sea at night and just landed on Lesbos the same morning. They tell about the vexations suffered during their youth in exile, their lack of trust in the political and economic future of Afghanistan, and their feeling of being invested by their families with the crucial social mission to succeed, get a legal status somewhere, in Germany or Sweden, and then found a family with a girl from their village. They keep repeating, as if to convince themselves: "It is not Europe here, it could not be Europe!" Thomas Faist talks about the cognitive dissonance among peoples in Europe to describe the tension between knowledge and action. These two young men also experience discrepancy between their hope and what they face. More than disappointed, they seem surprised. They expected something else from Europe and their first reaction is a protective denial ... they have not reached the heart of Europe yet.

Summer 2015, I spend some time in Tarcento, my father's village of origin, in Friuli, northeast of Italy. I am surprised to see that two small local hotels are filled up with more than forty Afghan asylum seekers. Having got acquainted with them, I invite on the 8th of August Akmal, from Kandahar, Gul Agha, from Wardak, and Mahmud, from Nangarhar to accompany me with my two children aged 10 and 8 to a concert in Stella, an abandoned hamlet up the mountain. On the way, I talk about local history, the conflicts of the past, the migration of many Friulians around the world, the 1976 earthquake, the American reconstruction aid during the Cold War. The road climbs the slopes in tight turns, the view opens on the vast plain. "On a clear day, you can see the sea in the distance!" Gul Agha sighs, he would so much like to go to the beach, listen to the sound of the waves and watch the endless horizon. Akmal abruptly interrupts him: "The sea? I saw enough of it when I was in Turkey!" Mahmud, nestled in the trunk, remains silent. Gul Agha and Akmal are more talkative. They marvel at the landscape: "What a beautiful place, so green!" They are bewildered by the abandoned cherry orchards, by so much land left unexploited. They laugh without real joy: "They should bring us here rather than in hotels where we are left to languish. We know how to take care of fruit trees." Arrived at Stella, many acquaintances greet me. But no one pays attention to my companions, nobody welcomes them, nobody expresses interest in exchanging a few words with them. We eat chicken legs, polenta and beans. Akmal is lost in his thoughts. He looks at my son with tenderness. He finally takes him on his knees, hugs him gently in his arms and then starts talking about the family he left behind in Afghanistan. I bring the three companions back to their hotel. Standing at the entrance to the terrace, two carabinieri peacefully con-verse with guests. Akmal jumps out of the trunk of my car. A part of me wants the men in uniform to approach me, question me about my overloaded vehicle, my ties with these Afghans ... but they only glance at us, indifferent. As in Stella, my new Afghan friends are invisible. Akmal thanks me with an energetic but quick accolade: "You do not behave like the people here ... you are like an Afghan." Solidarity, hospitality and a sense of honour are values that he hardly noticed among the Europeans he met along the road of the Balkans and in Italy. He fled a conflict that is not his anymore, an armed combat between a government from which he does not receive much benefit and an insurgency that is now divided and increasingly brutal; he was hoping for better living conditions. But his experience of the West was not that of humanistic benevolence. He is beyond the initial denial of Reza and Mahdi in Lesbos. He dares an ethical judgment: European people do not behave properly; Afghans have higher moral standards.

Friday 13 November 2015, I am in Calais, in the North of France, to visit the so-called jungle. It is late afternoon when I arrive on the site, east of the town. It is already dark; the wind is blowing hard. After moving past a few vehicles of the riot control forces of the French National Police, I notice a group of men, Sudanese from Darfur, lining up behind a white van. A retired couple distributes loaves of bread. We exchange a few words. They cooperate with a local association and have been helping refugees and asylum seekers for fifteen years. "Where may I find Afghans?" do I ask. "Do not go there, they might be aggressive?" answers the elderly man.

In the previous days, asylum seekers and human rights activists have pro-tested against the precarious living conditions. Indeed the jungle is presented in the media as an informal settlement where hardly any service is available, where up to 5,000 people from Afghanistan, Iraq, Syria, Eritrea or Sudan con-verge in the hope to cross the Channel and set foot on British soil. Is it a place of exception, where the rule of law is suspended, where the state's involvement does not go beyond containment?

I pass some mobile toilets and walk on the muddy path between the tents and the makeshift shelters. I reach an Eritrean-Ethiopian church made of tarpaulins nailed on wooden frames and then some shops: a tandoor, sev-eral grocery stores and restaurants. Most shopkeepers appear to be Afghans. I stand in a queue to buy some bread and take the opportunity to start a con-versation. Beside Kurdish and Arab speaking patrons from Iraq or Syria, the Afghans are mostly Pashtuns from the South and East. In a gesture of hospi-tality, the baker does not want at first to take money from me. I have to insist. Even in this space of supposed social vacuum, the sense of pride and honour is not lost.

In the same evening, a series of coordinated terrorist attacks occurred in Paris. Suspicion falls immediately on Islamic militant groups. On the next day, all the conversations turned around the potential policy consequences on the asylum seekers and refugees, many of whom are Muslims. A fire broke out in the jungle during the night and many wonder if it was an act of retali-ation by some far right groups. I go to a restaurant that I quickly visited the previous night. Three partners run it; they are Pashto speakers from different provinces of Afghanistan. More than by geographical origin or tribal affili-ation, they are united by a common experience of long-term mobility. One of them, Ehsanullah, spent seven years in England but has circulated widely in other European countries. He spontaneously shows me an Italian identity card for foreigners, which allows him to travel legally within the Schengen Area. "How is it that you stay here, in the jungle, and do not try your chance in a more welcoming setting?", I ask. "Here, that's true, I sleep under a tent, it is cold and windy. But I run my own business, I can make some money. One day, hopefully, I will be able to save enough and bring my family." His tone is half playful, half afflicted. The quest for autonomy comes with a cost. His goal is not to go to England and settle there; not yet at least. He inhabits mobility. A place such as the jungle offers to people like him an economic niche. It cannot be solely depicted as a dead end for migrants; it is a microcosm, a site where people on the move reinvent social relations. Many come here knowing that they will be among people with whom they share the experience of displacement, knowing that they will be able to collect information on the migration routes and the ever-changing asylum regimes of EU countries.

Lesbos, Friuli, Calais, three sites on a long journey from uncertain presents towards uncertain futures, a journey without final destination. These three vignettes also illustrate the moral journey undertaken by the people I met, from the initial defensive denial of Reza and Mahdi that could not admit that Europe was mistreating people like them, to the negative ethical judgment of Akmal against Europeans, and then Ehsanullah's loss of faith in Europe and subsequent entrepreneurial effort on the fringe of the surrounding society. We paradoxically reach a form of cosmopolitanism from bellow, what the Italian philosopher Paolo Virno has called "engaged withdrawal" (2004): an exodus defined as defection from the state, an act of resistance towards established power. It is not a new positioning if we refer to James Scott's description of "the art of not being governed" (2009). Reza, Mahdi, Akmal and Ehsanullah have experienced in their bodies the global landscape of exclusion I mentioned at the beginning of this paper. All of them fled violence or injustice; all of them aspire to a better life. More than putting them under a label, that of migrant in search of employment or refugee in need of protection, I see them as living witnesses of the growing unequal world in which we live.

In this brief paper, I take inspiration from Thomas Faist's invitation to bring together various scholarly traditions and think outside the existing boxes. Considering that we live in a post-post Cold War world, seemingly the most unequal ever in human history, I suggest that it is time to reexamine our conceptual framework of human mobility, cross-dress forced migration and find a way to reveal the human cost of existing dichotomous categories. The massive arrival in Europe of Syrians, Afghans, Iraqis, Eritreans, Sub-Saharan Africans do not only result from a series of regional conflicts or an individual quest for labour. The people knocking at the door of Europe tell something that needs to be listened to, they tell their moral fatigue towards the growing gap between the wealthiest and poorest segments of humanity. They are active participants in the global moral polity in showing how immoral it is. Their mobility represents a protest against the global distribution of wealth and security, as well as a subversion of classical forms of political territoriality. As such, it can be conceived – through its structural consequences more than individual intentions – as a political act.

## References

Donini, Antonio, Alessandro Monsutti, and Giulia Scalettaris. 2016. *Afghans on the Move: Seeking Protection and Refuge in Europe.* (Global Migration Research Paper No. 17). Geneva: The Graduate Institute

Faist, Thomas. 2008. "Migrants as Transnational Development Agents: An Inquiry into the Newest Round of the Migration–Development Nexus." *Population, Space and Place* 14: 21–42.

Hage, Ghassan. 2016. "État de Siège: A Dying Domesticating Colonialism?" *American Ethnologist* 43, no. 1: 38–49.

Hoerder, Dirk. 2002. *Culture in Contact: World Migrations in the Second Millenium.* Durham: Duke University Press.

McKeown, Adam. 2004. "Global Migration, 1846–1940." *Journal of World History* 15, no. 2 :155–189.

Monsutti, Alessandro. 2008. "Afghan Migratory Strategies and the Three Solutions to the Refugee Problem." *Refugee Survey Quarterly* 27, no. 1: 58–73.

Oxfam. 2017. *An Economy for the 99%.* Oxford: Oxfam International (Oxfam Briefing Paper).

Scott, James C. 2009. *The Art of Not Being Governed: An Anarchist History of Upland Southeast Asia.* New Haven: Yale University Press.

Swing, William Lacy. 2013. *Statement.* New York: International Organization for Migration (11th Coordination Meeting on International Migration).

Virno, Paolo. 2004. *Virtuosity and Revolution.* Accessed June 9, 2017. http://www.generation-online.org/c/fcmultitude2.html, 2004.

Zucman, Gabriel. 2015. *The Hidden Wealth of Nations: The Scourge of Tax Heavens.* Chicago: University of Chicago.

# Palestinian Diaspora or Exile? Affective and Experiential Dimensions of (Im)mobility

*Leonardo Schiocchet*

## Introduction

I have a confession to make: I regret having used the term diaspora in an edited volume I published in Portuguese, entitled *Between the Old and the New Worlds: The Palestinian Diaspora from the Middle East to Latin America* (2015). This chapter explains why and how the use of the term at large, and my regret in particular, are tied to questions about refugee regimes and refugee agency.

In refugee studies, "the refugee regime" is very often expressed in singular. This usage implies the terms "global/international" and "legal", which in turn means that "the regime" has been analyzed as a complex but single institution, or as a multi-level structure (Betts 2010; Kleist 2018). However, actual situations of flight and the intrinsically interwoven multipolar regulations and restrictions on human (im)mobility suggest that "the refugee regime" is in fact a much more complex meshwork of social relations and political principles, but also moral imperatives, dispositions, and experiences replete with affect. With this in mind, This chapter draws on the emerging literature on "regime complexity", referring to "the way in which two or more institutions intersect in terms of their scope and purpose" (Betts 2010, 20 and 35) and offers a more nuanced approach to the study of what I prefer to call "refugee regimes", in plural, including but not limited to: the United Nations; the Geneva Convention and its amendments; Nation states' forced migration policies; the humanitarian intervention at large, including NGOs. In sum, refugee regimes are sets of norms, rules, principles, and decision-making procedures – what I call instruments (deliberate) or more broadly mechanisms (both deliberate and unintentional) – to regulate refugees.

The argument above suggests that we must problematize how even the academic discussion on refugee regimes may be embedded in, and often unintentionally may help to reinforce, mechanisms of refugee control (see for example Cabot 2019; Szanton 2004). As part of such considerations, this chapter discusses the academic mobilization of the term "diaspora" to characterize the Palestinian exile. To achieve this goal, it first considers the Palestinian global dispersal and social belonging subjectivity as a background for a debate around conceptualizations of the term "diaspora". These two parts then inform a discussion on how fitting this term is for the Palestinian case, and what it may leave out of the picture.

*

Many Palestinian and non-Palestinian authors working on Palestinian displacement stand by the use of the term "diaspora", and their reasoning is not easily dismissed (see, for example, Doraï 2002; Lindholm Schulz 2003; Shiblak 2005; Hanafi 2005, 2003; Khalidi 2010; Zaidan 2012; Suleiman 2016). Finding myself among such fine authors in itself is a statement that this chapter is not a tribunal for condemnation, but an invitation to academic reflection.

I used the term diaspora in *Between the Old and the New Worlds* because the book drew significantly on case studies of Palestinians who for the most part had migrated to Latin America in the beginning of the Twentieth Century, and therefore before the first mass displacement of Palestinian refugees in 1948. These established migrants, some of third of even fourth generation, often employ the term diaspora themselves to express how they connect home country to homeland. Their migration narratives partially overlap with those of much larger Lebanese and Syrian communities in Latin America, who dominate the Arab milieu of a whole genre which we can provisionally call here "migrant literature". This literature is mostly written by migrants and for migrants, and is characterised by two interlocked tropes: longing for the homeland and a rhetoric of what Sonia Hamid (2015), in her chapter in *Between the Old and New World*, aptly called a "pedagogy of social ascension". Pedagogy of social ascension refers to the narrative that migrants, in this case, Arabs, migrated to Latin America decades ago without anything. In having to fend for their lives, they became very successful owing to their own tireless efforts and strong moral character, all while playing a central role in the nation-building processes in that continent. Having grown up looking at large-sized, easy-to-read table-top books with fantastic photos of their homelands, and hearing about the heroic feats of heroes from their home country and homeland, these established generations of migrants typically celebrate a continuum between nation of origin and nation of residence, while eschewing other groups that take their place in the host nation and nation of origin for granted.[1] It is also important to note, however, that some authors (myself, as well as Rosemary Sayigh, Ilana Feldman, Anaheed Al-Hardan[2] and Amanda Dias) in that book used the term diaspora also when referring to Palestinians outside of Latin America, mostly as an umbrella term within which more precise variations relating to different contexts of (im)mobility could fit. The general principle behind the use of the term then, I think, was trying to account at once for the experiences and expressions of Palestinian who had largely migrated to Latin America before 1948 and those of Palestinians living as refugees in the Middle East. While I cannot speak for others, it seems reasonable to me to suppose that the contemporary catch-all definition of the term diaspora seemed promising in that regard to many authors besides myself.

Today, however, I have come to agree overall with Julie Peteet's (2007) more cautious assessment of the use of the term diaspora for the Palestinian case, apart from a few considerations. First, unlike her, I do not claim that the term diaspora may not fit the Palestinian case, while agreeing with her premise that it may not be the best term to express the Palestinian dispersal worldwide. In this chapter, I play devil's advocate and explore the extent to which the term diaspora can be applied to the Palestinian case, while also questioning a few alternatives. While Peteet singles out limitations among the many staple definitions of "diaspora", I look for definitions that are inclusionary enough to support the usage for the Palestinian case. As was the case for Peteet, however, this chapter is not about finding – or not – a suitable definition per se, but is rather about what we may learn in the process: problematizing the advantages and disadvantages of applying such a definition. Second, like her,

---

1   The chapters in *Between the Old and New World* (2015) about Brazil (Sônia Hamid; Denise Jardim), Peru (Denis Cuche), Chile (Cecília Baeza), Argentina (Sílvia Montenegro and Damián Setton), and Paraguay (John Tofiq Karam) particularly illustrate this point.

2   Al-Hardan's use was perhaps the most cautious among those I mention. Yet, while she problematised other authors' usage, pointing to their own justifications, she employed the concept herself once. Since her chapter in the book was a translation (Al-Hardan 2012), I will quote the original article directly in English: "The Palestinian Right of Return Movement (RoRM) emerged among diaspora refugee communities following the Oslo accords and the perceived threat to the right of return" (Al-Hardan 2012, 62).

my main argument departs from comparing the terms diaspora (*shatat*) and exile (*ghurba*). But while her argument for supporting the term *ghurba* departs from political positioning with a solid ethnographic support, mine is first and foremost ethnographic, with political implications. This chapter suggests the usage of "exile" – not primarily due to political positioning, but rather from proposing an anthropological perspective that puts experience and affect at the centre of analysis. In doing so, I focus on these terms' capacities not only to relate to various forms of Palestinian (im)mobility, but also to relate intimately to the varied experiences of Palestinians. Thus, my approach shifts the discussion from politics to agency. While agency and politics are ineluctably interwoven, the former is more overtly committed to our research interlocutors' own experiences and expressions, rather than to a political positioning that may be extrinsic to them.[3]

## Dispersal

At the end of the First World War, the victorious allies partitioned the newly conquered Middle East. The outcome of this partitioning was a series of treaties relating to the breakdown of the Ottoman Empire, and among them the secret Sykes-Picot agreement (1916) and the Balfour Declaration (1917). According to the Sykes-Picot agreement, the British created mandates in Palestine and Mesopotamia. The mandate of Palestine was soon divided into Palestine and Transjordan (today Israel, the Occupied Territories and Jordan). In turn, the Balfour Declaration was a letter from the British government addressed to Baron Rothschild – one of the leaders of the Jewish community in Britain. While the correspondence promised "a Jewish home" in Palestine, it did not specify how the Jewish settlement would proceed nor whether it

---

3    Here it must be noted that the differences between our approaches are more methodological than practical. On the one hand, I understand that Peteet's groundbreaking article decisively puts Palestinians' own considerations at the forefront. On the other hand, as much as I may try to give a central consideration to the experiences and expressions of Palestinians, I am not Palestinian, and I can only hope that my ethnographic assessment is correct. In this regard, I take stock on my conversations with numerous Palestinian studies specialists and on the academic publications I read, but also – and especially – on my experience since 2006 among non-academic Palestinians in the Middle East, Latin America and Europe.

would be a national state.[4] The declaration also pledged not to harm "the rights and political status of non-Jewish communities in Palestine" (Encyclopaedia Britannica, [s.d.]). At the time, most Arabs in Palestine viewed the Zionist plans with suspicion, as they had witnessed since the late 19th century the arrival of Zionist Jews with intentions to repopulate the entire country. During this period, Jews bought Arab land – sold mostly by absent landowners many of whom were not even Palestinian – while the peasants, who were then the vast majority of the Palestinian population, found themselves jobless and landless as Jewish labour replaced them (Khalidi 1998). Nevertheless, the lack of clarity in the Balfour declaration allowed the British to negotiate with Arabs and Zionist Jews simultaneously, without being completely unmasked by either. Both Zionists and Arabs had signed the Treaty of Sèvres (UNISPAL 2011) but the Arab elite who had signed the document were far from representing all Arabs. The British mandate over Palestine was registered at the League of Nations in 1920 in the San Remo Conference. In 1922 the mandatory power, Britain, through the so-called memorandum of Transjordan, then separated the territory of Transjordan (those to the east of the Jordan River) from Palestine (to the west of the Jordan River). The right to autonomy was granted to Transjordan (which later became Jordan), and Abdullah I bin Al-Hussein was appointed ruler of the new kingdom. Meanwhile in Palestine, Britain imposed direct rule, which lasted until 1948 with the creation of the State of Israel – at British recommendation and by approval at a meeting of the new international entity created from the League of Nations, the Organization of the United Nations (UN).

In 1947, Resolution No.181 of the UN General Assembly decided to divide Palestine in two, while Jerusalem would be under international mandate on behalf of the UN itself. However, only the Zionists accepted the proposal. This was the beginning of the main phase of the conflict that continues to this day, with about 250,000 Palestinians fleeing or being expelled from Palestine. When the terms of the mandate expired in 1948, Ben Gurion declared Israel's independence, causing a declaration of war by a junta of Arab countries comprising Lebanon, Syria, Egypt, Iraq and Jordan. 700,000 Palestinians had to leave the region during the conflict. With the ceasefire in 1949, Egypt annexed the Gaza region (now known as the "Gaza Strip") and Transjordan

---

4    The history of Israel is directly related to the history of displaced persons in Europe – particularly the Holocaust (also known by the Hebrew term "Shoah", meaning catastrophe) – and therefore to the emergence of the so-called "International Refugee Regime".

annexed the West Bank, where East Jerusalem is located. After annexation of the West Bank, Transjordan was renamed simply Jordan (Pappe 2004; Sayigh 2007). While the independence of Israel (Hebrew, Yom Ha'atzmaut) is celebrated every year, the event that caused the exile of Palestinians from almost all the lands of the mandate to the neighbouring Arab countries was called by Palestinians and Arabs in general *"al-Nakba"*[5] (The Catastrophe). This event changed the Middle East forever, informing the social actions of individuals who somehow relate to the region (Schiocchet 2011a).

Yet, the Independence of Israel was not the last event generating the mass expulsion of Palestinians from their lands. In 1967, the Six-Day War broke out. It was largely motivated by the Suez Crisis, but also because one of the most important platforms of Nasser's Pan-Arabism was precisely the "liberation of Palestine". The trigger for the onset of the war was the expulsion of UN troops from the Sinai Peninsula (one of the banks of the Suez Canal), which according to the Israeli government justified an invasion. Not only was Egypt involved in the conflict, but also Jordan, Syria, Iraq and Lebanon. An effective peace accord was only reached in 1978, now in the middle of the Lebanese Civil War and with Egypt under the leadership of Anwar Sadat. Jordan sought the restoration of the West Bank as part of its own territory, only giving up in 1988 on behalf of the PLO. Both the Gaza Strip and the West Bank would from then be under the military control of Israel. As time passed, Israel gradually left the interior of these territories so as to more effectively control their borders, and during this period has made only periodic military incursions into them. However, East Jerusalem, the Shebaa Farms and the Golan Heights were never completely returned to their own governments and are still today at the centre of the Arab-Israeli conflict (Pappe 2004). The aftermath of the Six-Day War produced around 250,000 more Palestinian refugees (Segev 2007, 15). The overall number of Palestinian refugees today has soared, and UNRWA – the UN Relief and Works Agency for Palestine Refugees – counts 5.6 million registered Palestinian refugees in the Middle East (UNRWA September 4, 2020).

Far from being circumscribed to the Palestinian case, to live, conceive, and express collective experiences of (im)mobility through affective relations be-

---

5    It is worth noting, however, that many scholars have since then proposed using "Nakba" to refer to, not only the events leading to the Israeli independence, but also the series of events leading up to the continuous Palestinian displacement and dispossession. In other words, they speak today of an "ongoing Nakba".

tween community, place and displacement is a human trope. Anthropological categories aiming to characterise forms of human (im)mobility must reflect on this premise. Palestinian refugees and their descendants are legally considered refugees by the UN, which acknowledges their "right of return" since 1948, as UN General Assembly's Resolution 194, article 11 (1948), attests. In practice, however, Palestinian refugees and their descendants have not been allowed by Israel to return to their places of origin. Instead of enforcing this right, the UN and the international community have sought to appeal to permanent resettlement in a third country, or simply maintaining humanitarian aid through the UNRWA when the former solution is not possible.

## A Polyvocal Arena of Social Belonging

My long-term personal research program focuses on the nexus between the subjunctive space of Palestinianness and the diversity of expressions that vary according to subject and context. This subjunctive space – that is, shared and idealized, mingling past, present and future – must be seen as a public arena of negotiation of values, practices, dispositions, techniques, affects and embodies sensibilities expressed through complex motivations irreducible to practical reasoning and conscious strategies on the one hand, or to moral imperatives and unconsciousness on the other. This idea of such subjunctive space comes from memory studies and especially from Lena Jayyusi (2007), who argues that Palestinian refugees tend to conflate the present time with an imagined past before the Nakba. To Jayyusi, contemporary memory articulates a "past condition", a "bibliographical event", and a "historical facticity", but always from the point of view of "present interests", "viewpoints," and "subjective (even also subjunctive) modalities." Yet, in English, the subjunctive mood is not limited to the articulation of past and present, since it denotes expressions of what is dreamed, imagined or wished. In other words, the subjunctive mood articulates the present to idealized past *and* future. Thus, my own usage of the term "subjunctive space" of Palestinianness departs from Jayyusi's subjunctive mood, adding to the equation a moral destination (Malkki 1992), often an utopian future, based on dreams of return to an idealized Palestine.

Between pre-1948 Palestine and what was left of it today, and between the Middle East, Europe and Latin America, the contextual space for the negotiation of Palestinianness is far and wide, and the experience of Palestinianness varies greatly. A given Palestinian subject's social belonging is not limited to their Palestinianness, while Palestinianness is also not only engendered by Palestinians themselves. Part of my research has been to understand how, for example, part of the Latin American, European and Middle Eastern political left understands the idea of the "Palestinian cause" as being universal, secular and often socialist, and puts this sense into the very idea of Palestinianness. Approaching something as complex as the Palestinian dispersion in the world, entails encountering a dialectical relationship between the polyvocal, shared and disputed idea of Palestinianness and unique forms of being Palestinian.

Being Palestinian in the West Bank is not the same as being Palestinian in the Lebanese refugee camps, in a small city in Denmark, in the Austrian capital, or when resettled from Iraq to Brazil. My fieldwork among Palestinians in all these settings has taught me about unique contextual and subjective dimensions, while it also taught me how important tendencies of social belonging processes form within this subjunctive arena of Palestinianness. How is it possible to conceptualize, then, this shared but inherently disputed space of social belonging? In these terms, to what extent can it be called a "Palestinian diaspora"?

## The Palestinians in the World

The Occupied Palestinian Territories and Israel are still largely imagined by many Palestinians as a part of Palestine. However, conceptualizing this idealized territory, this moral destination as such does not necessarily imply the non-acceptance of the state of Israel. To many, Israel is an independent state, no less recognized as a country as the USA, for example, and at the same time is Palestinian territory. To understand this logic, it is necessary to remember that an overwhelming majority of the more than five million Palestine refugees and their descendants (UNRWA n/a) originally came from what is today Israel, and not from the Gaza Strip or the West Bank. Moreover, many Palestinian migrants who left the country before the Israeli independence in 1948 came from villages in today's Israel or cities such as Haifa or Jaffa (Yaffa – today a part of Tel Aviv). That is, beyond a Palestinian state, a Palestinian imagined *nation* stretches from the West Bank and the Gaza Strip to the state of Israel, especially among refugees and immigrants.

The overwhelming majority of Palestinian refugees, who for more than 70 years have not been able to return to their villages and cities of origin –

today within Israeli territory – live in the Mashreq (the Arabic name for a region roughly equivalent to the Near East). To be more precise: in 2010, 37.5% of Palestinians "resided in the Palestinian Territories (4,108,631 individuals), 12.4% in Israel (1,360,214 individuals), 44% in Arab countries (4,876,489 individuals) and only 5.7% in "foreign countries" (626,824 individuals) (Palestinian Bureau of Statistics 2010). That is, more than half of the entire Palestinian population lived outside of the geographical area of pre-1948 Palestine, while many of these living in the Palestinian Territories did so as refugees and, as non-refugees, lived (and still live) under Israeli occupation. In other words, in 2010, only about 50% of Palestinians lived within that which many Palestinians define as Palestinian territory, while 44% of them were displaced from it, but still lived physically around it, and only a fraction (5.7%) lived further away.[6]

Today, Lebanon harbours what until the Syrian war was considered the most vulnerable Palestinian population in the world, with about half of them still living in refugee camps and constituting one of the oldest ongoing and most protracted refugee situations in the world. Only once, immediately following the arrival of Palestinian refugees in Lebanon, was Lebanese citizenship offered on a large scale to Palestinian Christians (and then only to them).[7] An overwhelming majority of Palestinian refugees in Lebanon do not have any kind of citizenship and do not have access to basic human rights, such as: to live free and in security; to not be discriminated; to not be subject to exile; to freedom of movement; to a nationality; to not be deprived of their own property; to work, and others (UN n/a; LPDC n/a). Due to their stateless conditions, the legal concept of reciprocity employed within Lebanese Law discriminates Palestinians even in relation to other refugees and migrants. They can only leave Lebanon upon Lebanese authorisation (decided ad hoc, on a case-by-case basis), which is difficult to obtain and is risky, given that there are many cases of those who left Lebanon then not being allowed to come back.

Despite this situation, many of the Palestinians registered in Al-Jalil – one of the camps in which I resided during my first fieldwork in Lebanon (2006-2009) and continue to visit up until the present day – had already managed to emigrate to Scandinavia in the 1980s. Most of those coming from this camp

---

6    Unfortunately, I was not able to obtain more recent reliable data on this subject.
7    My fieldwork among Christian Palestinian refugees in Lebanon demonstrated that even among the less informed and less wealthy Christians acquiring Lebanese citizenship was not an easy or a straightforward process (Schiocchet 2011b).

settled in Aarhus, Denmark, where I did six months of fieldwork in 2013. Al-Jalil is known among other Palestinian refugees in Lebanon as "the Danish camp" (al-mukhayyam al-denmarky). Despite what the Danish government had imagined when conceding them immigrant status and subsequently citizenship, and despite what even many Palestinian refugees imagine (even in Al-Jalil), many of the Palestinians in Denmark do not feel content and satisfied to live in that country. The majority of them live in Gellerupparken, known in Aarhus as a "ghetto", along with Kurds from Iraq and Syria, Somalis, and other Muslims. During my fieldwork in that setting, Islam predominated among the youth in vernacular expressions of belonging, much more so than among most other Palestinian-dominated settings I knew then. While expressions of Palestinianness still abounded, especially among the first generation of Palestinian migrants in Gellerupparken, they were less prevalent among the youth, frequently appearing among the latter group as a further indexation of their Muslim identity. There was only one Christian Palestinian family in that area, having originated from the Dbayeh refugee camp in Lebanon.[8]

A large shed in Gellerupparken, called Bazar Vest[9] (West Bazar, in Danish) supplied much of the community's demand products, work, and community life, while two mosques served as religious centres. In Aarhus, Gellerupparken was not only shared by Palestinians with other Muslim minorities, but the Danish also tended to stereotype Muslims, belittling national and ethnic categories of belonging. In homogenizing Muslims, the Danish context pushed the imposition of Islam as the main category of identification for Palestinians and other minorities. In this way, local centres of sociability became more associated with religious and economic activities than with culture and nationhood, favouring the identification of the second generation of immigrants with transnational (many of which are neofundamentalist) Muslim movements, rather than national ones. As Islamic neofundamentalist movements I refer here to Olivier Roy's (2004) concept characterizing relatively recent groups such as Al-Qaeda and Da'esh,[10] which seek the pu-

---

8    Dbayeh was one of my primary fieldwork sites, along with Al-Jalil camp, between 2006 and 2009.

9    Although fewer Turks lived in Gellerupparken itself, many had shops in the Bazar. They migrated to Aarhus earlier, and most had moved to wealthier neighborhoods.

10    It can of course be claimed that this was not the case of Da'esh. Nonetheless, this objective was enshrined in the group's discourses and much of their followers' motivations to join the group.

rification of Islam via the purging of politics, which are considered dirty. In this way, Islamic neofundamentalist movements would essentially be different than Islamist movements, such as Hamas or Hezbollah, which are in turn characterized by formal political involvement in their countries of origin and beyond. Incidentally, this description of neofundamentalism resonates with Bruno Latour's (1993) conception of the purification process derived from the tentative secularisation of the world characteristic of the utopian project of modernity. Latour defines the project of "modernity" according to two mutually reinforcing practices: a) "translation", which separates nature and culture, creating hybrids; and b) "purification", which creates two ontological zones, that of human being and that of nonhumans. Separation between subject and object, and between religion and politics was also intrinsic to the modernist project. However, Latour cautions us that this project was never fully realized, since humans never really managed to maintain these separations in practice. Inspired by Latour, I suggest that what Roy describes and calls secularization thought religion is an important impulse echoing the encounter of Islam with the project of European modernity (Schiocchet 2016).

This "Islamisation" process of Palestinians in Denmark did not occur with the same strength in Austria, where Palestinians first arrived, especially in the 1970s, as students (and not refugees) and then established themselves as liberal professionals, such as doctors, dentists and lawyers, engaging with local civil society politically, socially and culturally through the political left. Historically, this relationship had already started in the years of Chancellor Bruno Kreisky (1970s), who outside of the Arab world was directly responsible for the legitimation of the PLO as the only representative of Palestinians (as opposed, for example, to the Jordanian government). While he may never actually have intended it, his acknowledgement of the PLO – as he saw this group as his only chance for dialogue with the Palestinian side – ended up legitimising the group to the rest of the world. This, in turn, paved the way for the formulation of the so-called "Palestinian cause" as being universal, secular, and socialist to much of the European left. After 2015, however, the large number of refugees from the Afghan and Syrian conflicts (in the Syrian case, bringing to Austria and especially to Vienna, hundreds of Palestinians), started to change the Austrian context in ways that cannot yet be fully comprehended. From what I have been able to infer so far, the influence of Austrian activists and of established generations of Palestinians (and other Arabs) in Austria continues to reinforce a sense of Palestinianness that is less demarcated by Islam than seen in Denmark. Politically engaged Palestinians in Austria do not tend to be mobilized in the direction of what Roy called Islamic neofundamentalist movements.

In Brazil likewise, neofundamentalism and religious orthodoxy did not attract much of a following, neither within the group initially comprising 114 Palestinian refugees resettled from Iraq in 2007, nor amongst the established generations of Palestinians and other Arabs who had arrived in Brazil especially in the first half of the Twentieth Century. Pan-Arabism, however, appears to have seduced them more so than in Denmark or Austria. Almost all Palestinian refugees from Iraq came from the Rwayshed refugee camp in Jordan, where they were sent after having been persecuted following the fall of Saddam Hussein in 2003 (Schiocchet 2019). Almost all of these refugees were Muslims, with the exception of one family. Moreover, almost all, including the Christian family, praised Saddam Hussein as a great popular secular leader, many of them having found employment in the Iraqi administrative machine governed by the Baath party. This connection happened especially because Saddam Hussein labelled the "Palestinian Cause" his own, politically mobilizing during the Lebanese Civil War (1975-1990) against Syria (one of the PLO's main enemies then) and treating the few Palestinians in Iraq with positive distinction. This, in turn, reinforced a complementary sense of Palestinianness and Arabness over religion, especially given that many of the forces opposing Saddam Hussein mobilized an Islamic rhetoric as opposed to the Baath secular and anti-Imperialist rhetoric. Moreover, the group never really came together as a community while in Rwayshed. A common sense of social belonging within this group of Palestinian refugees was not mainly articulated in Rwayshed nor any other refugee camp setting (as it was in Lebanon) or within a Palestinian symbolic territory. Instead, it was mainly articulated in Iraq and then significantly rearticulated in Brazil. Arabness, as an iteration of Palestinianness, was maintained as a central element to the majority of the families composing the group as it had already been during the Iran-Iraq conflict (1980-1988).

As I have shown so far, not all Palestinians in the world are refugees or exiles, and the Latin-American case is emblematic for being shaped mainly by a pre-exile dispersion, and the experience of Palestinianness varies greatly according to context and subject. However, the force and appeal of the subjunctive space of Palestinianness, especially when institutionally supported by political parties, social movements and cultural and sport clubs, pushes Palestinians in the world at large to share idealized notions of Palestinianness connected to the tropes of refuge and exile that, in one way or another,

tend to influence social belonging processes and patterns of social organisation of Palestinians world-wide. These notions of Palestinianness, in turn,
have been largely conceived and transformed in response to the Palestinian
refugee plight and the refugee regimes imposed historically upon them. The
very notion of "Palestinian cause", in all the richness of its innumerable contextual iterations as this section demonstrates, can be interpreted as an attempt to regain agency and some measure of control over such regimes.

## Conceptualizing Diaspora

Based on what has been presented so far, to what extent can we speak of a
Palestinian diaspora? To answer this question, we must turn to the term's
definition. According to Judith Shuval, the term diaspora comes from the
Hebrew original *galut*, and initially referred to setting out colonies outside
of Palestine after the Jewish Babylonian exile, which implied the meaning of
settling away from the homeland (2000, 42). Near the middle of the third
Century BC, the Greek translated Deuteronomy, 28:25, as *"esē diaspora en pa-
sais basileias tēs gēs"*, [Thou shalt be a diaspora in all kingdoms of the Earth].
The term diaspora here comes from the Greek *diaspeirein* (disperse), formed
by the junction of the preposition *dia* (across) and the verb *speirein* (to scatter)
(Oxford Reference n/a), through which the Greek, as with the Hebrew, understood the term as meaning migration and colonisation; that is, a migration
that takes root. Yet, the term only came into use in the social sciences in the
1980s, having been reappropriated from its Jewish origins in the Torah (or, as
Christians would say, from the Old Testament). From its original meaning,
implying settlement and not just temporary migration, a new meaning was
attributed based on the Jewish mythology and experience of exile. Longing
for the homeland, and ideas about a utopian return to it, became intrinsic to
most definitions, albeit some authors today reason that this is not a necessary characteristic of a diaspora, so as to broaden the term to include virtually
any kind of long-term migration. In *Modern Diasporas in International Politics*,
Gabriel Sheffer (1986) argues, for example, that a diaspora implies simply: a)
the maintenance and development of a collective identity; b) the existence of
an internal organisation distinct from those of the country of origin and the
host country; and c) significative contact with the "homeland", whether "real"
or "symbolic". And according to Stanley Tambiah (2000) the popularity of the
term diaspora "courts the danger of inordinately stretching it", corroborating

James Clifford's branding of the diaspora as "a traveling term". According to Tambiah, "In the face of these multiple as well as fluid connotations it would be wise not to strive toward a tight, inclusive definition embracing general criteria" (2000, 169).

Clifford's classic *Diasporas* (1994) is among the most popular definitions of the term among contemporary anthropologists. This definition was based on that of Willian Safran (1991), which in turn was modified from the original definition by Walker Connor (1986). In *Diasporas in Modern Society* (1991), Safran suggested enlarging Connor's definition so that a diaspora is defined by a "minority community" sharing several of these characteristics:

1) they, or their ancestors, have been dispersed from a specific original "center"; 2) they retain a collective memory (...) about their original homeland; 3) they believe that they are not (...) fully accepted by their host society; 4) they regard their ancestral homeland as their true, ideal home and as the place (...) [of] return; 5) they believe that they should, collectively, be committed to the (...) restoration of their original homeland; and 6) they continue to relate (...) to that homeland (...) and their ethnocommunal consciousness and solidarity are importantly defined by the existence of such a relationship (Safran 1991: 83).

For Safran then, it would be legitimate to speak of "the Armenian, Maghrebi, Turkish, Palestinian, Cuban, Greek, and perhaps Chinese diasporas at present and of the Polish diaspora of the past, although none of them fully conforms to the 'ideal type' of the Jewish Diaspora" (Safran 1991, 84).

With the explosion of interest in the concept of diaspora by the end of the 1980s, there was what Roger Brubaker called "a diaspora of diasporas", that is, "a dispersal of the meaning of the term in the semantic, conceptual and disciplinary spaces" (2005, 1). And, as James Clifford suggests,

> We should be wary of constructing our working definition of a term like diaspora by recourse to an "ideal type", with the consequence that groups become identified as more or less diasporic, having only two, or three, or four of the basic six features (...) we should be able to recognize the strong entailment of Jewish history on the language of diaspora without making that history a definitive model. Jewish (and Greek and Armenian) diasporas can be taken as nonnormative starting points for a discourse that is traveling or hybridizing in new world conditions (Clifford 1994, 306).

Although the classic definitions by Sheffer, Safran and Clifford are not identical, they share some of the same basic characteristics (Shuval 2000).

Somewhat similarly to Clifford in the above quotation, I suggest that it is constructive to identify that the concept of diaspora has two different basic strands, from which the multiple meanings derive: a normative and a descriptive strand. While the normative strand conditions all applications of the term to fulfilling objective criteria of the "must be/should be" sort, the descriptive strand makes no assumptions of what a description of diaspora "must be" in relation to an ideal type. Both strands derive from the Jewish[11] ideal type (Safran 1991, 83-84; Clifford 1994, 306; Cohen 1997; Brubaker 2005, 2), but while the normative strand is still intrinsically tied to it, the descriptive strand transformed the concept into a broad anthropological category. In practice, however, the myriad definitions of the concept of diaspora today may be found within these two basic strands, and identifying these strands is relevant insofar as it allows us to discuss the advantages and disadvantages of staying closer to or distant from each.

In its most extreme understanding, the normative strand is mostly not academic, and is characterized by Jewish exceptionalism, according to which the only case that can be called diaspora is that of the community formed by the world Jewry. This usage has not been common in the social sciences since the 1990s, having been relegated to one possible understanding of the concept among the Jewish community itself, rather than among scholars (Cohen 1997; Anteby-Yemini and Berthomière 2005). In turn, the extreme of the descriptive strand is utilised simply as a synonym for any community of immigrants – in this way, it is possible to hear about, for example, of the Filipino diaspora in Los Angeles, of the Brazilian diaspora in Massachusetts, or the French diaspora in Lebanon. In both extremes, the concept of diaspora loses its classificatory and explicatory power, particularly as the descriptive trend overlaps with the concept of transnationalism (Anteby-Yemini and Berthomière 2005, 265), as I will develop in what follows. Thus, any meaningful conceptualisation of the term must define a class of human mobility phenomena located between the particular and the general. To understand the extent to which it is productive to speak of a Palestinian diaspora, we must first redirect my initial question in the following sense: which class of phenomena can be defined as being characterized by a diaspora so that this concept can instrumentalise

---

11    Deliberately following the Jewish case, at least in some of its empirical aspects, secondary ideal types have commonly included, for example, the Armenian, Greek, Chinese, Indian, and Lebanese (Brubaker 2005, 2).

us to speak of a specific form of human mobility not contemplated in other concepts?

Without limiting ourselves to the six characteristics enunciated by Safran and reiterated by Clifford and Brubaker, among the most basic characteristics associated with definitions of diaspora is a notion of less territorialized identities than those more generally associated to nation states. According to Safran (1991), Robin Cohen (1997), Shuval (2000) and others, diaspora typically involves an idea of homeland and an actual geographically inhabited nation state. However, I argue that this homeland can be only idealized (not empirical) and that it does not need to be at the centre of the given imagined diasporic community (see, for example, Balzani 2020). As Liisa Malkki argues (1992, 35), Homeland can sometimes be only a "moral destination", marked by idealized images of a homeland, conveyed by a well-organized community with a strong sense of social belonging. Besides, a temporal dimension of a certain depth is also necessary, implying the existence of the imagined community (Anderson 2016) as historically established and as a lasting condition. Finally, even when only moral, this destination must evoke in one way or another an original existence before dispersion or displacement. That is, the dispersion itself tends to be the nexus of the shared, subjunctive, imaginary of the diasporic community. Thus, the diaspora in itself does not end in a pre-dispersion, or another post-dispersal moment, but reaffirms a transnational existence.

On the one hand, the concept of diaspora demonstrates that a homeland is not necessary to maintain a given imagined community, contrarily to what evokes the concept of nationalism. On the other hand, that which connects the diasporic community is exactly the longing caused by the lacuna left by the original territory from where the diaspora departed, or the symbolic place of a homeland that thus does not need to represent a national entity. According to Helena Lindholm Schulz (2003, 09), it is not territory that defines a diaspora, but its very absence. Going one step further, I propose to think, however, that it is not this absence of territory per se either that defines a diaspora, but the longing generated by its intangibility, its distance.

More normative conceptualisations of diaspora imply a more or less global dispersion, while more descriptive conceptualisations could potentially even be employed to define cases of an imagined community mostly inhabiting only two countries. Thus, one of the main challenges in considering a purposeful concept of diaspora is in determining where most of its explicatory potential resides: the importance not only of the form of dislocation, but also of its scale, one weaved onto the other. Otherwise, one could characterize the Argentinian migration to the south of Brazil as a diaspora, or else speak of a Brazilian diaspora in Massachusetts/USA. And if this were the case, then what is unique about the Jewish, Palestinian, Lebanese or Armenian diasporas, for example, both in terms of scale and in terms of the organisation of social imaginaries, would be lost, and the concept of diaspora would lose its evocative and explicative power. Thus, by definition, I suggest that it is important that not any and all migration of a given ethnic or religious minority be considered as a diaspora; that is, the concept of diaspora should not be simply used as a rough synonym for migration. In practice, thus, in what way does a diaspora differ from other forms of human (im)mobility such as hybridizsation, transnationalism, forced migration, or exile?

Diasporas tend to create social relations marked by the transnational flux of people, things, information, values, attitudes, conceptions, and behaviour. Thus, it is common to think that a diasporic condition necessarily encloses the traversing of borders characteristic of transnationalism. But diasporas are not defined solely by transnationalism and do not always involve transnational relations. It is evident that something can be transnational and not diasporic, for example, the flux of capital from an international bank or company. It is less evident that a diaspora may not be transnational, but this also occurs, especially in the context of violence. According to the normative strand of diaspora, the concept is often associated with a catastrophic dispersion, while according to the more descriptive strand, this notion is widened to encompass dispersions motivated by trade, work, or even culture (Lindholm Schulz 2003). While the normative strand contends that the violence-motivated diaspora is the ideal type, such cases are contemplated even among proponents of the descriptive strand.

Hybridisation evokes new forms of social belonging through the connection between an original social belonging to another/others. In the work of Homi Bhabha (1995) and Stuart Hall (1990), for example, forms of identification in the diaspora were taken as the epitome of hybridized identities (see, for example, Tambiah 2000, 178). One of the advantages of the concept is that it shows the plasticity of identification processes, while one of its most severe disadvantages is the over-valorisation of the hybrid as being new, to the detriment of the influence of national poles.[12] Once again, this becomes more

---

12    It is possible to find traces of this false premise even in Clifford's concept of diaspora. See, for example, the excerpt cited on page 84 (Clifford, 1994, 306).

important in the cases of forced migrations, when belonging to an original community tends to be valorised while belonging to the host community may even be shunned, when not morally prohibitive, but then permeably absorbed in practice. Concomitantly, and paradoxically, this process of hybridisation, far from always being harmonious or a product of practical reason, can be the result of contestation and moral and existential imperatives connected to the impossibility of maintaining a now stigmatised original identity. The inverse of this limitation is also problematic: a hybrid identity often implies the existence of two independent and static terms to be mixed, that is the essentialisation of the pre-hybridisation units of belonging (Lindholm Schultz 2003, 14).

Transnationalism, in turn, has been intimately connected to diaspora almost since the re-emergence of the latter term in the social sciences. As early as in 1991, Khachig Tölölyan famously declared that "diasporas are the exemplary communities of the transnational moment" (1991, 5). This statement was published in the first issue of the journal he found and served as main editor, *Diaspora: A Journal of Transnational Studies*, which in turn served as one of the most important fora for the scholarly debate around the term diaspora. In the words of Steven Vertovec and Cohen (1999, XIII), transnationalism is "a social morphology wherein ethnic diasporas become what Tölölyan (1991, 5) has memorably called 'the exemplary communities of the transnational moment'". In *Migration, Diasporas and Transnationalism*, these authors describe the three elements in the title as being intrinsically connected, and therefore place transnationalism as a "central concept" (Vertovec and Cohen 1999, XIII). "Diasporic strategies" are then "a positive means of bridging national and transnational economies, cultures and societies" (Vertovec and Cohen 1999, XIII). And ultimately, "'Diaspora' is the term often used today to describe practically any population which is considered 'deterritorialized' or 'transnational'" And "the rebirth of the notion of diaspora has stemmed from academics using it to characterize transnational ethnic groups and from intellectuals and activists from these populations who have found in the expression a positive way of constituting a 'hybrid' cultural and political identity" (Vertovec and Cohen 1999, XVI-XVII). In the foreword of a long, recent edited volume, Cohen celebrated that the concept of diaspora as employed there described:

> 'linear negotiations in costumes of culture', Muslim burial funds, school alumni associations, nomadic cyberspace, intimate cross-cultural liaisons, architectural permissiveness, multiple religious affiliations, Pentecostal-

ism, Yiddish anarchism, job-seeking networks, polygamy, carnival, skilled entrepreneurship, floating roots, anti-politics, counter-insurgency, international relations, global ecumenes, pan-Somali unity, Palestinian statelessness, bodies in motion, and much else besides (Cohen 2015, XVI).

Or, as the editors of *Diasporas Reimagined* state, the broadest definitions of diaspora, which are very popular today, have only two core elements "the loss of 'home' and the ongoing link to some notion of it" (Sigona et al. 2015, XIX). These quotations illustrate that the more the concept of diaspora has developed over time in the social sciences, the less normative and, ironically, closer to the basic Hebrew and Greek definitions it has become. Today, definitions of diaspora can typically include virtually any case of settlement away from an original homeland, and contrary to Jewish mythology, experience and collective memory surrounding their original exile, for example, by requiring that a diaspora must include longing for a return to the original homeland (see also Tambiah 2000). And the more that diaspora has evolved that way, the closer it has become to transnationalism.

Concomitantly, the notion of transnationalism has been increasingly associated with migration broadly speaking. And while most definitions of diaspora tend to incorporate forced migration, after all, they did originate from the Jewish archetype; during the main phase of development of the concept of diaspora in the 1990s, transnationalism was closely associated with the debate on globalisation. In anthropology, one of the most influential publications on the topic, was *Nations Unbound*, by Linda Bash, Nina Glick-Schiller, and Cristina Szanton Blanc (1994). In this book, the authors distance themselves from other popular conceptualisations of the term in the social sciences, especially those associated with the "postmodern" perspective of "transcultural cultural studies", epitomized by the works of authors such as Arjun Appadurai (1991). According to Bash et al., transnationalism there was used to signal "fluidity with which ideas, objects, capital, and people now move across borders and boundaries", making reference to "hybridity, hyperspace, displacement, disjuncture, decentring and diaspora" (1994, 27). Their main complaint, however, is that much of this work had "remained evocative, rather than analytical", while theirs aimed at linking the definition of transnationalism "to migration" and rooting their analysis in social relations, though which they could focus on "the manner in which migrants, through their life ways and daily practices, reconfigure space so that their lives are lived simultaneously within two or more nation-states" (Bash et al. 1994, 28). This celebration of mobility was a very important moment in the recent history of the social sciences, leading to the questioning of the boundedness of culture, social groups, identity, and ultimately nations to territory. Cuban and other Caribbean communities of migrants, along with Czechs, Irish, Slovaks, and others in the USA, transnationally participated in nation-building processes in their home countries, which in turn meant that these nations were unbound by territory.

However, Bash et al.'s strongly Marxist perspective emphasized social class and labour migration, thus underplaying forced migration. In their own words "the image of the 'uprooted' may be as questionable portrait of many earlier immigrant populations as it is of recent immigrants" (Bash et al. 1994, 24). According to them, "economic and political vulnerability, magnified by the factor of race, augment the likelihood that migrants will construct a transnational existence" (Bash et al. 1994, 27). Their work questioned, among other things, the popular genre on migration literature, largely written by migrants themselves, overemphasizing persecution rather than entrepreneurship in their voyages to the Americas. Inasmuch as I appreciate their point of departure and their contextual contribution at the time, especially by focusing back onto ethnography and social relations, one major limitation of their model is to have left forced migration cases largely out. And, in so doing, like with other concepts of transnationalism or the modernisation theory that they criticize, they have also overemphasized mobility to the detriment of experiences of immobility.

As I have illustrated, transnationalism tends to emphasize mobility, and when the concept of diaspora intersects with that of transnationalism, it inherits some of transnationalism's main problems, including the emphasis on geographical and symbolic mobility (despite a tendency toward class immobility, in the more Marxist strain of the concept). Overall, transnationalism evokes the idea of a fluid transit between at least two national poles, which is not necessarily the case when considering refugees and asylum seekers. Transnationalism, also, does not necessarily highlight the inherent asymmetry of forces involved in such a case, nor of the direction of displacement or all possible motivations. Refugees generally do not experience fluid transit from one place to another. In fact, by definition they cannot return to their original territory, or can do so only at the risk of violence, persecution or death. In other words, the literature on transnationalism, and by contagion much of that on diaspora, tend to emphasize mobility, even when the experience of immobility is what marks the (in this case, forced) displacement. Even if it is often hard to distinguish migration from forced migration (or exile) in practice, these represent two different and opposed ideal types of human (im)mobility. My point is not that the concepts of diaspora and transnationalism cannot or have not been used to emphasize the experience of immobility. There is a good number of studies that do just this, particularly those dealing with the original ideal typical cases, such as the Jewish, the Greek and Armenian. My point here is also not that such concepts cannot or have not been used to characterize the Palestinian case with relative fidelity. Rather, the situation is the opposite, as exemplified by Lindholm-Schultz's groundbreaking book (2003), but also Doraï (2002), Shiblak (2005), Hanafi (2005, 2003), Khalidi (2010), Zaidan (2012), and Suleiman (2016).[13] Instead, I have been arguing that these kinds of studies have become few and far between when compared to the plethora of much wider contemporary usages and applications of the term. Most of these usages have become almost synonymous with migration at large to the point that the overall ideas of diaspora and transnationalism in the social sciences today tends to strongly evoke mobility (see, for example, Ember, Ember and Skoggard 2005), having dispersed much of the explicative power they could have if they were limited to explaining a more defined form of human (im)mobility.

As opposed to the concepts above, exile and forced migration directly evoke instability, insecurity, and ephemerality, while diaspora evokes flux, but not necessarily implies ephemerality, flight, or even instability. The social belonging experience of Italians in New York or Boston, for example, is not necessarily marked today by flight, instability, ephemerality or insecurity. Exile, flight, refuge, and forced migration on the other hand, imply removal, while the descriptive, much wider, concept of diaspora does not.[14] As such, Tutsi motivations to leave for Burundi following the genocide perpetrated by an extremist faction among the Hutu would be invisibilised if this displacement were to be called simply called "the Tutsi diaspora in Burundi". Therefore, the

---

13    However, it must still be noted that, despite the many references I am citing, proponents of the term "Palestinian diaspora" today are much fewer than those who overtly criticise the term (as Peteet 2007) of simply prefer to employ other terms.

14    Here, I accept Brubaker's (2005, 2) suggestion that the concept of diaspora must extend beyond removal marked by violence, displacement or dislocation marked by other motivations, such as economic (often also involving physical or symbolic violence) and other factors. My motivation here, as before, is to circumscribe, as an anthropological category, the concept of diaspora to another form of human (im)mobility, that is simultaneously broader than just the Jewish ideal type and narrower than the inclusion of any form of migration.

concept of diaspora, even when utilized widely, may efface the emphasis on forced (im)mobility and on the dispossession highlighted by concepts such as exile, forced migration, flight and refuge. This effacement, in turn, exonerates the concept of diaspora of binding legal processes and mechanisms that aim to address the conditions of the displaced. As we have seen, refugee regimes have, in practice, been far from optimal solutions to forced displacement and dispossession, and the protraction of the Palestinian case, after more than 70 years, strongly attests to this. Their fundamental flaw can be said to be the – often-blatant – lack of acknowledgement of the displaced subject's own subjunctive space and, with it, the interrelation of understandings of the past, present predicaments, and hopes and visions for the future. Simply put, refugee regimes tend to be imposed from the top downwards, severely limiting the scope of refugee agency, as the Palestinian cases I presented above illustrate. However, the complete obliteration of legal flight and refuge mechanisms would go even further in preventing refugee agency. Refugee regimes need fixing, but the right direction is acknowledgement of refugee predicaments and empowerment of their agency, rather than conceptual alienation and practical disregard.

*

The concept of diaspora is seen today as challenging nation state normativity, since it affirms that state and nation need not to coincide. It is important to note, however, that diaspora does not preclude the idea of strong bonds between state and nation. In fact, it depends on it to the point that even in exile what connects the imagined community is a yearning for a common past centred around a common territory – a subjunctive articulation that often leads to a strong attachment to an envisioned reunion between nation and state, as for example among Kurds and Palestinians. If there was never a modern Kurdish nation state before, the imagined community was previously never so divided into sovereign territories as it is today. What stands between past and present is less about being spread across various states, and more about how the modern idea of sovereignty has created impenetrable frontiers where once, often, there had only stood porous borders, interjecting and interrupting ways of living. The Palestinian case is similar. Methodological nationalism assumes that the prior existence of a territory circumscribed to a state that governed the imagined nation is legitimising of a given nation state order. In fact, this presence or absence is irrelevant, given the relatively recent invention of the nation state model and the realisation that it was preceded by other forms of social communal belonging. In general terms then, what matters to diasporic communal experiences is the imagined territorial and/or symbolic contiguity of social relations in an idealized past, made somewhat intangible by present dispersal.

But the experience of flight and refuge is above all one of immobility. Even when forced migrants traverse continents and seas, engage with various languages and embody unique cultural competences, they cannot remain where they belong; that is, their moral but not geographical destination (Schiocchet 2017). In addressing refugees and exiles in this way, the main limitation of the concept of diaspora is its focus on mobility, just as with the concepts of transnationalism and even hybridism. Its descriptive strand – the one that has been used as an anthropological category – much too often highlights geographic mobility to the detriment of experiences of immobility as lived and narrated by refugees and exiles. As Ismat Zaidan states:

> The contemporary celebration of travel and mobility of transnational migrants with hybrid identities may be different for those stateless Palestinians who have terrifying experiences whenever they attempt to cross checkpoints in their country or try to enter another country at an airport. Such Palestinian Diaspora experience significant restrictions on their movements and, thus, limited mobility (Zaidan 2012, 92-93).

To reiterate: a constructive definition of diaspora must depart from its less normative strand yet restrict itself to human mobility phenomena of significant scale, as the existence of a significant part of a nation state's population being spread into other nation states, or the very inexistence of a nation state that corresponds to this population. Such a concept of diaspora would not need to be restricted to populations under forced displacement, but would be general to the point of including more specific forms of mobility such as refuge and exile. Finally, for a diaspora to exist, it must have a strong communitarian bond, reinforced by the appeal of an original community and its original territorial imagery, even when such a territory is but a moral destination. Given this definition, is it possible to speak of a Palestinian diaspora?

## A Palestinian Diaspora?

As I have argued, it is very well-established within the discussion on diaspora that exile could lead to the formation of a diasporic community, so long
as the basic criteria are met and the willingness to apply the term exists. In
*Problematizing a Palestinian Diaspora* (2007), Peteet brings to the forefront some
important challenges in utilising the concept of diaspora in the Palestinian
case. Perhaps the most important of these issues is the tension between tran-
sience and permanence, or between protraction and stability. This issue is
particularly prominent in Avtar Brah's (1996) definition of diaspora, as noted
by Peteet.

For Brah, a diaspora is "essentially about settling down, about putting
roots 'elsewhere'" (1996, 182); that is, there must be some permanence. And,
as Peteet notes, "Refugee status is supposed to be temporary, and most host
countries strive to prevent permanent integration" (2007, 636). Similarly, in
his introduction to *Being Palestinian* (2016), Yasir Suleiman suggests that "lim-
inality" is a key element in "Palestinian identity", which then "exists in a state
of constant alert, waiting to come to the fore at every pulling of a trigger"
(Suleiman 2016, 4). Abbas Shiblak also notes that "some" Palestinian and Arab
scholars contend that the term diaspora is problematic for the Palestinian case
because "the Palestinian diaspora is a new and recent phenomenon", and that
these authors assumed that the use of the term would be "an implicit acceptance of the dispersal of the Palestinian community, assuming that they were
no longer refugees uprooted from their country by force and unable to receive
permission to return to their homes" (2005, 8); that is, diaspora would tacitly
reiterate the permanence of the Palestinian exile for, as Lindholm Schulz tes-
tifies, "Exile is contrary to what is stable, secure, and static. It is not the equivalent of life after movement, but represents movement itself" (2003, 10). For
this reason, Hanafi (2003) also claimed that Palestinians in Syria are "partially
diasporized", between an established diaspora like those in the Americas, and
a protracted refugee community, like those in Lebanon.

Interestingly, inverting both Brah's and Hanafi's logic, Mohammed Kamel
Doraï's quite unique argument contends that "from within the united Palestinian diaspora there is emerging a new transnational community" (2002, 88).
That is, there is a Palestinian diaspora, albeit only partially transnationalised.
Utilising a version of Gabriel Sheffer's definition of diaspora, for which the
potential group requires a common ethnic identity, some internal organisation, and a significant level of contact with the homeland, Doraï claims that

the difference between diaspora and transnational community "lies in the nature of the relationship with the homeland (...) for the former, they are symbolic; for the latter, they are real" (2002, 88). However, one does not need to
follow Doraï's uncommon definition to be aware of the tension between protraction and stability and still support the use of the expression Palestinian
diaspora. In fact, all of the authors cited in the previous paragraph do so. Shiblak, for example, answers the predicament he enunciated by claiming that it
"does not conceal the fact that the Palestinian Diaspora has been in formation
over the past century (...) with the mass expulsion of Palestinians following the
establishment of the State of Israel" (2005, 8). And Lindholm Schulz answers
her own conundrum by claiming that the term diaspora itself, or "life away
from one's homeland, is life in flux; it implies an unstable and ephemeral,
fugitive condition" (2003, 10). In addition, going beyond the Palestinian case
and returning to more general definitions of diaspora, this tension between
protraction and stability is not as decisive as in the other definitions that I
have illustrated in more detail here, such as Safran's or Cohen's. Ultimately,
the question of applying the definition of diaspora or not to the Palestinian
case cannot be reduced to one of splitting hairs in trying to make the Palestinian case fit or not into one or another general definition of the term. As
Brah herself affirms: "These journeys must be historicised if the concept of
diaspora has to serve as a useful heuristic devise (...) What regimes of power
inscribe the formation of a specific diaspora?" (Brah 1996, 182). And, "diaspora
is a heterogeneous category. (...) The concept of intersectionality is critical in
engaging with the complexity of such differentiations and divisions" (Brah,
cited in Roman and Henry 2015, 252).

Overall, despite the world-wide vast literature on Palestinians and the
numerous studies I cite in this chapter, studies on a "Palestinian diaspora"
are relatively few. Given what was presented here, especially in the relation
between diaspora and exile, the reasons for such relative absence are evident. In Zaidan's words, "the terms exile and refugee are more prominent
as these terms emphasise the forced nature of the dispersal and the necessity of returning home, regardless of how symbolic or realistic this return is"
(Zaidan 2012, 26). So, "defining the Palestinian Diaspora is equally as problematic as defining Diaspora" (ibid.). The "dilemma" being, in his opinion,
"political and moral". Up until the last 10 years, 4,816,500 Palestinians lived in
the Palestinian Occupied Territories (Palestinian Central Bureau of Statistics
2016) and 5,149,742 were registered as refugees with UNRWA. Among the latter, around 2,032,000 resided outside of the Gaza Strip and the West Bank.

To these may be added around 500,000 Palestinians who lived in Latin America (Baeza 2014), around 1,500,000 in Israel (Palestinian Bureau of Statistics 2010) and others in other places, it is understood that only 37.5% of Palestinians resided in the Palestinian Territories (Palestinian Bureau of Statistics 2010) until relatively recently. That is, the Palestinian displacement certainly qualifies in comparison as a diaspora, even according to the normative strand of the concept.

Palestinians, today, have only a shrinking and increasingly disempowered proto-state, harbouring only a minority of the Palestinian population. With a few notable exceptions, this proto-state has been legally acknowledged by most nation states in the global south, and not recognised by global north nation states and the highly dependent global south nation states. The dispersal of most Palestinians, who departed from what was once the British Mandate of Palestine, was prompted by the violence engendered by the Zionist colonisation project and the Independence of Israel, and took the form of exile. Despite this dispersal, today there exists among Palestinians a strong feeling of social belonging and communitarian attachment to each other, reinforced by a powerful imagery of an original Palestine made tangible by the utopian collective return chased thorough the idea of "Palestinian cause", which in turn marks Palestine as a moral destination. After 1948, it was initially from Jordan, then Lebanon, and then Tunisia that Palestinian nationalism, and along with it, a Palestinian nation was significantly rethought in a way that exile itself became a crux to the very idea of Palestinianness, transnationally negotiated in relation to the lost, intangible land.

In face of this, the major paradox of the concept of diaspora is perhaps the Jewish exceptionalism position, its extension to Israel, and the subsequent impediment to using the concept in relation to the Palestinian case, albeit this approach is typically not taken by academics, and was, instead, characteristic of part of the Jewish community's own concerns with issues of cultural appropriation.[15] The creation of Israel occupies an important place in the Jewish narrative of diaspora, but it was the very creation of Israel that caused the Palestinian exile. Ironically, then, the Palestinian case checks absolutely all the boxes listed even by the Jewish exceptionalist narrative (the most radical form of the normative strand) to characterise the Jewish diaspora. So why,

---

15    See, for example, Robin Cohen's encounter with a Rabbi who accused him of having "stolen" the term diaspora from the Jews, in the Foreword to *Diasporas Reimagined* (2015, XV).

then, has the term diaspora not been accepted or utilised by more specialists on Palestinian dispersal and Palestinians themselves?

Apart from other possible general reasons, such as scholars avoiding polemic statements, or Palestinians avoiding being associated with the Jewish narrative, there is fact one major reason for why many Palestinians themselves avoid the usage of the term. Simply put, as I have highlighted throughout this chapter, the concept of diaspora when utilised in its more descriptive, sociological strand – thus far from being tied to the Jewish ideal type – conceals the "forced" aspect of their displacement. It turns displace- ment – a body moving to another place though the action of another body – into dispersal and mobility – bodies spreading to other locations or simply moving from one place to another. In other words, it conceals the agency responsible for the forced relocation.

The commonly used academic form of term for diaspora in Arabic is *shatāt*, literally meaning "dispersed", "separated", "dissolved", "spread". How- ever, Arabs express their dispersal from a given original nation state diversely. For example, the Syrian and Lebanese dispersal to the Americas is known to Syrians and Lebanese (in Brazil, often Syrian-Lebanese) as *mahjar*, literally meaning "place of migration", "refuge" and "sanctuary". For them, however, the term also came to mean the community of immigrants itself and to evoke sensibilities, dispositions and affects connected both to the land of origin and that which was then a destination (Khater 2001; Mahdi 2013; Pastor 2017). Through my ethnographic experience among Palestinians in Latin Amer- ica, the Middle East and Europe, I learned another term of high currency, less used among intellectuals and more so among poets and my refugee interlocutors: *ghurba*, meaning literally "absence of a homeland", "separation form homeland", "banishment", "exile", and broadly speaking, "life away from home". This term is close to the German term *Heimweh*, (*Heim* = home; *weh* = pain), with the absence of home being implicit in the term and home referring to *Heimat*, meaning homeland. Ghurba also evokes sensibilities and affects similar to those evoked by the Portuguese term *saudade* (nostalgic melancholic longing for something or someone absent), but perhaps with more emphasis on the arbitrariness of the rupture, separation.

As we have seen, not all Palestinians dispersed thought the world are refugees or exiles, and the Latin American case is emblematic here, since it is mostly characterised by a pre-exile dispersal. However, as I have previously mentioned, the strength of the appeal of the subjunctive space of Palestinian- ness, especially when supported by institutions such as political parties, social movements, or civil society (for example, cultural and sports clubs), drives Palestinians around the world, regardless of their social statuses, is to share notions of Palestinianness which are intrinsically tied to the trope of exile. In Lebanon, most Palestinian refugees do not cross state boundaries, and in many cases have their whole existence geographically restricted to Lebanon, without necessarily feeling Lebanese. In some refugee camps, such as 'Ain el-Helweh, they need to cross Lebanese checkpoints even to leave or enter the camp. These Palestinians, therefore, do not live transnational – or at least not cosmopolitan – lives, even if they are inscribed into a foreign territory. In Europe likewise, their situation reflects immobility at least as much as mobility. The first significant flux of Palestinians into Europe took place only in the 1970s, first in Germany and Scandinavia, and then more intensively only in the 1980s (Lindholm-Shulz 2003). In the cases of Austria and Denmark, the majority came from Lebanon, at least before the influx of refugee from the Syrian conflict in 2015. Despite taking up European citizenship, many Palestinians, particularly in Denmark, locate themselves as being clearly distinct from a Danish nation, which entails a necessary reflection on transnationalism and its emphasis on the celebration of hybridism and/or mobility. To characterise these examples as diaspora and maintain the emphasis on forced displacement, it would be necessary to reform its descriptive strand and thereby avoid its general disregard for asymmetries and subjective dimensions of the experience of exile. But this effort is the exact opposite direction and reasoning that the current usage of the term has taken in the social sciences, which was exactly to make the term less normative so it could be applied to a highly diverse variety of cases. In lieu of this, the problem could be approached from the opposite angle, and the normative notion of diaspora broadened to make it less normatively tied to the ideal types from which it emerges. However, it is doubtful that, whichever the angle, such a notion of diaspora would concomitantly retain its power to characterise a specific form of human (im)mobility that is not simply a synonym to others such as exile. Such effort would be at least convoluted, and possibly pointless.

Alternatively, my Palestinian interlocutors – Muslim or Christian – sometimes referred to their displacement thought the Arabic term "*hijra*". However, this was not very common, given that in Latin America we mostly spoke in Portuguese with each other, and elsewhere I have mostly carried out research among refugees who tended to prefer the term *ghurba*. With regard to *hijra*, in a personal email exchange while I was writing this article, Rosemary Sayigh told me that she had sometimes heard this term used among Palestinians "in the early days", when Palestinians were expelled to Jordan. According to her, colleagues of her explained then that this was "a way of associating their experience with that of the Prophet Muhammad when he moved from Mecca to Medina" and that "Hijra also carried an optimistic note, since the Prophet Muhammad eventually was able to return to Mecca". Of course, it is first necessary to understand that *hijra* can be used as a simple synonym for "migration". But I agree with her that there may be more to this usage, especially when comparisons are actively pursued. After all, *Hijra* is also a cultural model available in the Palestinian repertoire, and is one that probably resonates more than diaspora, which in turn evokes the Jewish exile. Ironically, I found at least a couple of instances when academics working on the Palestinian displacement used the term "Exodus" (not exile) (see, for example, Doraï 2002, 92; Nazzal 1978). Inasmuch as these instances are rare, they were only used by academics who otherwise use the term diaspora themselves, which may reflect the effort of re-signifying the term from its Jewish ideal-type to use it in the Palestinian case. But such effort further strengthens the association of the term with the Jewish case, and distances from Palestinian experiences and expressions. In the same communication, Sayigh also told me that she sometimes heard Palestinians residing in refugee camps using the word "*iqtila'a*", meaning "uprooting" for the events following 1948.

It seems very likely to me that Sayigh is right on all accounts, and my own ethnographic experience resonates with her insights. But whichever multiplicity of terms were used in the past, and may be still used today, *ghurba* has tended to gain more currency among Palestinians across the board, from the Middle East to Europe and Latin America. The main reason for this, I would suggest, is not a conscious semantic usage, or political positioning, but rather affective appeal. In the introduction to *Between the Old and New World*, I had translated *ghurba* as "diaspora", which is not an uncommon translation (see Peteet 2007, 627), albeit according to what I have presented so far, it is somewhat imprecise. Yet, I had also pointed to the most important element about the definition of this concept: it is "not a technical synonym for the term diaspora. This Arabic concept is charged with sentimental elements"[16] (Schiocchet 2015, 21, note 23). Elsewhere (Schiocchet 2019), I have discussed how *ghurba* is also often mobilised in the context of mental health among refugees. In

---

16    In the Portuguese original: "não é um sinônimo técnico para o termo diáspora. Este conceito árabe é carregado de elementos sentimentais. Tal como entendo, inclui alguns dos sentimentos evocados pelo conceito português de 'saudade'".

this present chapter, however, what is important to highlight is that *ghurba* is an affective complex at once expressing longing, loss, and desire to reconnect, while emphasizing exile. There are other (possibly more technical) terms for exile, such as "*manfa*" (from the root "*nafa*", meaning among other things "negation" and "banishment"), but *ghurba* is the most widely used term among Palestinians, especially – but not only – among refugees, due to the twofold impact of its possible technical usage and its affective appeal.

Therefore, it seems logical to characterise the Palestinian dispersal not through the concept of diaspora, but though one that takes into consideration Palestinian – and especially Palestinian refugee – agency and colloquial expressions of their situation, such as *ghurba*. It could still be argued that the experience of Palestinians in Latin America is generally adequately expressed by the term diaspora, given that this dispersal is mostly characterized by pre-exile human fluxes, even if that would not account for the particular experience of the group of refugees resettled in Brazil that I presented previously. What brings further complexity to this characterisation, however, is the nature of the subjunctive space of the nation, by definition collective, shared and contested. Even among non-refugees, exile and longing for a return to Palestine as a moral destination is embedded in notions and feelings of Palestinianness, regardless of first-hand experiences of border-crossing. Thus, even if diaspora may retain some conceptual space, particularly among established generations of Palestinians in Latin America, it is not broad enough to define "the Palestinian diaspora" world-wide, and not as well-suited a term as exile. And even if exile must be used with caution for the Latin American case, it possesses fundamental value not only due to its legal and political dimension, but also because it is rooted in the shared experience of Palestinianness, given its proximity to the idea of *ghurba*.

In sum, *ghurba*, expresses what *shatāt* does not. While the latter is closely associated with the most commonly used anthropological usage of the term diaspora, and expressing mostly geographic human distribution, the first points to an affective experience of exile, acknowledging a subject's own experiences and framing of this geographic distribution. Thus, I suggest that *ghurba*, or exile, is better suited to characterise the form of human (im)mobility experienced by Palestinians world-wide. Unlike diaspora, exile captures the relationship between the refugee regimes imposed on Palestinians well, and how Palestinians grapple with it – conceptually and practically – in their daily lives.

## Conclusion

In this chapter, I have considered "normative" and "descriptive" strands of the concept of diaspora, noting that while the normative strand has been increasingly falling in disuse in the social sciences, the descriptive strand has become as broad as to lose some of its *raison d'être*. While the concept of diaspora may still be usefully employed depending on the topic at hand, it is equally important to be aware of its limitations. As I have shown, on the one hand, the theoretical discussion on diaspora is intrinsically related to those on migration and transnationalism. On the other hand, my non-academic Palestinian interlocutors in the Middle East, Latin America and Europe typically related their experiences of displacement through Arabic terms for migration and exile, but not through diaspora and transnationalism. The most important reason for this is that the latter two terms were fairly recently popularised within the social sciences. The former was resignified from its Jewish ideal type to characterise other cases in the late 1980s and then, more strongly, in the 1990s, while the latter was already established in the realm of international relations before that. However, both terms were, until quite recently, somewhat tied to academic usage, and even today have much less currency outside of academia than other terms do. This lack of expression in common parlance in itself should not prevent us from utilizing these terms if they have heuristic value when applied to the contexts that we seek to describe and discuss. However, as I have also shown, these terms in their common academic form today are too wide to describe in detail the experiences of my Palestinian interlocutors, and to resonate with their expressions.

In retrospect, even though *Between the Old and the New World* was about Palestinians in Latin America at least as much as it was about Palestinians in the Middle East, utilising the term exile to characterise the general Palestinian displacement would have been more suitable than utilising the term diaspora. Like shatat, ghurba also expresses a general meaning. But unlike shatat, which expresses a general condition of geographic dispersal, in this context, ghurba primarily expresses feelings and emotions related to loss and longing for a homeland. In this chapter, in turn, in line with contemporary anthropological practice, I have suggested that focusing on the experiential dimension of the particular contexts' we analyse is a suitable compass for conceptual usage. In the Palestinian case, this focus on context and experience reveals affective dimensions of displacement intrinsic to a subjunctive space that must be acknowledged in order for scholars to find effective ways to characterise the Palestinian predicament, and for policy makers to address it. In English, the term diaspora has come to emphasise geographical dispersal and mobility to a greater extent than it does exile and the experience of being forced to leave a homeland, which Palestinians typically relate to experiences of immobility. Whenever my Palestinian interlocutors throughout the world had something to say about their own displacement, they usually turned to highlighting exile, even when celebrating their transnational communal existence. I do not often heard the term shatat, which most commonly translates as dispersal, or diaspora. Instead, I often heard the term ghurba, and people overwhelmingly expressed emotions associated with the term, even when not mentioning the term itself. Ghurba can be also be translated as exile, although it encompasses a much denser affective complex. The more descriptive strand of the concept of diaspora, today dominant in the social sciences, traded this concept's earlier emphasis on exile for very wide, catch-all, definitions. Thus, in the Palestinian case, unlike diaspora, exile is firmly rooted to people's experiences and expressions.

The anthropological emphasis on experience and affect entails addressing the relation between refugee regimes and agency, both that of refugees themselves and that of us scholars, who often have an active role in creating, transforming and reproducing the terms of engagement. As I have shown, it could be easily argued that the Palestinian case checks of the boxes not only of basic requirements, even among of some of the most demanding definitions. Yet, concomitantly and contradictorily, the protracted Palestinian exile – one of the world's longest – has also led to the outmost refusal of the transnational character of a nation unbound by territory. The Palestinian subjunctive space is fuelled by an encompassing longing for being bound together again in its own national territory, as much as by utmost repudiation of the (trans)national refugee regimes that bound them to places where they are often not welcomed and feel they do not belong.

There seems to be no consensus among Palestinian scholars themselves regarding which is the most appropriate term to use. As such, we scholars can choose our angle: either privilege the celebration of the community's transnational existence and resilience despite all the odds, or else to highlight its predicament. While it is possible to do both concomitantly, I have justified that Palestinian experiences of displacement are highlighted and empowered by the concept of exile, while concealed and disempowered by the concept of diaspora. With relation to policy, neither maintaining humanitarian aid in or outside of refugee camps, nor resettlement in a third country addresses the fundamental affective dimension of exile I have presented in this chapter. As a result, based on humanitarianism, a regime of knowledge that came to support the depoliticisation of the refugee condition in order to circumvent the principle of national sovereignty that characterises the current nation state-dominated order of the world (Fassin 2012; Agier 2008, 2012; Feldman and Ticktin 2010), the international refugee regime effectively imposed on Palestinian refugees is characterised by more than 70 years of protraction and it is no closer to a permanent solution today than it was at the outset of this displacement. The concept of diaspora, unlike those of forced migration and exile, does not evoke a legal binding nor does it effectively underline and challenge violence and dispossession. In speaking of a Palestinian diaspora, academicians may risk unwittingly concealing and preventing Palestinian agency, becoming themselves complicit to, and conceptually part of, the refugee regimes they are supposed to question.

## References

Agier, Michel. 2012. *Managing the Undesirables: Refugee Camps and Humanitarian Government*. Cambridge: Polity Press.

Agier, Michel. 2008. *On the Margins of the World: The Refugee Experience Today*. Cambridge: Polity Press.

Al-Hardan, Anaheed. 2012. "The Right of Return Movement in Syria: Building a Culture of Return, Mobilizing Memories for the Return". *Journal of Palestine Studies* 41, no. 2: 62–79.

Anderson, Benedict. 2016. *Imagined Communities: Reflections on the Origin and Spread of Nationalism*. London: Verso Books.

Anteby-Yemini, Lisa, and William Berthomière. 2005. "Diaspora: A Look Back on a Concept". Jerusalem: *Bulletin du Centre de recherche français à Jérusalem*, 16:262-270.

Appadurai, Arjun. 1991. "Global Ethnospaces: Notes and queries for a Transnational Anthropology." In *Recapturing Anthropology*, edited by Richard Fox, 191-210. Santa Fe: School of American Research Press.

Baeza, Cecília. 2014. "Between Assimilation and Long-Distance Nationalism". *Journal of Palestine Studies* 43, no. 2:59-72 .

Balzani, Marzia. 2020. *Ahmadiyya Islam and the End of Days: The Muslim Diaspora Living at the End of the Days*. London: Routledge.

Basch, Linda, Glick-Schiller, Nina, and Cristina Szanton Blanc eds.. 1994. *Nations Unbound: Transnational Projects, Postcolonial Predicaments, Deterritorialized Nation-states*. New York, Gordon and Breach.

Bhabha, Homi. 1995. *Location of Culture*. London: Routledge.

Brah, Avtar. 1996. *Cartographies of Diaspora: Contesting Identities* (Gender, Race, Ethnicity). London: Routledge.

Rogers Brubaker. 2005. "The 'Diaspora' Diaspora." *Ethnic and Racial Studies* 28, no. 1: 1-19.

Clifford, James. "Diasporas." *Cultural Anthropology* 9, no. 3: 302-338.

Cohen, Robin. 2015. "Foreword". In *Diasporas Reimagined: Spaces, Practices and Belonging*, edited by Sigona, Nando, Gamlen, Alan, Liberatore, Giulia and Hélène Neveu Kringelbach, XV-XVI. Oxford: Oxford Diasporas Programme.

Cohen, Robin. 1997. *Global Diasporas: An Introduction*. London: UCL Press.

Connor, Walker. 1986. "The Impact of Homelands upon Diasporas". In *Modern Diasporas in International Politics*, edited by Sheffer, Gabi, 16-46. New York: St. Martin's.

Doraï, Mohamed Kamel. 2002. "The meaning of homeland for the Palestinian diaspora: revival and transformation." In *New approaches to migration? transnational communities and the transformation of home*, edited by Al-Ali, Nadje Sadig, and Khalid Koser, 87-95. London: Routledge.

Ember, Melvin, Ember, Carol R. and Ian Skoggard, eds.. 2005. *Encyclopedia of Diasporas: Immigrant and Refugee Cultures Around the World*. Volume I: Overviews and Topics; Volume II: Diaspora Communities: Overviews and Topics v. 1. New York: Springer.

Encyclopedia Britannica. *Balfour declaration*. [s.d.]. http://www.britannica.com/EBchecked/topic/50162/Balfour-Declaration. Accessed on November 19, 2020.

Fassin, Didier. 2012. *Humanitarian Reason: A Moral Order of the Present*. Berkeley: University of California Press.

Feldman, Ilana, and Mirian Ticktin. 2010. *In the Name of Humanity: The Government of Threat and Care*. London: Duke University Press.

Hall, Stuart. 1990. "Cultural Identity and Diaspora". In *Identity: Community, Culture, Difference*, edited by Rutherford, J., 222–237. London: Lawrence & Wishart.

Hamid, Sonia. 2015. "Árabes Estabelecidos e Refugiados Palestinos Recém-Chegados ao Brasil: tensões referentes ao "direito de retorno" e a uma "pedagogia deascensão social". In *Entre o Velho e o Novo Mundo: A Diáspora*

*Palestina desde o Oriente Médio à América Latina*, edited by Leonardo Schiocchet, 449-486,Lisboa: Chiado Editora.

Hanafi, Sari. 2005. "Physical Return, Virtual Return: The Palestinian Diaspora
and the Homeland". In *The Palestinian Diaspora in Europe: Challenges of Dual
Identity and Adaptation*, edited by Abbas Shiblak, 141-153. Palestine: SAMA.

Hanafi, Sari. 2003. "Rethinking the Palestinians Abroad as a Diaspora: The Relationship Between the Diaspora and the Palestinian Territories." *HAGAR:
International Social Science Review* 4, no. 1–2: 157–182.

Khalidi, Rashid. 1998. *Palestinian identity*. New York: Columbia University
Press.

Khalidi, Walid. 2010. *Before their Diaspora: A Photographic History of The Palestinians, 1876-1948*. Washington D.C.: Institute for Palestine Studies.

Khater, Akram Fouad. 2001. *Inventing Home: Emigration, Gender, and the Middle
Class in Lebanon, 1870-1920*. Los Angeles: University of California Press.

Jayyusi, Lena. 2007. "Iterability, Cumulativity, and Presence". In *Nakba: Palestine, 1948, and the Claims of Memory*, edited by Sa'di, Ahmad and Lila Abu-
Lughod, 107-134. New York: Columbia University Press.

Latour, Bruno. 1993. *We Have Never Been Modern*. Cambridge: Harvard University Press.

Lebanese Palestinian Dialogue Committee (LPDC). n/a. *Palestinian Refugee:
Property Ownership*. http://www.lpdc.gov.lb/property-ownership/the-pale
stinian-refugee-and-the-property-ownership/56/en. Accessed on November 19, 2020.

Lindholm Shulz, Helena. 2003. *The Palestinian Diaspora: Formation of identities
and Politics of Homeland*. London: Routledge.

Mahdi, Waleed F. 2013. "Mahjar." In *Multicultural America: A Multimedia Encyclopedia*, edited by Carlos E. Cortés, 1397-99. London: Sage.

Malkki, Liisa. 1992. "National Geographic: the Rooting of Peoples and the Territorialization of National Identity among Scholars and Refugees". *Cultural Anthropology* 7, no.1: 24-44.

Nazzal, Nafez. 1978. *The Palestinian exodus from Galilee, 1948*. Beirut: Institute
for Palestine Studies.

Oxford Reference. n/a. *Diaspora*. https://www.oxfordreference.com/view/10.
1093/oi/authority.20110803095716263. Accessed on November 21, 2020.

Palestinian Central Bureau of Statistics. 2016. *Estimated Population in the Palestinian Territory Mid-Year by Governorate, 1997-2016*. http://www.pcbs.gov.ps/
Portals/_Rainbow/Documents/gover_e.htm. Accessed on July 27, 2016.

Pappe, Ilan. 2004. *A history of modern Palestine: one land, two peoples*. Cambridge: Cambridge University Press.

Pastor, Camila. 2017. *The Mexican Mahjar: Transnational Maronites, Jews, and Arabs under the French Mandate*. Austin: Texas University Press.

Peteet, Julie. 2007. "Problematizing a Palestinian Diaspora." *International Journal of Middle East Studies* 39, no. 4: 627-646.

Roman, Leslie G. and Henry Annette. 2015. "Diasporic reasoning, affect, memory and cultural politics" (Interview with Avtar Brah). *Discourse: Studies in the Cultural Politics of Education* 36, no. 2: 243-263.

Roy, Oliver. 2002. *Globalized Islam: The Search for a New Ummah*. New York: Columbia University Press.

Safran, William. 1991. "Diasporas in Modern Societies. Myths of Homeland and Return". *Diaspora: A Journal of Transnational Studies* 1, no. 1: 83-99.

Sayigh, Rosemary. 2007. *The Palestinians: from peasants to revolutionaries*. London: Zed Books.

Schiocchet, Leonardo. 2017. "The Middle East and its Refugees". In *Facetten von Flucht aus dem Nahen und Mittleren Osten*, edited by Gebhard Fartacek and Susanne Binder, 101–122. Vienna: Facultas-Verlag.

Sheffer, Gabriel, editor. 1986. *Modern Diasporas in International Politics*. New York: Crom Helm.

Schiocchet, Leonardo. 2019. "Wellbeing as a Key Site for the Encounter between Arab-speaking Refugees and Austria." In *Die Lange Dauer der Flucht – Analysen aus Wissenschaft und Praxis*, edited by Josef Kohlbacher and Maria Six-Hohenbalken, 231-262. Vienna: Verlag der Österreichischen Akademie der Wissenschaften.

Schiocchet, Leonardo. 2016. "On the Brink of a State of Exception? Austria, Europe, and the Refugee Crisis". *Critique and Humanism* 46, no. 2: 211-248.

Schiocchet, Leonardo. 2015. *Entre o Velho e o Novo Mundo: A Diáspora Palestina desde o Oriente Médio à América Latina*. Lisboa: Chiado Editora.

Schiocchet, Leonardo. 2011b. *Refugee lives: ritual and belonging in two Palestinian refugee camps in Lebanon*. 2011. PhD Dissertation. Department of Anthropology, Boston University, Boston.

Schiocchet,Leonardo.2011a."FarMiddleEast,BraveNewWorld:TheBuildingoftheMiddleEastandtheArabSpring".ThePerspectiveoftheWorldReviewBrasilia/Brazil:IPEA3,no.2:37-80.

Segev, Tom. 2007. "The June 1967 War and the Palestinian Refugee Problem". *Journal of Palestine Studies* 36, no. 3: 6-22.

Shiblak, Abbas. 2005. *The Palestinian Diaspora in Europe: Challenges of Dual Identity and Adaptation*. Palestine: SAMA.

Shuval, Judith. 2000. "Diaspora Migration: Definitional Ambiguities and a Theoretical Paradigm". *International Migration* 38, no. 5: 41-57.

Sigona, Nando, Gamlen, Alan, Liberatore, Giulia, and Hélène Neveu Kringelbach. 2015. "Introduction". In *Diasporas Reimagined: Spaces, Practices and Belonging*, edited by Sigona, Nando, Gamlen, Alan, Liberatore, Giulia and Hélène Neveu Kringelbach, Oxford: Oxford Diasporas Programme.

Suleiman, Yasir. 2016. *Being Palestinian: Personal Reflections on Palestinian Identity in the Diaspora*. Edinburgh: Edinburgh University Press.

Tambiah, Stanley. 2000. "Transnational Movements, Diaspora, and Multiple Modernities". *Daedalus* 129, no. 1: 163-194.

Tölölyan, Khachig. 1991. "The Nation-State and Its Others: In Lieu of a Preface". *Diaspora: A Journal of Transnational Studies* 1, no. 1: 3-7.

United Nations. n/a. *The Universal Declaration of Human Rights*. https://www.un.org/en/universal-declaration-human-rights/. Accessed on November 19, 2020.

UNISPAL (*United Nations Information System on the Question of Palestine*). Online Official File. 2011. http://domino.un.org/unispal.nsf/9a798adbf322aff38525617b006d88d7/5bff 833964edb9bf85256ced00673d1f?OpenDocument&Highlight=2,faisal. Accessed on November 19, 2020.

United Nations General Assembly. 194 (III). *Palestine – Progress Report of the United Nations Mediator*. https://unispal.un.org/DPA/DPR/unispal.nsf/0/C758572B78D1CD0085256BCF0077E51A. Accessed on September 29, 2020.

UNRWA. September 4, 2020. *UN agency for Palestinian refugees launches $95 million appeal to keep COVID at bay*. https://news.un.org/en/story/2020/09/1071702. Accessed on November 19, 2020.

UNRWA. n/a. *Where we work*. http://www.unrwa.org/where-we-work. Accessed on July 27, 2016.

Vertovec, Steve and Cohen, Robin. 1999. "Introduction". In *Migration, Diasporas and Transnationalism*. Cheltenham: Edward Elgar Publishing Ltda.

Zaidan, Ismat. 2012. *Palestinian Diaspora in Transnational Worlds: Intergenerational Differences in Negotiating Identity, Belonging and Home*. Ramallah: Birzeit University.

# PART 2: Complexity and Selectivity in Refugee Regimes

# Intermingling and Overlapping of Refugee Regimes in Their Transnational Connections and Agencies: Yezidi Refugees From Iraq

*Maria Six-Hohenbalken*

In this contribution I will discuss some examples of refugee regimes which are at stake when we speak about Iraq, thus the case of the Yezidis. Using Iraq as an example, it can be shown that differences in the refugee regimes emerged, which are often contradicting and I will show how these contradictions interfere in the lives of those affected by them. The chapter elaborates on how a demographically rather small community cannot be considered in isolation, but is embedded in different regimes that overlap and that require different strategies and set conditions for agency. In various international and national statistics asylum seekers, such as the Yezidis are reduced to their citizenship and labelled, here as "Iraqi refugees". The receiving countries perspectives' hardly acknowledge that since the founding of the modern Iraqi state different refugee regimes have emerged, partly influenced by historical developments.[1]

As outlined in the introduction multiple refugee regimes are existing on the national and international level simultaneously, either side by side or overlapping or opposing each other. In terms of theory, the complexity, multipolarity and various political principles which determine the (im)mobility of people in one nation state is discussed. The complexity of refugee regimes will be shown here on the example of Iraq in general and with a specific focus on the situation of the Yezidis since 2015. Herein some of the mechanisms

---

1   I am grateful to Sabine Bauer-Amin and Leonardo Schiocchet for their valuable comments on a previous version of this article; this article was brought into being through a year-long, very fruitful cooperation, within a collegial atmosphere with them in Refuge Studies projects.

which regulate the movements on the regional (Yezidi/Kurdish), on the national (Iraq) and international level as well as the multiplicity of political, legal and social instruments will be scrutinized.

In this chapter instead of tackling the question of humanitarianism, humanitarian intervention and agencies' for which Iraq would provide a plethora of examples and development, I will focus on the role of transnational networks which became in some cases a considerable factor in refugee regimes. The transnational (ethnic and/or religious) networks are social actors and can be part of and become active within humanitarian practices and strategies for agency. The Iraqi and Yezidi case – as it will be shown – is not only an extraordinary example for the complexity and multipolarity of refugee regimes but shows how refugee regimes overlap, intermingle and counteract each other.

I will briefly sketch the political backgrounds and challenges which are deeply rooted in Iraqi history and discuss some of the features, ambiguities and ambivalences in the multipolarity of movements for refuge within, from and to Iraq. Different refugee regimes evolved – due to the historical and recent political situation, which as I will show cannot be seen only in the binary relation of sending and emitting nation states, but rather each has its various international implications. Furthermore, in the last decades an increased transnationalisation of some of the Iraqi communities of concern has influenced the individual actors, Non Government Organisations (NGOs) and policy makers to develop their agency. Through an empirically based investigation, I shall show the necessity of having transnational networks in focus when scrutinizing the agency of refugees.

My intention here is to discuss how some of these refugee regimes exist side by side, overlap or intermingle, showing the challenges for the nation states involved as well as for NGOs and the refugees themselves. Within the framework of this article, it is impossible to discuss the single refugee regimes in depth. It is only possible to shed light on some of the developments and discuss some of the interdependencies in this multipolarity. This encompassing approach should help to scrutinize whether and how these complex refugee regimes limit or enable refugees' agency. I refer here to various "field-sites" which span transnational relations between Iraq, Armenia, Austria and Germany.

This paper has a threefold structure: firstly, I sketch the situation in Iraq as a target, transit and emitting country for displaced people. Here, a brief reflection on the history of the Iraqi state is necessary to understand the overlapping and intermingling of refugee regimes. Secondly, based on empirical research, I focus on the situation and agency of Iraqi refugees from various backgrounds in Austria, and discuss their aims and prospects. I also show the consequences and impacts of the multipolar Iraqi refugee regimes. Of specific interest here is the position of the Austrian state within these regimes. The Austrian asylum system examined here is of specific concern as it oscillates between the acceptance and non-acceptance of the multicultural diversity – and thus the multi-layered reasons for the refuge of Iraqi citizens. As I shall show, it is not a question of arbitrariness but more the question of lobbying by and of policy makers and, increasingly, the importance of transnational communities. These two chapters provide the context of the multipolarity and complexity of the following case study. Thus, thirdly, I will focus on the situation of Yezidis from Sinjar (Iraq), their situation as Internally Displaced Persons (IDPs) and asylum seekers in Europe and beyond, the meaning of the transnationalisation of the Yezidi community and, within several premises, their agency. The example shows that due to the transnational networks with Yezidi and Kurdish diaspora groups, that refugee groups do not stand in isolation, but interact with each other.

## Iraq in focus

As a successor state of the Ottoman Empire established out of the three former Ottoman vilayets Mosul, Baghdad and Basra, Iraq gained its independence in 1932, when a monarchy was declared following the de facto end of the British protectorate in 1930. Iraq came into being as a result of post WWI negotiations and colonial interests and, from the beginning, was a heterogenous state with concern to the ethnic and religious belonging. The Arabic Shiite population in the southern provinces, the Arabic Sunni population in the centre, and the Kurdish, predominantly Sunni, in the north are the demographically largest groups. Besides the Arabic and Kurdish populations several ethnic and religious minorities were also scattered all over the country, as for example members of various Christian denominations, Yezidis, Shabak, Yaresan, Jews or Bahai.[2] Religious and/or ethnic belonging became much more decisive in

---

2    For the historical developments of the displacement of the Nestorians in Iraq see e.g. Chatty 2010, chapter 4. For the Kurdish related historical developments since the fall of the Ottoman Empire, see Chatty 2010, chapter 6 and for the history in the last 50 years

the last decade(s) in the spiral of violence. While the Iraqi regime tried to suppress, downplay or ignore religious or ethnic belonging, after the fall of the regime, various forces came into play which instrumentalized religion to mobilize people.

Géraldine Chatelard (2012) critically remarks that there are hardly any all-embracing and longitudinal studies on (forced) migration and displacement in Iraq since the founding of the state. The existing studies focus on single ethnic and religious groups, or on minority issues. The frameworks of these studies are often ideologically-driven, use specific terminologies and lead to certain ideologically-loaded interpretations. It becomes obvious, as Chatelard shows, that the driver for the numerous migration movements and forced displacement policies was always the state and a policy which had already started in the 1930s. For a comprehensive analysis, the historical context must therefore be taken into account and "...what is lacking [is] a conceptual attempt to link various types and episodes of involuntary migration together to try to make sense either of the recurrence of the phenomenon or of a certain regularity in the ways it occurs." (Chatelard 2012, 362). She refers to Aristide Zolberg's approach, that the formation of a new state can be linked closely to refugee generating processes, displacements and attempts to "homogenize" a population (Zolberg 1983 in Chatelard 2012, 363).

Iraq is a specific example that under the guise of a modernisation paradigm, the suppression of ethno-national movements and politically undesirable movements occurred, marked by displacement and forced migration on the one hand and restrictions of mobility on the other.[3] Thus, refugee movements out of Iraq of the various emigrant groups – comprising Arabs in opposition to the regime, Kurds, Christians, etc. – before, especially during and also after the Baath regime were "driven by a set of dynamics that cannot be reduced to their relations with the state, but in each instance, state policies were a determining factor that indirectly impacted their decision to leave Iraq" (Chatelard 2012, 363).

---

see Chatty 2010, 263 – 266. For the recent situation of religious groups in Iraq after ISIS - see e.g. Sevdeen and Schmidinger 2019 and for the situation in the Autonomous Kurdish Region, Schmidinger et al. 2019.

3   After the end of the British administration, the issuing of identity cards was dependent on the loyalty of citizens and their compliance with the regime. Furthermore, the food distribution system was an instrument to control mobility within Iraq.

Not only were the policies against individual minorities highly complex, multi-layered and subject to change within short time frames, but furthermore we have to analyse these interdependencies, and how these policies of forced migration and displacement were linked to each other. "The settlement of Arabs led to the displacement of Kurds and Turkmen through different administrative techniques entitling the former to food distribution, land and house ownership while depriving the others of those same entitlements (Romano, 2005)" (cf Chatelard 2012, 367).

In addition to these policy-driven displacements, we also have to take into account development induced migrations – that is for example instigated by concerns relating to the (under)development of infrastructure, etc. – within and to Iraq. Furthermore, the establishment of exile communities in Europe and America since the late 1950s became part of the refugee regimes. These historical and more-recent developments evoked a multipolarity of the Iraqi migration system, as Chatelard (2005) argues.

Furthermore, international politics were a driving force in displacement and refuge. For example, the Kurdish resistance in the north, which was able to take control of parts of the Kurdish settlement area between 1964 and 1975 was – at an international level – connected with the question of disputed territories in the South. When the long-standing conflict between Iraq and Iran over the question of drawing the border at Shatt al-Arab was settled at the OPEC conference in Algiers, the condition for Iraq's concession was that Iran gave up its support for the Kurdish movement in Iraq. As a consequence, more than 250,000 Kurdish refugees from Iraq sought refuge in Iran and the UN High Commissioner for Refugees appealed to Western states to accept refugees. Therefore, European states received contingents of Kurdish refugees, laying the ground for the shaping of a Kurdish transnational community, which showed its influence in Iraqi policy for decades after. When Saddam Hussein took power through a *coup d'état* in 1968, a "brain drain" had already started then, which caused a decrease in the Iraqi middle class in the following decades.[4]

What followed was a brutal regime in which the government pursued a "policy of terror" against its own population, against minorities, such as the Kurds and political oppositions. Thousands of villages were destroyed, mass

---

4    For the history of the Kurds in Iraq see e.g. Aziz 2011; Chaliand 1993; Bengio 2012; Ibrahim 1983; Izady 1992; Khalil 1985, Khalil 1989; Kreyenbroek and Sperl 1992; Makiya 1998; McDowall 2000 and Strohmeier and Yalçın 2000.

displacements organised, people expelled from the country (as for example the Faili from Baghdad[5]) and cultural rights were suspended. "The Republic of Fear", as Kanan Makiya (1998) labelled the Iraqi regime, also persecuted its opponents outside of Iraq. During the Iraq-Iran War (1980-88), one million people were killed,[6] and Kurds,[7] Shiites,[8] and smaller minorities also faced displacement, expulsion and massive state violence. In the shadow of the war the Baath regime executed a genocidal policy (Anfal processes) against the Kurdish population, in which more than 200,000 Kurds lost their lives in poison gas attacks, mass executions and tremendous state violence.[9] This genocidal policy, the Gulf War and the policy of the authoritarian state evoked a massive emigration which had its peak in 1990/91 when a Kurdish uprising was overthrown and two million refugees transgressed the Turkish and Iranian border.[10]

The developments after the Gulf War led to two UN resolutions and, based on these, to the establishment of two protection zones, under UN observation (Stansfield 2003, 79ff.). The northern one in the mainly Kurdish inhabited territory and one in the south, with a predominantly Shiite population. The international embargo on Iraq hit these zones tremendously and evoked further emigration. After the fall of the Saddam regime, the power vacuum, the destroyed infrastructure and the political instability perpetuated flight movements to the West.[11] When the invasion of allied US, UK, Australian and Polish forces started in 2003, it is estimated that between two to four million people had already left the country, which was already undergoing an

---

5    For the case of the Faili see e.g. Institute of Statelessness and Inclusion 2019; Minority Rights Group International 2017.

6    Pelletiere argues, that due to missing statistics the number of death could raise up to 1,5 million people (2007, 115).

7    See Izady 2004. Yildiz estimates that more than one million Kurds were displaced within Iraq, mostly under the Baath regime (2007, 64).

8    In the early 1970s, a total of 90,000 Iraqi Shiites were expelled from the country. After the Algier Agreement, these deportations were briefly suspended, but at the end of the 1970s, on the eve of the Iraq-Iran war, some 200,000 people of Shiite faith were again expelled and/or deported.

9    For the Anfal processes see e.g. Hiltermann 2008; Middle East Watch Report 1993; van Bruinessen 1994; Hardi 2011.

10   "Nearly 1,5 million Kurds passed into Iran. Another 500,000 massed on the Turkish border, with only about 200,000 being allowed in by the Turks, who closed their borders after two days" (Izady 2004, 85).

11   For the Post-Saddam era see e.g. (Tejel et al, 2012).

enormous "brain drain" (Sassoon 2012, 379). Further factors for emigration were the collapsed economy and infrastructure, impoverishment, low levels of services and basic needs (like electricity, water and supply), high levels of unemployment and inflation, and corruption. "The internal displacement in which more than 2,7 million lost their homes created another 'push' factor for the brain drain" (Sassoon 2012, 381). Unemployment rates were between 25% and 40%, and even higher among young people.[12]

In 2012 Chatelard argued that, "In the last few years, a multiplicity of collective actors has directed violence against the confessional, ethnic and class composition of entire urban and rural areas, displacing populations inside and outside the country, and forcing others to be immobilized" (2012, 375). From 2002 onwards the security situation had worsened, the (sectarian) violence exercised by militias increased, which lead to, for example, the kidnapping of individual people, for sectarian reasons or to enforce ransom payment, and to a high assassination rate of academics. Violence against people working in the medical sector, especially, was a driving force for destabilisation, as doctors were a soft target (Sassoon 2012, 383); as a consequence more than 35% left the country. Terror and violence against people in the educational sector fuelled further emigration. Many students and professionals decided to settle in the securer Kurdish autonomous region in the north, to continue their work.

Emigration was fuelled by the uneven socio-spatial distribution of security inside Iraq due to militias and armed groups, the internalisation of the ethno-sectarian territorial divide, the government policies to maintain displaced populations in the areas to which they have been directed or displaced, strategies of retaliation "a displacement for a displacement" in between the various ethnic/religious/political groups (Chatelard 2012, 376 f.); all of which made "mobility a security strategy for many individuals and collectivities" (378).

---

12    "A survey conducted in 2004 by the United Nations Development Program (UNDP) and the Iraqi Ministry of Planning showed that unemployment reached an astonishing 37,2% among young men with secondary or higher education (UNDP 2005, 133)." (Sassoon 2012, 381).

Based on the annual reports of the UNHCR from between 1999 and 2013 "Iraq was the highest-ranking country of origin for asylum seekers in industrialized countries"[13] (Paasche 2016, 94).

What followed in the years thereafter was an uneven development inside Iraq and a change in the refuge regimes towards neighbouring countries. The better security conditions in the Kurdistan Region and the establishment of a democratic system[14] was not only an argument in individual asylum procedures against granting asylum status, but also became a decisive factor in the refugee regimes of European states towards "Iraqi refugees". In 2013, those persons with a temporary subsidiary protection status were forced by EU member states to return, numbering some 95,000 people, the majority of whom were Kurds (Paasche 2016, 94). At the same time, from 2012 onwards, Iraq also became a receiving country for refugees following the outbreak of war in Syria. Until December 2019, UNHCR in Iraq registered 245,810 Syrian refugees, of whom 99% were staying in the Kurdistan Region of Iraq (KRI).[15]

In the year after this enforced return of Iraqi refugees from Europe, the situation in Iraq did not turn to the better, but rather worse. Not only the absence of the state (al-ladaula see below), but also the threat from the so-

---

13    In these accounts the migration movements from the former Yugoslavia is not included

14    Furthermore, the Kurdish Regional Government (KRG) developed a diversity policy and conveyed an experiment in pluralism; they also promoted a Kurdistani rather than Kurdish identity, which encompasses the ethnic identities of Kurds, Assyrians, Turkmens and Arabs (Stansfield 2007, 141). This form of civic nationalism, and almost more significantly the – although politically different – self-administrative experiment in Rojava with its focus on the participation of women in politics, is a model for governance for leftist groups in the Middle East.

15    UNHCR 2020. https://reliefweb.int/report/syrian-arab-republic/information-kit-syrian-refugees-iraq-humanitarian-inter-agency.

called "Islamic State"[16] and its expansion, its genocidal policy against religious minorities and the overall suppression and persecutions evoked mass refuge, especially from Mosul and Sinjar, and long-lasting displacement.

As outlined above in the history of Iraq, the state was the main driving force for displacement and forced migration. The recurrent instability in Iraq, the competition of various ideas of nationalism, the division of ethno-national and religious communities and their various competing militias evoked a political development which is categorized as a non-state, or in Arabic *al-ladaula*.[17] The Iraqi political situation of non-state governance is characterized with the concept of *ladaula*, which

> refers neither to a deep state nor a parallel state, but rather a mixed constellation of actors inside and outside the state organization whose operations include formal policy, extra-governmental violence, and polarizing popular rhetoric... [which] contains a spectrum of different forces and groups: political parties' militias, criminal groups, armed tribal groups, and others. In this sense, ladaula is not beyond the state, nor does it aim at ending the state; it is both inside and outside the state (Aziz 2020).

Thus, the relationship between the existing state structures and *ladaula* is not one of opposition, but rather they are entangled in multiple ways, thus complicating scenarios for getting out of this situation.

But what do these various political developments and demographic regimes mean for individual asylum applicants? All of them are seen as "Iraqi refugees" – statistics do not differentiate between the various ethnic or religious groups, many of them have experienced displacement and forced migration more than once and also their family biographies are marked by (enforced) migratory experiences. The younger generations of Iraqi refugees,

---

16    The so called "Islamic State" or the preceding names ISIS "Islamic State of Iraq and al-Sham" (i.e. Greater Syria)" or the Arabic acronym DAISH (Al-Dawla al-Islamiya fi al-Iraq wa al-Sham)], or ISIL (Islamic State of Iraq and the Levant) is a Salafist terror organisation, which has never organized a state according to international law. They controlled part of Iraq (until 2017) and parts of Syria (until 2019) and executed genocides against the Non-Muslim population, destroyed cultural heritage sites and carried out war crimes in civil wars in the region. Internationally IS is ranked as a terrorist organisation, which has recruited fighters internationally. The IS has spread and executed its terrorist activities far beyond Iraq and Syria, in the Middle East, Central and Southeast Asia, Africa and Europe.

17    In correct Arabic transliteration "al-lā-daula".

especially, were raised in war situations and can hardly remember years without warfare. In the following discussion, results of qualitative research projects with refugees from Iraq in Austria, conducted between 2015 and 2019 are presented. I shall critically discuss here, how the current refugee regime in Austria allows them a space for elaborating agency and imagining their futures.

## Refugees from Iraq in Austria

In the course of 2016 during the refugee movements from the Middle East and Central Asia to Europe, several strategies were employed to grant or not grant asylum to applicants. In Austria, somewhat similar to the situation in other European countries, refugees from Syria were able to gain asylum more easily and quickly than people from Iraq were.

The Austrian refugee regime for Iraqi asylum applicants extends back to the mid-1970s. In 1975, following the defeat of the Kurdish resistance movement (as a consequence of the Shatt al-Arab treaty, see above) and refugee movement, the Austrian government accepted 103 Kurdish refugees due to an appeal of the UN High Commissioner. In the following decade between twenty and sixty persons from Iraq applied for asylum annually.[18]

It is estimated that during the regime of Saddam Hussein about 4,000 to 5,000 people from Iraq came to Austria: these were predominantly Kurds, but also Arabs who were in resistance against the regime and Christians of various denominations. There was an increase of applications during the Iraq-Iran war (1980 – 88) and due to the genocidal policy against the Kurds (1988/89). Another state-led admission program arose due to the defeat of the Kurdish resistance and the mass exodus in 1991, when about 200 people were accepted. As the Austrian refugee regime became more rigid, however, many people were only able to seek refuge via human trafficking. There was an increase of applications in between 2001 and 2003 (especially of people from Iraq).[19] Another resettlement program was organized in 2011 for thirty Christians, who were fleeing the violent persecution of Islamic extremists and already

---

18    So, for example, sixty-two in 1980, thirty-three in 1981, fifty-one in 1982, and thirty-seven in 1983 (see Fercher 1995, 70). As the Austrian statistics do not reflect the ethnic or religious belonging, we only have information regarding former citizenship.

19    In addition to Afghanistan, Serbia, Russia and Turkey (see Berger and Strohner 2016).

had family members or relatives in Austria.[20] The quota[21] of cases which were recognised decreased in the following decade, e.g. to only 25% in 2016.

The Austrian government recognized ethnic and religious factors in the specific resettlement programs during the beginning phases of the arrival of Iraqi refugees. However, in later years the refugee regime did not distinguish accordingly between the various ethnic or religious groups, although in Iraq the multipolarity of refuge accelerated. In Austria, refugees were then seen as Iraqi citizens, therefore no specific statistics exist which inform about the ethnic or religious belonging and the respective rates of acceptance. What is obvious here is the difference and contradictions between national categorizations ("Iraqi refugees") and regional, religious, political and/or ethno-linguistic identifications of the refugees themselves. Labelled as "Iraqi refugees", they see themselves not only or not as predominantly Iraqi, but rather as Kurds, Yezidis, Turkmen, Sunnis or Shiites. These different logics of categorizing become especially pertinent in the case of people from the de facto-autonomous Kurdish Northern Iraq and the Yezidis who seem to have a strong sense of groupness and identification.

The refugees reflect the diversity within Iraq, which can also be seen in the various political associations, diasporic groups and religious communities.

From 2015 onwards many of the Iraqi applicants received a "white card", which means that the asylum procedure was accepted and that, usually, a residence permit card would be issued. This card confirms that the asylum seeker now has a right of residence for the duration of the procedure. However, the residence permit card is not an identity document, but only serves as proof of identity in proceedings before the Federal Office for Foreigners and Asylum (BFA).

Even before the refugee movement from 2015 onwards, Austrian asylum procedures were protracted and applicants had to wait – in some cases several years. Thus, the Iraqi refugees were aware that their procedures in Austria could take a long time, and with an unfortunate outcome they might only gain a temporary residence status or, at worst, have to leave the country. What many of them had in common was, that they had started in Turkey, managed to cross the Mediterranean in inflatable boats and made their way, via Greece, Macedonia, Serbia and Hungary, or Croatia/Slovenia to Central Europe. Only those who could afford between 8,000 and 10,000 Euro managed their refuge

---

20    See Knapp 2001.
21    Berger and Strohner 2016, graphic 4.

hidden in trucks all the way from Turkey. Some Iraqi citizens who came before 2014 sought refuge via the UN, family reunion procedures or through kin who helped them to get a visa – then they could manage the way via plane from Iraq or neighbouring countries.

Reasons for refuge from 2014 onwards were multifaceted. Young men got caught in between the various militias in central and southern Iraq and were forced to join these paramilitary groups – coercive methods employed include torture, the kidnapping of younger family members, assassination of kin, physical and psychological pressure at the work place and expropriation. Baghdad and larger cities were constantly hit by bomb attacks committed by the various combatants. The forces of al-Qaeda and the IS exercised genocidal persecution, fuelled hatred and forced people to combat against each other. The instrumentalisation of religious belonging and sectarianism was also enforced by other belligerent parties, mainly the several militias which had arisen. Especially those informants who were the offspring of bicultural or bireligious families (mostly from Sunni and Shiia denominations), were constantly attacked, discriminated against and could hardly make their living between Shia or Sunni dominated and politicised quarters. In 2014 when the so-called Islamic State captured various regions in Iraq, the genocidal policy against the Christian and the Yezidi population evoked a mass flight. While many of the Christians from Mosul and the Ninive plains could not hope for a further existence in Iraq, and tried to leave the country, more than 200,000 Yezidi refugees from the Sinjar province stayed as IDPs in the refugee camps in the Kurdish Autonomous Region of Iraq (see below).

In Austria during a pilot study undertaken in 2016,[22] many of our informants had been awarded a white card. At best, some Iraqi refugees had gained subsidiary protection, which means that the protection status is granted by decision and for an unlimited period, while their residence permit is limited in time and has to be extended (bi)annually. In case the political conditions in the country of origin changes, the residence permit can be revoked. This was the case with people from the Yezidi denomination – some of whom had come even before the genocidal persecution by the so-called Islamic State in

---

22    The pilot study was realized at the Institute for Social Anthropology and the Institute for Urban and Regional Research of the Austrian Academy of Sciences (ÖAW), Vienna. Sixty narrative interviews in the respective mother tongues were conducted. The focus was on: the reasons for refuge; the managing of the refuge itself; educational, occupational and family backgrounds; and their expectations in Austria.

2014. This was also the case for those Iraqi citizens who could prove additional reasons (severe illnesses or gender-specific violence) beyond the overall turmoil and constant, highly dangerous situation. Others who had been in an assailable position (such as in the secret service, critical journalists, opposition party members, etc.), were still holders of a white card. So many of our interlocutors were in limbo, aware that their legal issues would not be settled in due course, and slowly realising that they had hardly any outlook for family reunions. It was mostly men who were sent first, having left their family members in Turkey or in Iraq where they awaited the possibility to follow. The relative safety of the autonomous Kurdistan Region of Iraq (KRI), then the northern provinces, were a main argument used in the asylum procedures when people were not granted asylum. They would have a safe region within Iraq where they could return to – although enough regard was not given to the prerequisites required for settling in the KRI, such as the acceptance of the person by high ranking officials, etc.

Hardly anybody brought up the losses of their basis of life through warfare, dispossession and displacement during our interviews – it seemed that it was taken to be a part of the fate of Iraqi citizens, an already taken for granted element which nobody really stressed in specific. Our younger interlocutors explained that they had constantly lived in a war-torn society and connected their biographical stages to the wars they went through.

In a study conducted in 2017/18,[23] we again interviewed people from Iraq,[24] who had applied for asylum in Austria. At that point, the majority had already stayed in Austria for two, three years and for many their procedure was not settled yet. They were still holding white cards and were in the midst of the asylum procedure. Several complained that they were still waiting for their interviews, and thus the next step for decision in their applications. They were in a limbo; one of our informants said it is "empty time" for him, during which he could hardly make a living. Some of them had also gained migratory experiences, as they had lived for several years in Syria, Egypt or in other countries of the Middle East. Consequently, the "condemnation of

---

23    See the Innovation Funds Project Loslassen–Durchstehen–Ankommen, at the Institute for Social Anthropology and the Institute for Urban and Regional Research. The interviews with Iraqi refugees were conducted by Sabine Bauer-Amin and Leonardo Schiocchet. I am thankful to refer to this empirical work in this chapter.

24    These were different interlocutors than from the first study.

waiting" expressed as "empty time" might also relate to their former migratory experiences, where they had experiences in acquiring new competencies in their adaptation to a new country.

Some of the younger men interviewed had finished an academic education, but could not find an academic position and had worked in various craft trades, as a carpenter, baker or confectioner in Iraq. While they were trained to work in these occupations, they did not gain a certificate of an apprenticeship comparable to those in Austria. The procedures of learning a craft cannot be compared with strict apprenticeship programs, which are very locally bound systems in Europe. In Austria, to go through the nostrification procedure to acknowledge academic education is costly, so several did not see the sense in undergoing the process before their asylum application was settled. Although the Employment Service Austria[25] – the state institution for service at the labour market – has established training programs, based on so called *Kompetenzchecks* for refugees. However, gaining a vocational qualification, based on their previous jobs, was hardly doable for those in limbo, who could not access all the prescribed German courses and language steps.

The people interviewed were forced to rely on social benefits, as they were unable to find jobs as, in addition to their white card, they also need an employment permit. Instead, they experienced competition and repression in the illegal working market, where they were exploited in restaurants or in the cleaning sector.

Without additional resources it is almost impossible to find a flat in and around Vienna, where most of them had moved to from the assigned accommodation in the countryside, in order to have better possibilities in the housing and working market. What many faced in these two or three years of stay in Austria was the issue of dequalification of their education and expertise. Only a few had managed to do a vocational training and if so, still faced joblessness.

Compared to the Syrian refugees the agency of Iraqi asylum seekers was limited due to the legal prescriptions, structural limitations and the protracted state of their asylum application. Some had decided to do an internship at NGOs, GOs or a voluntary service year or month – and they hoped that this would improve their chances for getting the asylum status. During the peak of the refugee movement in 2015 and 2016 some of our interlocutors were already engaged in associations which provided first support to

---

25    Arbeitsmarktservice (AMS) in German.

refugees. The *Train of Hope* was such a loose network, which emerged out of civil society, and which was active at railway stations where they supported newcomers or transiting people with their basic needs and in translations. Those who had good English competency, translated from Arabic, Kurdish or Farsi into English and allowed communication with the engaged civil society. Some of them continued these translation services – predominantly without any payment – for the newcomers over the following months. Close relations with Austrian voluntary workers enabled these engaged persons to establish personal networks with the civil society and widen their contacts. This helped them to find a room or a flat for a reasonable price, or as one informant expressed "Social relationship is the key of life". The repeated changes of residence and the overstretched housing market, especially in Vienna, was a further factor for family reunions being unrealizable.

Members of the Kurdish and Iraqi Arabic diasporic associations,[26] for example, were active at the beginning in supporting the newcomers arriving at train stations, refugee camps or in their first adaptations. This was based more on individual engagement and, to a lesser degree, on the diasporic/ association level.

Due to the extremely complex situation in Iraq with many belligerent parties being involved, some people did not easily trust the diasporic associations, or co-ethnics (from whom some felt exploited in housing or job issues) but instead relied more on Austrian NGOs and activists. A general argument was that relations which were predominantly in the diasporic community would not help them to improve their German language acquisition. For Iraqi refugees in Austria, there is a protracted temporariness inherent in the asylum regime which creates vulnerability and which hampers agency. Many of the interviewed Iraqi refugees have a transnationally dispersed family, with kin in various nation states in Europe and the Middle East. In this early application stage, without having identity cards to move freely wherever they want, they cannot uphold the kin networks in the ways that they had

---

26    Interestingly the established Kurdish diaspora gained its influence, coherence and a further momentum in self-organisation during the mass flights of Kurds from Iraq at the end of the 1980s and during the 1990s, when they were officially assigned with the caring for newcomers. The development was twofold, either out of these diasporic associations representatives for and of the autonomous region emerged or representatives of the Kurdish political parties in Austria became more active also in these diasporic organisations.

intended to. Psychological distress caused by the protracted asylum procedure, the difficult housing question, the experiences of dequalification in occupational concerns and the fading prospects of family reunification caused a constant feeling of being estranged. The possibilities which were established in the Austrian refugee regime, therefore, were not easily accessible for the Iraqi refugees in limbo, but only for those who had already gained asylum or a subsidiary protection status and who could then move on in the language acquisition program, nostrification of academic degrees, apprenticeships or trainings, etc.

This protracted temporariness was also found to be a decisive factor in a survey study of IOM about complex migration flows from Iraq to Europe, realized among Iraqi migrants in European countries in 2015 (IOM 2016).[27] A high number of interlocutors in this IOM study originated from the governorates of Anbar and Nineveh, and had already previous experiences of internal displacement within Iraq. In this survey the majority of respondents were from Arab Shiite (50%) or Sunnite (30%) origin, with only 13% being Sunni Kurds and 3% Yezidis. The majority were 30 years old or even younger, 93% were male and had university education (41%), or secondary education (47%), (IOM 2016, 5ff.). The high level of education is remarkable. 80% of the interlocutors had no hopes in their future in Iraq. From the people interviewed, 270 had expected a refugee status, but only half were granted asylum. More than 50% were still waiting for the asylum procedure to be processed and almost two thirds expressed their unwillingness to return to Iraq (IOM 2016, 21). Several factors seem to be the same as shown within our own studies (gender, education, protracted asylum procedure). But from such statistics alone the refugee regimes of and for the various Iraqi communities and social groups (ethnic, religious, socio-political) are hardly retraceable. Furthermore, statistics and numbers alone will not easily encompass all the impediments which come up in case of a a return migration (see below).

---

27    The informants were staying in Germany (180), Austria (172), Finland (55), Sweden (43) and Hungary (30).

## KRI – region of safety and transition[28]

In 2016 the KRG[29] announced that more than two million refugees and IDPs, originating from Syria and Iraq were housed in the Autonomous "Kurdistan Region of Iraq". In comparison, there were about 5,2 million inhabitants counted in the autonomous region. Within the refugee and IDP statistics, about two million people were counted, comprising IDPs from Iraq (mainly due to the IS occupation of Mosul), about 250,000 refugees from Syria, 300,000 Yezidis and about 100,000 Assyrians who sought refuge from ISIS, in addition to Sunnis who fled from Shiite territories, dominated by militias. For the young autonomy which was slowly establishing its economy, stability, and infrastructure this challenge of handling refugee movements and dis-placement fostered instability and hampered the way out of the decade long crisis (see Frantzmann 2016, 17).

In 2019 our research team learned that more than 50% of our interlocu-tors (from 2016) had already left Austria, many of them before their status was decided and before IS was defeated in all Iraqi provinces. The reasons and motivations for seeking asylum were divergent as also were the reasons for a return migration to Iraq in the last decade. Even the divergent motives of return are an important factor for refugee regimes. In addition to the better security situation in, and political autonomy of, the KRI, the economic growth and infrastructural development in the northern most regions probably also contributed to decisions for a return migration. This post-exile transition was also fostered by Iraqi Kurdish politicians. As Erlend Paasche in his study on return migration to Iraq outlines, returns could be temporary as well as per-manent, and with various scenarios in between; therefore new concepts are required, with more concrete sub-categories, which also encompass "return-visits", "long-term return", split up households with long-term returnees and return visitors (2016, 22). Paasche also explained the differences in return mi-gration in the Iraqi Kurdish case based on the length of stay in exile. The first wave of refugees were seen as elite pioneers (1974 – 1991), those coming to Europe between 1992 and 1998 were seen as reactive second-wavers and those proceeding between 1999 and 2014 as proactive third-wavers (Paasche 2016, 51 f.). "Asylum migration continued during the 2000s despite improved

---

28    KRI Kurdistan Region of Iraq.
29    KRG means Kurdish Regional Government, which is the official ruling body of the Au-tonomous Kurdistan Region of Iraq.

macrostructural conditions in Iraqi Kurdistan and worsened conditions for asylum seekers to Europe. Migration became more proactive, in other words, and self-perpetuated" (Paasche 2016, 93). Compared to asylum seekers from the rest of Iraq, residents of the KRI in the third wave did not flee from violent disorder like refugees from the rest of Iraq, but rather from the overall socio-economic and security situation, and on the basis of individual political decisions.

Paasche argues, that the return is as sensitive as the flight was, due to the high expectations of and for returnees, e.g. coming back with material or social capital, as successful businessmen or academics. "The experience of return among empty-handed, socially stigmatized forced returnees caused great distress. Future plans were a delicate subject because such returnees were often mired in debt, with grim prospects" (Paasche 2016, 51).

The refuge regimes discussed here have to deal with the ambivalence arising from this background of multiculturality/ethnicity/religiosity, and which cannot be compartmentalized into a single ethnic or religious belonging, but rather intermingles. Ignoring, or over-stating, exclusionary belongings therefore will not reflect the socio-political reality, which on the other hand is also undergoing enormous transitions in response to actions of the belligerent parties.[30] In some cases, the increasing importance of transnational networks and connections are visible, while for others these do not exist. For example, the Christian communities of the Middle East were the focus of church lead initiatives, programs and specific humanitarian associations, with their own advocates for their cause. People with bicultural origin, whose parents have both Sunni and Shiite backgrounds, could not rely on proponents or a lobby for their cause.

Those people in our study who gained asylum or permanent residence status were predominantly of non-Sunni Muslim denominations, above all the Christians and the Yezidis. While the Christian population gained specific support from church institutions in Austria (Catholic as well as various

---

30    Plebani refers to the interculturality in Iraq: "Mixed areas and mixed communities have always been one of the main features of the Iraqi social fabric (....) It is of outmost importance, then, to launch a series of confidence-building measures operating at all levels in direct coordination with Iraqi institutions and social groups, NGOs, and foundations, to restore the culture of diversity that has defined the Iraqi model for decades, to strengthen the bonds between communities inhabiting areas affected by significant ethno-sectarian polarisation, and to promote a serious dialogue over Iraq identity and future" (Plebani 2017, 162).

oriental Christian churches), it took time until the Yezidi received similar attention. For decades, Yezidi refugees in Austria were seen as Iraqi refugees and up until 2014 hardly any differentiation was made. Although the Yezidi community in Austria has increased since 2000, for a long time the specific reasons for their persecution were not recognized. On the contrary, some of my interlocutors, heads of a Yezidi association, argued that people were not granted asylum, with the official argument "that nobody knows who the Yezidis really are." [31] This changed over the course of the years, especially with official acknowledgements of the genocidal processes in Sinjar since 2014 and the elaboration of specific admission programs in Germany.

In the following I will briefly outline refugee regimes for the Yezidis and employ a comparative perspective to show intersections of these systems and the meaning of diasporic transnational connections.

## Yezidi refugees from Sinjar

I outlined the historicity and multipolarity of the Iraqi refugee regimes in the first section, focusing on the refugees from Iraq during and after the Saddam regime, and discussed the Austrian asylum system in relation to Iraqi refugees in the second. I shall now turn to the situation of the Iraqi Yezidi refugees in particular and will herein analyse the forces for and the meaning of the increased transnationalisation of Yezidis over the last two decades. These transnational networks are of growing importance, both in interfering in refugee regimes in host countries on the one hand and in the possibilities for agency on the other.

From August 2014 onwards, Yezidis from the region of Sinjar (kurdish Şingal, arabic: Sinğār) in the Nineveh Governorate in north-western Iraq became victims of the devastating attacks of the so-called "Islamic State". "The province Niniveh, as Sinjar was part of, was the most dangerous governorate already in 2009. The city of Mosul was ranking highest on the list of the most violent cities in Iraq. Sinjar became a 'peripheral area', from where people could hardly move to other zones in Iraq, due to the Public Distribution Systems (PDS) of nutrition rates" (Savelsberger et al. 2010). Even during the Baath regime they were displaced from rural areas, forced to live in so-called collective towns and experienced Arabisation, instrumentalisation, dispossession

---

31    Personal conversation with a Yezidi activist in August 2017.

and impoverishment. This region was and is outside KRG control, but is of particular interest for the KRI and the Iraqi state. The predominantly Kurdish speaking Yezidis were encompassed as Kurds, although many of them stress their own identity and belonging, based on their specific socio-religious structure.

When IS fighters were approaching in 2014, the defensive units hastily withdrew and left the civil population to the attackers. The majority of the population of Sinjar, numbering between 250,000 and 450,000 people, had to flee. Several hundred people, especially small children and the elderly, did not survive the strain of the escape. According to the United Nations, 5,000 Yezidi, mostly men and young adolescents, but also some children, have been executed and about 7,000 Yezidi girls and young women have been abducted. They were sold as slaves and experienced systematic sexual violence, forced Islamisation, and other forms of degrading treatment. Only half of them have been freed to date. The intentions of extermination were obvious, as the IS also systematically destroyed the Yezidi cultural heritage. The European Parliament, and several human rights organizations and governments have stated that the enormous brutality of displacement and persecution were acts of genocide. Within the framework of a broad-based anti-IS coalition, the terrorist organisation was largely driven out of the Sinjar region. But for the years thereafter Sinjar has remained a disputed territory between the various local power militias, the Kurdistan Region Iraq and Iraqi national forces, thus the situation has been too insecure and unstable for refugees to return (see Kaválek 2017).

"According to the UN High Commissioner for Refugees, in 2005 some 550,000 Yazidis resided in Iraq, more than two-thirds in Sinjar district itself (UNHCR 2005, 6). The precise number nowadays is unknown, but it is surely significantly lower with many Yazidis having emigrated" (Kaválek 2017, 13). Estimations are thus between 250,000 and 400,000 (see UN Habitat 2015, 4 in Kaválek 2017,13 and Cerny 2020, 2) and as Kaválek notes, that about 275,000 IDPs (including non-Yezidis) sought refuge in the autonomous Kurdistan Region of Iraq.

"Estimated seventy thousand of them then became refugees and left for Europe" (Černý 2020, 2; in reference to Rudaw 20 March 2017). Driving forces for migrations were insufficient aid, the overall economic crisis in Iraq, the economic decline in the Kurdish Region and the poor distribution of aid, the overall insecurity for Yezidis, the demand for space in refugee camps, unsuitable social conditions, distrust in state institutions and towards Muslims, and that their homeland was for years a disputed territory (Černý 2020, 2-5). In the aftermath, the struggle for Yezidi loyalties,[32] the discussion about ethnic belonging and identities, as well as splits in political and military loyalties worsened the overall situation (see Černý 2020, 12). In 2017 only 29,000 people had returned (Kaválek 2017, 13; referring to IOM 2017, 11).

Even after the defeat of IS, official sources from the KRG[33] mention that, in February 2020, 264,720 individuals were registered as refugees (predominantly from Syria, but also from Turkey and Iran), and 787,705 individuals as IDPs. Therefore, all together more than one million IDPs and refugees still remain in the KRI, with almost half in the governorate of Erbil, 30% in Duhok and the rest in Sulaimaniya. About 40% of the IDPs are Sunni Arabs, 30% Yezidis, in addition to Kurdish Muslims from provinces outside the KRI, Christians and "others" (as for example, Turkman, Armenians and Shabaks). In 2021 due to official numbers from the Kurdistan Regional Government the numbers of refugees and IDPs has hardly decreased.[34]

Only a small percentage of the Yezidis managed to take refuge in Europe, while the majority were doomed to remain as IDPs in the refugee camps in the Kurdistan region. The situation only changed years later, with an agree-

---

32    The KRG has been actively promoting the Kurdish ethnic identity of Yezidis living in disputed territories, especially in the post-2003 period (see also Musings on Iraq, 2014; Savelsberg, Hajo and Dulz, 2010). "Consequently, the Yazidi leadership was increasingly caught between the KRG and Baghdad and ended up increasingly politically divided (ICG, 2009; Human Rights Watch, 2009; PAX for Peace, 2016, 20-21)." (see Kaválek 2017, 14). Even in the time of the Baath Regime a strong Arabisation politic was enforced (Priest 2019, 200).

33    http://jcc.gov.krd/contents/files/25-02-2020/1582612800.Humanitarian%20Situational %20Report%20(2-20)%20for%20February%20%20Kurdistan%20Region%20of%20Iraq.pdf.

34    Kurdistan Regional Governement 2021: Humanitarian Situational Report: No. 6 (IDP's: 664,561, 241,190 Syrian refugees, 8,450 Turkish, 10,510 Iranian, 738 Palestinian and 83 "other" refugees).

ment in September 2020, which allowed the IDPs to successively return.[35] The cumulative causes for seeking refuge in Europe shows several self-reinforcing mechanisms, which create new social dynamics and bring forth new drivers for migration (Černý 2020, 12 ff.). But seeking ways to apply for asylum, in Europe or beyond, was difficult to manage on an individual basis for Yezidis. According to our interviews Iraqi refugees spent between 6,000 and 8,000 US Dollars per person to manage the flight to Europe.

In the following I will scrutinize what influence Yezidi diasporic communities can have, to support people in their refuge and asylum application. Here I shall take a closer look at the importance of diasporic, transnational networks for managing refuge, for interfering in some of the state refugee regimes and for building up agency. I will scrutinize the question of agency on behalf of the refugees and of those already established, but who had fled decades ago themselves and who are now important agents in the transnational networks.

When in August 2014 the Yezidis in Sinjar faced genocidal persecution, Yezidis in Armenia followed the reports on the Internet and satellite TV. This Armenian Yezidi community – descendants of refugees of the persecutions lead against non-Islamic denominations in the Ottoman Empire during the First World War – comprised, at its peak, up to 60,000 persons.[36] The genocide in Sinjar 2014 had an enormous impact on Armenian Yezidis. There were a series of reactions from the Republic of Armenia, both from the state and civil society. It was the then Armenian President, Serzh Sargsyan, who made the persecution of the Yezidis a topic amongst international bodies, including the UN General Assembly. Concurrently, Armenians along with other Christians in Iraq as well as in Syria had to seek refuge, especially when IS attacked their livelihoods and cultural heritage. For (ethnic) Armenian refugees from

---

35  In October 2020 an agreement was settled between the Iraqi government and the Kurdish regional government over the future of Sinjar. Various militias should no longer control the region, the authority of the Iraqi central government should be restored and Yezidis should be integrated into the state forces. The stability should be restored and article 140 of the Iraqi constitution (which enables a referendum regarding the future political belonging) should be realized, as also a reconstruction of the infrastructure and new elections for mayors. Up until this time, details about the agreement have not been published and Yezidi associations long for codetermination in these processes (see Ezîdî Press, 11 October 2020, www.ezidipress.com)

36  Dalalyan 2012; Schulze and Schulze 2016; Six-Hohenbalken 2019

Iraq and Syria, the autonomous Kurdistan Region of Iraq was a transit country for proceeding to the Transcaucasian Republic of Armenia. Here a specific
refugee regime evolved, which was rather exclusive. Refugees with ethno-religious Armenian origin, verified through their denomination and language
skills, easily gained Armenian citizenship. Through this, they are integrated
within a transnational network in which the influential Armenian diaspora
has had a stronghold since the fall of the Soviet Union. For Armenian refugees,
the Republic of Armenia became not a resident but a transit country which
provided them with the necessary documents to commute further to North
America or other western destinations, where transnationally organized Armenian NGOs were active. None of these legal opportunities were open for
those Yezidi refugees from Iraq, who managed the refuge to the Republic of
Armenia. A few Yezidi families have managed the flight by taking the direct
plane from Erbil to Yerevan. When I conducted interviews with two families
who came from Sinjar, I learned that both families were from a village raided
by IS in 2014. Only through refuge to the mountains with thousands of others and, finally, with the help of the Kurdish YPG/YPJ[37] fighters from Rojava
(Kurdish region in Syria) were they saved and brought to refugee camps in the
autonomous Kurdistan Region of Iraq, as IDPs, or in Rojava.[38] Several tried
to move further as, intimidatingly, the distance between some of the refugee
camps and the IS fighters was only a few kilometres.

Family A numbered before the refuge 32 members, comprising the parents, the married and unmarried children and their grandchildren. The parents tried to gain asylum with half of their children and grandchildren in Armenia, while the others stayed as IDPs in the refugee camps in Kurdistan Iraq.
Likewise, family P, which once had ten people, managed refuge to Armenia
with five people. When I came in touch with them in 2015/2016 their residence
status in Armenia had not been clarified, as at that time they only had a temporary residence permit. This meant that the children were not enrolled in
school, they could not receive medical care and did not get any financial support. They were instead relying completely on private financial funding from
donors, on support by the very engaged Armenian Yezidi community, and on

---

37    *Yekîneyên Parastina Jin* [Women's Defence Units], *Yekîneyên Parastina Gel* [Peoples De-
      fence Units] (the male counterpart), the Kurdish militias in Syria, which are close to
      the PKK units in Turkey.
38    Rojava is the Kurdish term for West. It relates to the western parts of the Kurdish in-
      habited territory but also to an intended independent political unit.

occasional food donations from NGOs. They saw little future for themselves and their families – they were stuck. Further travel from Armenia to another country seemed impossible due to their lack of personal documents or financial means. In the course of 2016, family P managed to proceed to Turkey, while family A was still in Armenia before returning to Iraq two years later. Both families could hardly develop any agency, but were in a legal and social limbo. They could not accept the possibilities for making a living in Armenia, which had been offered to them by their Yezidi hosts: namely taking over one of the farms which was previously abandoned (due to the economically motivated high emigration rates) and renting animals to build up their own flock. Being formerly employed as workers in Iraqi oil companies, they could not see their future as livestock breeders in a remote village in Armenia without having the proper skills and language knowledge. Some of the Armenian Yezidis were disappointed when the refugees could not accept their offer and turn it into an agency, as they had imagined for them.

The Yezidi community with a more than a century existence in Armenia is the largest acknowledged minority, and faces the same socioeconomic conditions as the majority population there. Having received a lot of cultural promotion during the Soviet Times and up until the present day, the inequality became obvious in the exclusive refuge regime in Armenia which was integrated into international politics along with an influential worldwide Armenian diasporic national identity. Yezidi refugees from Iraq, Turkey or Syria, however, were excluded from this refugee regime, which was solely based on (ethno-religious) Armenianness.

While the oldest Yezidi diaspora had been established in Armenia after WWI, the largest Yezidi diaspora today came into being in Germany during the last few decades and has already become established demographically as the country with the second largest Yezidi population worldwide.[39] Soon after the persecution in Şingal 2014, the Central Council of the Yezidis (*Zentralrat der Êzîden*) actively sought dialogue with NGOs, media and politicians in Germany to organize immediate help for the refugees and those still captured by IS. The German Federal State of Baden-Württemberg managed to accomplish a remarkable humanitarian undertaking, namely the Special Quota Project, through which 1,100 victims of IS, primarily Yezidi but also Chris-

39    See e.g. Tagay and Ortaç. 2016 and the Society of Yezidi Academics in Germany, Gesellschaft Yezidischer AkademikerInnen gea-ev.net.

tians, were brought from the camps in Kurdistan Iraq to Germany.[40] Trauma-tized women and children especially were in particularly bad situations fol-lowing the death or disappearance of their husbands or fathers. Women and children were under multiple threats and with hardly any chance of reaching Europe on their own. The project was supported by German members of the government, representatives of all parliamentary factions, cities and munic-ipalities, churches and civil society. The realisation of this pilot project was only possible through the lead of, and collaboration with, Yezidi diasporic or-ganisations and their activists (politicians, psychologists, physicians, lawyers) and the highest Yezidi religious representatives in Iraq. The project's inten-tion was to provide specific medical and psychological care, as there are only a few institutions in Kurdistan Iraq to take up this task.[41] This initiative was possible due to the decades long supportive relationship between German in-stitutions[42] and the Yezidi communities and, especially, the upcoming gener-ations, who are active in community based and integration projects and have gained leading positions in health care and social institutions.

In addition to that, Yezidi female activists in Germany initiated several re-lief projects for Iraq. Worldwide attention was gained for the Yezidi girls and women who were freed from IS and who were able to speak about their ex-periences in public, above all Nadia Murat, who was awarded the Nobel Peace prize in 2018. But many others also gave testimony in public, publishing their ordeals and becoming spokeswomen for their community. They transgressed the patriarchal traditions and found their own ways to speak out, to represent Yezidi women and to gain a voice in the international public. This concurred with the agency of Yezidi women in diaspora, who were themselves refugees or the offspring of displaced people. Even before IS, the young Yezidi gener-ations in the homeland and in diaspora argued for a rethinking of strict reli-gious prescriptions in Yezidism – the product of self-protection in a century-long hostile environment (such as strict endogamy) – which causes tensions and even violence in families.[43]

---

40    Blume 2016, see also gea-ev.net.

41    Therefore, the follow-up project comprised the training of experts in the KRI, such as trauma therapy courses held at the University of Dohuk.

42    This is mainly based in Nordrhein-Westfahlen and Baden- Württemberg.

43    "Yazidi women acquire new aspirations and replace (or rather complement) Yazidi men in fulfilling their traditional roles and obligations. For example, Yazidi women from the highly conservative and isolated Sinjar region learn new skills in refugee camp workshops (for example sewing) and, for the first time, even enter the labour

Consequently, the new agency of women arising due to these tremendous violent incidents and all the suffering in the aftermath, encompasses even older claims as well as incredible coping strategies with genocidal violence against women. Unspeakable sexual violence, questions of sexual (im)purity, of honour and of the position of women in society are at stake and, specifically, within this Yezidi women in residence countries and, likewise, as IDPs have gained a strong voice. The protection of the Syrian Kurdish fighting units, the YPG and especially the YPJ, the female Syrian Kurdish fighters who contributed enormously to the defeat of IS, are also of particular importance for the internal societal transformation and external representation.

## Conclusion

An integrated view on some of the single developments of refuge from, within and to Iraq has shown the necessity to have a multi-layered and gradual approach in figuring out characteristics and transformations of the multiple refugee regimes affecting Iraqi refugees. Analysis of the single regimes, their recent developments and historical depths, as well as transformations within this and their concurrence with other sub-regimes is necessary to grasp the multipolarity of the Iraqi refugee system as a whole. The next step to be analysed comprises the specific policies of the receiving states, their preparedness and political agenda in order to recognize the framework of interdependencies between the sub-regimes. Elaborating on these steps is also a prerequisite for understanding the scope for agency of the people. In addition to discussing the opportunity structure in a receiving state, we must also determine the prerequisites and scope of agency: avoiding the states of legal limbo – in which many refugees live - and granting secure living environments and prospects for enabling trust. This is a necessary step to develop agency: an agency of individuals as well as of associations for a sustainable adaptation.

As has been shown above, some of the Iraqi refugees are reluctant to be connected with Arabic or Kurdish diasporic associations, especially those whose belonging is bicultural (Sunni/Shia) or from a marginalized minority. But transnational associations of minorities can have an important influence in interfering in refugee regimes, in trust building processes and, in the long

---

market (very often as employees of domestic or international NGOs and humanitarian organizations)" (Černý, 2020, 11).

run, in supporting the agency of individuals. Through the comparison of the Armenian and German cases it becomes obvious that some of the refugee regimes are competing each other in the receiving state, and it is dependent on socio-economic possibilities and national ideologies as to whether a diasporic community can build up a stronghold for people seeking asylum. The concurrence of state policies and transnational associations' attempts to impact on these regimes has, up until now, not been studied in comparison. The Yezidi-German case also shows that agency for and of the newly arrived asylum seekers can have its impacts in transition processes of a transnational community. These interdependencies require further research and conceptualisation.

## References

Amnesty International. 2014. "Ethnic cleansing on a historic scale: The Islamic State's systematic targeting of minorities in northern Iraq". London. https://www.es.amnesty.org/uploads/media/Iraq_ethnic_cleansing _final_formatted.pdf.

Aziz, Mahir A. 2011. *The Kurds of Iraq: Nationalism and Identity in Iraqi Kurdistan.* London, New York: Tauris.

Aziz, Sardar. 2020. "On the Non-state (Ladaula) in Iraq." September 25, 2020. https://www.washingtoninstitute.org/fikraforum/view/non-state-l adaula-iraq.

Berger, Johannes, and Ludwig Strohner. 2016. "Schwerpunkt Migration und Integration: Gegenwart und Zukunft." *Wirtschaftspolitische Blätter* 63, no. 3: 509–524.

Bengio, Ofra. 2012. *The Kurds of Iraq: Building a State Within a State.* Boulder: Lynne Rienner Publishers.

Blume, Michael. 2016. "Das Baden-Württemberger Sonderkontingent für besonders Schutzbedürftige aus dem Nordirak. Mit Ausblicken zur Zukunft des Êzîdentums." In *Şingal 2014: Der Angriff des'Islamischen Staates,' der Genozid an den Êzîdî und die Folgen,* edited by Brizić, Katharina, Agnes Grond, Christoph Osztovics, Thomas Schmidinger, and Maria Six-Hohenbalken , 61–70. Wiener Jahrbuch für Kurdische Studien 4, Vienna: Ceasarpress.

Bruinessen, van Martin. 1994. "Genocide in Kurdistan? The Suppression of the Dersim Rebellion in Turkey (1937–38) and the Chemical War Against the Iraqi Kurds." In *Conceptual and Historical Dimensions of Genocide,* edited by

George J. Andreopoulos. 141–170. Pennsylvania: University of Pennsylvania Press.

Chaliand, Gerard, ed. 1993. *A People Without a Country: The Kurds and Kurdistan.* Brooklyn, NY: Olive Branch Press.

Chatelard, Géraldine. 2005. Iraqi Asylum Migrants in Jordan: Conditions, Religious Networks and the Smuggling Process. In *Poverty, International Migration and Asylum*, edited by George Borjas and Jeff Crisp, 341-370. London: Palgrave Macmillan. DOI:10.1057/9780230522534_16

Chatelard, Géraldine. 2012. "The Politics of Population Movements in Contemporary Iraq: A Research Agenda." In *Writing the Modern History of Iraq*, edited by Jordi Tejel, Peter Sluglett, Riccardo Bocco and Hamit Bozarslan, 359–378. Singapour: Worldwide Scientific Publishing.

Chatty, Dawn. 2010. *Displacement and Dispossession in the Modern Middle East.* Cambridge, N.Y.: Cambridge University Press.

Černý, Karel. 2020. "Iraqi Yazidis: Complex Drivers for Migrating Abroad after the Genocide." In *Vom Taurus in die Tauern: kurdisches Leben in den österreichischen Bundesländern. Teil 1: From the Taurus to the Tauern: Kurdish Life in the Austrian Federal Provinces. Part 1*, edited by Grond, Agnes, Katharina Brizić, Christoph Osztovics and Thomas Schmidinger, 127 – 150, Wiener Jahrbuch für Kurdische Studien 8, Vienna: Praesens Verlag.

Dalalyan, Tork. 2012. "Construction of Kurdish and Yezidi Identities among the Kurmanji speaking Population of the Republic of Armenia." In *Changing Identities: Armenia, Azerbaijan, Georgia* (Collection of Selected Works), ed. Heinrich Böll Foundation South Caucasus, 177–201. Tbilisi: Heinrich Böll Foundation South Caucasus.

Duclos, Diane. 2012. "Cosmopolitanism and Iraqi Migration." In *Writing the Modern History of Iraq*, edited by Jordi Tejel, Peter Sluglett, Riccardo Bocco and Hamit Bozarslan, 391 – 401. Singapour: Worldwide Scientific Publishing.

Fercher, Harald Gernot. 1995. *Die österreichische Asylpolitik und die Kurden.* Diploma thesis, University of Vienna.

Frantzman, Seth J. 2016. "Kurdistan After Islamic State: Six Crises Facing the Kurds in Iraq." *Middle East Review of International Affairs* 20, no. 3: 12 – 23.

Hardi, Choman. 2011. *Gendered Experiences of Genocide: Anfal Survivors in Kurdistan-Iraq.* Farnham: Ashgate.

Hiltermann, Joost. 2008. "The 1988 Anfal Campaign in Iraqi Kurdistan, Mass Violence and Resistance."[online], published on: 3 February,

2008. http://bo-k2s.sciences-po.fr/mass-violence-war-massacre-resista nce/en/document/1988-anfal-campaign-iraqi-kurdistan

Human Rights Watch. 1993. *Genocide in Iraq: The Anfal Campaign Against the Kurds*. New York: Human Rights Watch, 1993. Available online: http://ww w.unhcr.org/refworld/country„HRW„IRQ„47fdfb1d0,0.html [1.12.2018].

Human Rights Watch. 1994. *Bureaucracy of Repression. The Iraqi Government in its Own Words*. New York: Human Rights Watch.

Human Rights Watch. 2014a. "Iraq: Forced Marriage, Conversion for Yezidis: Victims, Witnesses Describe Islamic State's Brutality to Captives." October 11, 2014. https://www.hrw.org/news/2014/10/11/iraq-forced-marriage-con version-yezidis

Human Rights Watch. 2014b. "ISIL's Reign of Terror: Confronting the Grow ing Humanitarian Crisis in Iraq and Syria, Testimony of Sarah Margon." December 9, 2014. https://www.hrw.org/news/2014/12/09/isils-reign-terr or-confronting-growing-humanitarian-crisis-iraq-and-syria-testimony

Ibrahim, Ferhad. 1983. *Die kurdische Nationalbewegung im Irak*. Berlin: Schwarz.

Institute For International Law And Human Rights. 2015. *Between the Mill stones: The State of Iraq's Minorities Since the Fall of Mosul*. Report. Brussels, 2015. http://minorityrights.org/wp-content/uploads/2015/03/MRG_Rep_I raq_ONLINE.pdf

Institute of Statelessness and Inclusion. 2019. *Statelessness in Iraq Country Po sition Paper* November 2019. https://statelessjourneys.org/wp-content/upl oads/StatelessJourneys Iraq-final.pdf

International Organization for Migration (IOM). 2016. "Iraq Mission: Migra tion Flows from Iraq to Europe. Displacement Tracking & Monitoring." DTM, February 2016.

Izady, Mehrad R. 1992. *The Kurds: A Concise Handbook*. London, New York: Ty lor&Francis.

Izady, Merhad. 2004. "Between Iraq and a Hard Place: The Kurdish Predica ment." In *Iran, Iraq, and the Legacies of War*, edited by Potter, Lawrenceand Gary Sick, 71–100. New York: Palgrave Macmillan, 2004.

Kaválek, Tomáš. 2017. "Competing Interests in Shingal District: Examining the PKK-linked Structures, Defusing Tensions." *MERI Policy Report*. The Middle East Research Institute.

Khalil, Fadel. 1992. *Kurden heute*. Wien, Zürich: Europaverlag.

Khalil, Samir al- 1989. *Republic of Fear. The Politics of Iraq*. Berkely: University of California Press.

Knapp, Anni and Asylkoordination Österreich. 2001. "Geschützte Einreise von Flüchtlingen in Österreich. " Vienna, 2001. http://archiv.asyl.at/projekte/et_legal_entry_austria.pdf.

Kreyenbroek, Philip G., and Stefan Sperl, eds.. 1992. *The Kurds: A Contemporary Overview*. New York: Routledge.

Kurdistan Regional Government, Ministry of Interior, Joint Crisis Coordination Centre. 2021: *Humanitarian Situational Report: No. 6*. https://jcckrg.org/en/article/read/405.

Makiya, Kanan. 1998. *Republic of Fear*. Berkeley: University of California Press.

McDowall, David. 2000. *A Modern History of the Kurds*. London: I.B. Tauris.

Middle East Watch Report. 1993. *Genocide in Iraq. The Anfal Campaign Against the Kurds* New York, Washington, Los Angeles, London.

Minority Rights Group International. 2017. *Iraq – Faili Kurds*, November 2017, available at: https://minorityrights.org/minorities/faili-kurds/

Paasche, Erlend. 2016. *Return Migration and Corruption: Experiences of Iraqi Kurds*. PhD theses, Faculty of Social Sciences, University of Oslo.

Pelletiere, Stephen. 2007: *Losing Iraq. Insurgency and Politics*. Westport, London: Praeger.

Plebani, Andrea. 2017. "Policy Recommendations for the EU." In *After Mosul: Re-Inventing Iraq*, edited by Andrea Plebani, 159–165. Milano: Ledizioni LediPublishing.

Priest, Benjamin. 2019. *Kurdish Nationalism and Islam: An Ethnography of Modern Iraqi and Turkish Kurdistan* PhD thesis, Indiana University, 2019.

Savelsberger, Eva, Siamend, Hajo, and Irene Dulz. 2010. "Effectively Urbanized. Yezidis in the Collective Towns of Sheikhan and Sinjar." *Études rurales* 186: 101–116.

Sassoon, Joseph. 2012. "The Brain Drain in Iraq after the 2003 Invasion." In *Writing the Modern History of Iraq*, edited by Jordi Tejel, Peter Sluglett, Riccardo Bocco and Hamit Bozarslan, 379–390. Singapour: Worldwide Scientific Publishing.

Schulze, Ilona, and Wolfgang Schulze. 2016. *A Handbook of the Minorities of Armenia. A Sociocultural and Sociolinguistic Survey*. In collaboration with Garnik Asatrian, Viktoria Arakelova, Vardan Voskanian, and others. SOCIALIA – Studienreihe soziologische Forschungsergebnisse, Band 144. Hamburg: Kovac.

Sevdeen, Bayar Mustafa, and Thomas Schmidinger. 2019. *Beyond ISIS History and Future of Religious Minorities in Iraq*. London: Transnational Press.

Six-Hohenbalken, Maria. 2019. "May I be a sacrifice for my grandchildren—transgenerational transmission and women's narratives of the Yezidi ferman". DialecticalAnthropology 43, no. 2. DOI:10.1007/s10624-01 8-9506-9

Stansfield, Gareth, and Hashem Ahmadzadeh. 2007. "Kurdish or Kurdistanis? Conceptualising Regionalism in the North of Iraq." In *An Iraq of Its Regions. Cornerstones of a Federal Democracy?*, edited by Reider Visser and Gareth Stansfield, 123–149. London: Hurst and Company.

Strohmeier, Martin, and Yalçın-Heckmann, Lale. 2000. *Die Kurden. Geschichte, Politik, Kultur*. München: C.H. Beck.

Tagay, Sefik, and Serhat Ortaç. 2016. *Die Eziden und das Ezidentum. Geschichte und Gegenwart einer vom Untergang bedrohten Religion*. Hamburg: Landeszentrale für politische Bildung Hamburg.

Jordi, Sluglett, Peter, Bocco, Riccardo, and Hamit Bozarslan, eds. 2012. *Writing the Modern Historiy of Iraq. Historiographical and Political Challenges*. London: World Scientific Publisher.

United Nations. 2015. "Report of the Office of the United Nations High Commissioner for Human Rights on the human rights situation in Iraq in the light of abuses committed by the so-called Islamic State in Iraq and the Levant and associated groups." Human Rights Council, Twenty-eighth session, Annual report of the United Nations High Commissioner for Human Rights and reports of the Office of the High Commissioner and the Secretary-General, A/HRC/28/18. March 27, 2015. http://www.ohchr.org/ EN/HRBodies/HRC/RegularSessions/Session28/Pages/ListReports.aspx.

UNHCR. 2020. "Information Kit – Syrian Refugees – Iraq: Humanitarian Inter-Agency Achievements. (December 2019)". https://reliefweb.int/repo rt/syrian-arab-republic/information-kit-syrian-refugees-iraq-humanita rian-inter-agency.

Yildiz, Kerim. 2007. *The Kurds in Iraq. Past, Present and Future.* London: Pluto Press.

# On Incorporating Refugee Integration Into Refugee Regime: South Korean Case

*Seo Yeon Park*

## Introduction

In comparison to some countries across the world that have received large number of asylum-seekers in recent decades, South Korea is not a major refugee-hosting country. Following the statistics from 2019 Germany received 165,938 asylum applications, France received 132,614 and Canada 29,365 applications while South Korea received about 16,000 refugee applications in 2019 (CBSA 2020). When the conflict and humanitarian crisis broke out in Syria in 2013, around 430,000 Syrians sought protection in Europe that same year alone, and by the end of 2020, some 5.6 million Syrians have sought international protection, with another 6.2 million being internally displaced (UNHCR 2015; World Vision 2020). The conflict in the region still persists, with about 900,000 people in northwest Syria being displaced in 2019 due to continuing conflicts in Idlib (World Vision 2020; BBC News 2020).

On the basis of these statistics alone, South Korea might therefore appear to be a peripheral host country. However, South Korea is rapidly becoming an attractive destination country for some asylum-seeking populations in the world, as the number of refugee applications has skyrocketed over the last decade. When South Korea passed the Refugee Act in 2012 and established its own independent refugee regime, the number of applications remained less than 1,000 per year. In 2014, applications reached around 3,000 and then in 2018 and 2019, it climbed up to 16,173 and 15,452 respectively (Ministry of Justice 2021a). Presumably, this rapid change can be explained by the fact that the South Korean legal and institutional system for asylum seekers came to be known to foreign populations during a time when other countries were implementing stricter border controls. The so-called "securitization" of refugees has generated what media reports call the "European Refugee Crisis," referring to divisions in domestic politics in several European countries around refugee issues and the challenges these issues pose to policy makers (Esses, Hamilton and Gaucher 2017; Greussing and Boomgaarden 2017). While it is well-known that the majority of asylum seekers find refuge in neighboring countries like Turkey, Pakistan, Uganda and Sudan, refugee migration nevertheless presents a burden for some European countries, generating xenophobia and ultranationalism in and beyond Europe (Buchowski 2016; Greussing and Boomgaarden 2017). In recent years, the United States has also significantly reduced its annual intake of asylum applications in tandem with a policy discourse about "security" (Pew Research Center 2019). While some 29 million remaining refugees are dispersed throughout the world about 4.1 million refugees exist in Asia and Pacific region (UNHCR 2020). In this international humanitarian environment, some applicants, especially those from the Middle East and North Africa (MENA) region have gradually turned their eyes to a small country in the East: South Korea. The number of MENA region applications has been on the rise throughout the 2010s, particularly from Syria, Egypt, Yemen and Morocco (Ministry of Justice 2020). The migration paths that these applicants take are known to be serial, which means they usually stay in other countries before coming to South Korea rather than coming directly from their countries of origin. The majority of applicants to South Korea have always been from the Asian region, with people from origin countries such as Kazakhstan, Malaysia, India and China being particularly high over the past 3, 4 years, constituting more than half of the applications. This is partly because the major East Asian countries neighboring South Korea have not been very active in accepting refugee applications nor in providing asylum to those in need of protection – China, for instance, has been a member state to the Refugee Convention and has historically accepted some asylum seekers from Europe, Vietnam or Myanmar, but it has never established its own domestic law to define a refugee or to have provisions on the procedures for determining refugee status (Peterson 2012; Song 2018). Japan, on the other hand, recognizes only a very small number of refugees, even after it passed the related "Immigration Control and Refugee Recognition Act" in 2004 (Flowers 2009; Japan Ministry of Justice 2015). The numbers of refugee applications in South Korea in 2020 and 2021 decreased due to the Covid-19 pandemic, but it is well expected that the number of refugee applications will rise dramatically in the post-Covid period, owing to the abovementioned reasons.

Notably, in 2018 South Korea experienced a significant event in terms of refugee migration: what media outlets called the "Yemeni Refugee Incident".

This event generated a dramatic social debate about refugees for the first time in South Korea. Some 500 Yemeni asylum seekers landed on Jeju island (a southern resort island of South Korea) through economic flights connecting Kuala Lumpur and Jeju that had been launched just a few months before the relevant media reports started. Public discourses of security and xenophobia, but also of hospitality began circulating within South Korean society, having a large effect on South Korea's overall refugee policy, institutions and subsequent scholarly engagement.

In the following sections, I first analyze the characteristics of the South Korean refugee regime, which has evolved over the years along with the country's migration institutions. The first part of this study will include some of the dramatic changes that have been made in the years following the 2018 Yemeni Refugee Incident. This will show how the Korean refugee regime – understood to be rigid, unchanging and strict, at least according to some critics – has actually been quite flexible and changeable. I then discuss how discrepant integrations among asylum seeker groups have materialized and what these materializations mean for the South Korean refugee regime. I claim that a more integrated, proactive and holistic approach to refugee policies is needed. I also argue that the South Korean refugee institution needs to set its own direction in terms of migration/refugee policies which can only be possible through reflecting upon, and analyzing, the current refugee-related situations in South Korea.

## South Korean refugee regime

International refugee regimes are based upon the 1951 Convention on the Status of Refugees (also known as the UN Geneva Convention) and the establishment and workings of the United Nations High Commissioner for Refugees (UNHCR). The principles guiding refugee regimes comprise of non-refoulement and protection of refugees, which require that member states take on two major obligations: providing asylum and burden sharing (Betts 2015). Providing asylum refers to the responsibility that each state takes toward asylum seekers who have reached its territory, while burden sharing refers to the responsibility towards refugees outside of its territory. However, the norms and principles of the refugee regime have been debated among political theorists and refugee theorists alike, as have the discretionary practices of each country, and their policies toward refugees (Betts 2009; 2015).

South Korea became a signatory to the 1951 UN Geneva Convention and the 1967 Protocol in 1992. It is not a coincidence that the country became a signatory to the Convention when the South Korean government took a more open stance toward "globalization" and the acceptance of foreign populations. South Korea's democratization movement, coupled with the country's aspiration to become "more global" epitomized in the 1988 Seoul Olympics, brought a new socio-political horizon to the country (Koo 1997; Song 2000). The 1992 signing occurred in the context of a change in national leadership in 1987, the collapse of the Soviet Bloc in 1989 and the subsequent changes in diplomatic relationships with former communist countries, both North and South Korea joining the UN in 1991, and the beginning of a foreign labor recruiting system that same year, and the *Segyehwa* (globalization in Korean) campaign of the Kim administration from 1991-1997 all pointed towards an opening up of the country to the wider world and a desire to position South Korea within the global order. Becoming a party to the Refugee Convention can be viewed as another example in this series of the nation's efforts to pursue "globalization" and aspiration of implementing the "global standard" in the global human rights regime. Even to this day, the South Korean government has appealed to the general public regarding the acceptance of refugees with rhetoric about maintaining the country's "global standard" and "global citizenry". One can witness this aspect through the Ministry's announcements on cases like that of the Yemenis in 2018 and Afghans in 2021 (Ministry of Justice 2018; 2021b). The Convention is legally binding, as there are 146 member states which have ratified it. As many scholars and practitioners have observed, however, it is up to each country's discretion to determine how to ensure the protection of an individual applicant, even as countries share the same legal commitments as spelled out in the Convention. South Korea had its first refugee recognized in 2001, a decade after it first ratified the Convention. The first refugee recognition was made in the same year that the South Korean government had signed up for the UNHCR's Executive Committee as a member state - according to some of the officials that I have met.[1] Since then, the South Korean government has largely granted refugee status to Ethiopians and Bangladeshis, who make up about 50% of South Korea's entire recognized refugee population (Ministry of Justice 2021a).

Prior to 2018, refugee issues in South Korea were largely debated by specialists interested in and directly involved with refugee and migration policies

---

1    This signing contributed to the recognition of the first refugee.

and practices (Seol 2018). In the mid-2000s, a circle of specialists, composed mostly of lawyers and NGO workers, launched a plan to establish a specific law pertaining to refugees. Refugee advocates unyieldingly claimed that the Immigration Control Act should not dictate the refugee status determination process because the Act mainly purported to regulate the inflow of migrants (Kim 2006; Oh 2012). In response, 24 congressional representatives then proposed the Refugee Act on the status and treatment of refugees and asylum-seekers to the 18th national assembly (2008-2012), and after a series of institutional evaluations, the bill was finally enacted in February 2012. This enactment marks the establishment of the first independent refugee law in Asia.

Similar to the refugee laws in other countries, the Refugee Act introduced the rights and duties of refugees, humanitarian status holders, and refugee claimants for the first time, specifying different benefits according to each status (Refugee Act, Article 2). It also highlights the principle of refoulement and allows for claimants to apply for refugee status at ports (Article 6), an accommodation which had not been possible under the Immigration Control Act. Refugee claimants have rights to have their own legal representatives in processing the claim (Article 12, 13), and they can also apply for living expenses support (Article 40). After 6 months from an initial application, a claimant can also work legally and without much restriction. The law also includes provisions of the Third Country Resettlement program (Article 24), one of the UNHCR's refugee programs which was established to share the burden of refugee crises internationally (Ministry of Justice 2020). Even with all these advancements in South Korean refugee policy, the bill has drawn criticism from civil society groups that saw the Act as favoring government interests by regulating the influx of foreigners rather than protecting asylum-seekers. From the government's side, it was still a brave move to have an independent refugee law which might conflict with the overall policy regulations on foreign populations (Choi and Kwon 2017; Oh 2012). Despite the criticism, the Refugee Act stipulated some crucial protection measures in its provisions. These provisions make up the backbone of South Korea's refugee law and the new protections which it ensures.

In addition to establishing the 2012 Refugee Act, South Korea has created institutional structures to determine the status of refugees, elaborate on overall refugee policy, and support the integration of refugees in the region. The South Korean government formed the Refugee Division of the Ministry of Justice in 2013 to address the determination of refugee status and overall policies. In 2015, the government established a refugee resettlement program, with particular focus on Burmese refugees (following a similar program that was begun in Japan in 2011). This program has received positive feedback from scholars and refugee advocates, giving it a good momentum for further expansion. There is also continued discussion regarding the emendation of the current Refugee Act. As of 2020, the South Korean government has 16 different regional offices set up to receive refugee applications, and two separate divisions for refugee matters in their headquarters: the Division of Refugee Policy and the Division of Refugee Appeals (Ministry of Justice 2020), which oversee the overall refugee policy and deal with refugee appeal cases, respectively. The number of Refugee Status Determination (RSD) officers have increased to about 90 across the country, and the Division of Refugee Appeals has recently recruited Country of Origin (COI) investigating specialists to build expertise in COI research.

The establishment of the Refugee Law also raised some concerns regarding the abuse of the refugee system, as South Korea has seen a large percentage of applications made by those who apply for refugee status based on circumstances that do not align with eligibility requirements as stipulated in the Refugee Convention. Due to this factor, the overall protection rate (rate of refugee status recognition and humanitarian stay issuance) has dropped significantly – which became a major target of criticism from civil society and human rights advocates – and the overall institutional stability. This situation is problematic as it puts unnecessary institutional burdens on the immigration and refugee processing system, as South Korea has not developed the system to sufficiently manage large number of application; moreover, it could possibly distort the overall refugee regime by delaying the process of refugee status determination and by encouraging more and more people who do not need such protection to apply for it as an easier way of avoiding immigration controls (Han 2014; Song 2016).

The nationalities and demographics of applicants show some noteworthy characteristics and trends of the South Korean refugee flows. In 2019, most refugee claims were made by Russians, followed by citizens from Kazakhstan, China and Malaysia. In 2016, the top three applicant citizenships were from China, Egypt, and Pakistan. Changes in the nationalities depend largely on South Korea's visa policy with the above-mentioned countries, as they can at least pass the Korean border easily with a visa-free agreement. The list of origin countries for people applying for refuge in Korea differs from the top three citizenships of refugees internationally: Syria, Afghanistan and Venezuela (UNHCR 2020). This difference can be explained in geographical and historical terms. Being geographically close to South Korea, Central Asians, Southeast Asians and Chinese applicants comprise a higher number of refugee applications than those from Africa or South America. These areas are also historically close for economic and social reasons. There are many Korean Chinese and Korean Kazakhs who have made it to South Korea since the 2000s due to the establishment of a relaxed entry system for ethnic Koreans from these regions. The rise of refugee applications from these regions is allegedly linked with the immigration of ethnic Koreans, even though to date a systematic study of this connection has not been conducted. Refugee migration is not an isolated human migration; rather, people often move along kinship ties and cultural/social/religious affinities, as has been witnessed in other refugee migration cases (Song 2018). Even with the efforts made in South Korean refugee system, it still shows a relatively low rate of refugee recognition – the low rate of acceptance could be explained in several ways, and one reason behind that is high number of Chinese refugee applicants whom the South Korean government is hesitant to give the status to, owing partly to diplomatic relations with China (Wolman 2013).

*Table 1: Refugee Claims by Nationality – only major countries included (Ministry of Justice 2021a)*

| Nationality | 1994-2012 | '14 | '15 | '16 | '18 | '19 |
|---|---|---|---|---|---|---|
| Kazakhstan | 2 | 1 | 45 | 539 | 2,496 | 2,236 |
| China | 359 | 360 | 401 | 1,062 | 1,200 | 2,000 |
| Russia | 17 | 7 | 27 | 323 | 1,916 | 2,830 |
| Total | 5,069 | 2,896 | 5,711 | 7,541 | 16,173 | 15,452 |

*Total number of applications include all the other nationalities that are not listed above.

*Table 2: Recognized Refugees by Nationality (Ministry of Justice 2021a)*

| Nationality | Total | 1994-2012 | '14 | '16 | '18 | '19 |
|---|---|---|---|---|---|---|
| Burma | 336 | 134 | 4 | 41 | 36 | 34 |
| Ethiopia | 133 | 19 | 43 | 12 | 14 | 6 |
| Bangladesh | 119 | 65 | 2 | 9 | 7 | 6 |

The top three nationalities of refugees who are recognized in South Korea are Myanmar (Burma), Ethiopia, and Bangladesh, which is somewhat consistent with the global trend. Burmese refugees are mostly ethnic minorities from Burma, mostly Karen, who have come to South Korea through the UNHCR's resettlement program (Hong 2019). Refugees from Bangladesh and Ethiopia are convention refugees, who have been granted refugee status through the individual refugee application system. These two groups have particular characteristics which, it is alleged, allow them to be more easily recognized as refugees than other groups. Refugees from Bangladesh are mostly Jumma people, an ethnic minority in Bangladesh, who are known to have been subjected to ethnic and religious violence. The Jumma people are mostly Buddhist, which is one of the major religions in South Korea. Ethiopians had some historical ties with South Korea, which has made a difference in the refugee status determination process as Ethiopians are well-known in South Korea as "brothers" who fought bravely in the Korean War in the 1950s (Nancen 2016).

## Refugee Discourse and Policy Changes in Recent Years

Major Western countries, especially those in the "Global North", have retracted the scope of their refugee protection efforts in recent years due to the proliferation of international migration institutions (Betts 2009; Zetter 2007), the global politics of counter-terrorism (Abbas 2019; Guild and Garlick 2010), and the rise of protectionist regimes (Miller and Chtouris 2018; Noll 2018). These changes have meant that the burden sharing of refugee protection has been shouldered more by the Global South and the neighboring states of contemporary conflict regions than by the countries in the Global North. The onset of the "European Refugee Crisis" since the mid-2010s and the subsequent push for the "securitization of refugees" are the result of, and simultaneously indicative of, changing landscapes of contemporary migration policies and practices in Europe and the larger Global North.

Shifts in refugee discourse have also had an effect outside of the West, with the "securitization of refugee" practices arriving later in South Korea. Mirroring the situation in Western countries, South Korean society became internally divided on the issue of refugee policy in 2018 when it was faced with hundreds of Yemeni asylum seekers who entered the island of Jeju, the southern resort island of South Korea. From major media outlets to social media platforms such as Facebook and Instagram, the "refugee" became a trending topic of discussion (Choi and Park 2019). Unlike the countries which were already accepting large number of refugees, or had been operating temporary refugee camps in their territories for many decades, South Korea had not seen a sudden influx of asylum seekers prior to 2018, due to only having established its refugee regime in 2012 and also because of its geographical distance from the popular asylum seeking groups.

The prime example of securitization discourses in South Korea is undeniably the 2018 "Yemeni incident". Media reports of Yemeni refugees coming to Jeju Island ambiguously depicted blurred images of young Arab men roaming around the Jeju Immigration Office building in a way that the South Korean public could not easily interpret. South Koreans are familiar with Southeast Asian and Chinese migrants as they have long been low wage male workers and female marriage migrants both in urban and rural areas. Korean-Chinese domestic workers, have increased in recent decades to compensate for labour shortages in service industries, fulfilling reproductive needs in contemporary South Korea. Institutional interventions such as the Employment Permit System (E-9 visa system) and institutionalized marriage migration have largely contributed to this influx of Southeast Asian and Chinese migrants (Kim 2012; Lee 2015; Seol 2005). Compared to these migrant communities, South Koreans have little contact with Middle Eastern Asians in their everyday lives, as there had been only a small group of wealthy Middle Eastern businessmen or families traveling to South Korea for medical purposes before 2018. Despite being aware of the "refugee crisis" in the Middle East starting from the early 2010s, one can say most South Koreans have had little contact with Middle Eastern asylum seekers.

The majority of Yemenis coming to South Korea in 2018 flew in from Malaysia and other Southeast Asian countries. This is unsurprising given that the Middle East has long-standing political, economic and religious connections with the Southeast Asian region (Khoo 2014; Mandal 2014), and both regions have seen the exchange of a significant mass of human movement (Mandal 2014). However, as Malaysia is not a signatory of the Refugee Convention, nor of the 1967 Protocol, refugees are not distinguished from migrants. Yemenis fleeing from the plight of civil war cannot find work or attend schools legally and stably. Naturally, these populations start to look for more sustainable and viable options to continue their education and work, seeking safety for themselves and for their families back home. South Korea has become one such viable option in recent years, especially after the advent of low-fare flights connecting Kuala Lumpur and Jeju Island in December 2017, a route intended to boost "Korean wave" tourism in the region (Cho 2010; Peichi 2013). By June 2018, more than 500 Yemenis took the flight to the island and requested asylum.

While the Yemeni Incident caused much public debate into refugee issues, South Korea's refugee regime was far from dormant prior to 2018. While it has been largely unknown by the public, approximately 1,000 Syrian nationals came into South Korea from 2014-2016, and most of whom were granted a humanitarian stay visa (Ministry of Justice 2020). Nonetheless, the South Korean discourse on refugee issues has been similar to that of the other major refugee-receiving countries in the West, reflecting what Polish anthropologist Michal Buchoski (2016) has observed in Eastern Europe: "Islamophobia without Muslims," where nationalist and xenophobic tones dominate public discourse, despite very few of the refugees actually being Muslims. Even though the overall population of South Korea was not completely swayed by the nationalist and Islamophobic discourse of anti-refugee movements in other nations, public discourse was somewhat affected by the negativity towards the new Other that these movements created. Since then, Korean media outlets have started to take a rather critical view of refugee matters, with the overall tone of their response to proposed legislation regarding refugees changing dramatically. Before the "Yemeni Refugee Incident" in 2018, even the right-leaning media covered the Syrian refugee crisis in a favorable light, going so far as to campaign for readers' donations (Jung 2016). Before 2018, refugee matters were conceived of as being a humanitarian issue and as a matter of protection of vulnerable populations, which would give South Korea a moral high ground as a developed country and as a responsible member of the global citizenry. After the "Yemeni Refugee Incident", however, political discourse around refugee issues changed dramatically with an increase in the number of anti-refugee petitions and legislation that were proposed in Congress meetings. In addition, refugee controversies have also revealed some of the "older" issues of Korean civil society and highlighted the (over-) politicization of everyday life matters (Song 2018).

After arriving on the island, most Yemenis applied for asylum. The Jeju Immigration Office was not ready for the sudden increase of refugee claims from this region, as they only had one Arabic interpreter and one Refugee officer. As many Yemenis tried to change their visa type so that they could travel to the mainland to seek out better living and working conditions, the Jeju Office quickly took action (Jeju Immigration Service Office 2018). On 30 April

2018, the Jeju Immigration Office ordered a mobility restriction for Yemenis entering the mainland of the Korean peninsula as a way to expedite asylum application processing time and also to soothe public anxiety around the "uncontrollability" of these new migrants. Yemeni asylum seekers had no choice but to wait on the island for their final status determination results. In addition to this mobility freeze, the South Korean government also removed Yemen from the list of visa-exempt countries on June, 1 due to concerns about more Yemenis flying in. Upon facing harsh criticism by a vocal public regarding the Yemenis asylum seekers, the Korean government began to implement these stricter measures.

The state's response during the Yemeni Refugee Incident is especially peculiar and drastic when compared with South Korea's acceptance of more than 1,000 Syrians as humanitarian status holders by the year 2017. Syrian refugees did not create any social controversy and South Koreans largely accepted this group on the basis of humanitarianism. The rise of anti-refugee opposition in 2018 is especially concerning. While the South Korean government stated it would not cede to the demand of anti-refugee groups to abolish the Refugee Act, it has nevertheless shifted to a more cautious and rigid stance towards Middle Eastern refugees. The Yemenis have been portrayed as people who require careful screening in determining their status, and hence they must come off as "unthreatening" to locals and docile to the state officials in order to successfully obtain asylum. As the geographer Alison Mountz (2010) has observed, immigration laws or policies often reflect how the relevant state views refugees and migrants. Those could be reflected in the number of asylum status given, categorization of a certain group of people, and/or the legal changes. The view of Yemeni refugees as "potentially uncontrollable" Arab men who are suspicious and threatening clashes greatly with that of Syrians as needing care and humanitarian support who have gone through unimaginable destruction from their home country.

It is important to note, however, that South Korean government did make some institutional changes in light of the Yemeni Incident. The Ministry of Justice further invested in institutional support for refugee screening by increasing the number of Refugee Status Determination (RSD) officers in Jeju from one to five. The Ministry of Justice also assigned four more interpreters to the Jeju Immigration Office (Lee 2018). As a result of these efforts, status determinations were issued within six months for most applicants, and all the applications from the influx of Yemenis in 2018 were completed by the end of the year (Jeju Immigration Service Office 2018). These processing times were unusually rapid, as South Korea refugee processing time was on average about a year at that time. In light of relevant scholarship and refugee advocates who have criticized for the slow pace of the process, this change is especially noteworthy (Heo 2018; Jeju Immigration Service Office 2018). In addition, by early 2019, the Ministry decided to hire more refugee officers who have prior experience in refugee law and refugee integration, as well as knowledge in the cultures of the asylum seekers' country of origin. As a result, there are over 70 workers currently working as RSD officers both in the primary application and appeals procedure, and about 20 of them are newly recruited outside of the common government official recruits. Thus, the state has taken a more positive step towards "competitive workforce" and "expedited refugee status determination" (Ministry of Justice 2020). The Ministry also took a proactive step towards supporting the asylum seekers' livelihood, as it allowed them to work in some industries in Jeju earlier than the six months' rule,[2] and it actively provided job opportunities to the applicants. Yemenis who could not find residence were provided shelters, with the help of some religious and civil society groups. These kinds of support were made possible through cooperation among governments of both central and regional, civil society organizations and local business owners. This could result in quite some momentum for the Korean refugee regime, and may lead to it being able to develop its system through real-life experiences and establish active cooperative networks among different stakeholders. The national-level crisis turned into something that can be cited as something positive and noteworthy in developing the refugee regime in South Korea. This aspect of refugee governance did not receive much attention in the national-level discourses, however. Policy makers, scholars and civil society organizations have instead paid more attention to what to do next; the larger number of influx of asylum seekers posed a difficult question to the nation.

As Song (2019) points out, refugee governance and integration requires more than bureaucratic reforms by the central government; it requires an active civil discourse, actual engagement by different actors within broader society. The Yemeni case in Korea revealed interesting and divergent trajectories, as the local refugee institutions to a degree gained valuable experiences in handling refugees and showed capacity of integrating refugees fairly

---

2     In principle, refugee applicants can legally work only after six months of their application submission.

– most of the Yemeni asylum seekers were given jobs and shelters to sustain them, and local Korean residents became more accepting throughout the period. However, a more balanced civil discourse was not achieved in South Korea at a national level during and after the 2018 Yemeni Incident. Pro-refugee and anti-refugee groups failed to reach any kind of social consensus, with the voices of anti-refugee groups becoming more extreme with a mix of false accusations and intensified nationalism and xenophobia, and pro-refugee groups failing to formulate a convincing counter discourse. Anti-refugee groups have called for abolishing the 2012 Refugee Act and withdrawing from the 1991 Refugee Convention. They even claimed that foreigners are taking away Korean traditions and hence are harming Korean society, which demonstrates a clear lack of understanding of the meaning of a refugee regime as constituted based on international convention, a nation-state's rights and duties, and the human rights regime regarding refugee applicants (Song 2019). Pro-refugee groups espoused the rhetoric of "universal human rights" and "a responsible global citizenry," but failed to effectively connect this rhetoric with the contexts of their specific refugee policy. As outlined in the previous section, refugee status decisions made in Korea reflect a rigid, or somewhat outdated immigration control. As pro-refugee groups never had a chance to proactively engage in larger public discussions or in policy debates with government officials and policy makers, they have had no choice but to passively react to the wave of anti-refugee protests in 2018.

In the next section of this chapter, I shall look into how refugee claimants are accepted and integrated in South Korea and will illustrate how and why this aspect of the refugee integration process should be considered as an important element in developing a more stable and integrated refugee regime. Furthermore, it attempts to show how refugee migration and integration are also closely connected to other kinds of migration. The discussion also suggests that policy makers and scholars in the field contemplate on how to mend the South Korean refugee regime in relation to migration regime that can work better for both the society and the migrants (including asylum seekers).

## Refugee agency: Posing possibilities? Or limitations?

In this chapter, I shall compare and contrast the refugee/migrant worker communities in Gimpo and Ansan, Seoul-metropolitan area. More specifically, the two groups under discussion are: the African community, composed of diverse African nationalities in Ansan, and the Bangladeshi community, which comprises mostly of Jummas granted refugee status in Gimpo. I contend that having diverse options in residency other than refugee-related visa status contributes to refugees' – inclusive of recognized refugees, refugee applicants and humanitarian stay holders – overall well-being, and more positive outlook in social integration. Further, these cases also purport to show how ethnic, cultural and religious politics play a role in social integration.

South Korea became one of the "Four Asian Dragons" in the 1990s due to rapid economic development and high growth rates from the 1960s. The 1990s were a period of economic achievement and celebratory optimism as the country prepared to move forward to the next phase of its industrial development. Major South Korean industries moved from manufacturing to more advanced technology and service industries. At the same time, small manufacturing factories had to compete with factories in less-developed countries prompting the recruitment of South Asian labour migrants. These labour migrants revived many "dead towns" in metropolitan areas such as Gimpo and Ansan, which were both manufacturing cities during the 1960s through 1970s and are now two of the most globalized cities in South Korea, with certain areas of the city containing mostly foreign workers.

Southeast Asian workers, mostly male, often made their initial journey to South Korea with the E-9 visa, a visa granted through the Employment Permit System (EPS) program and allowing applicants a maximum of four years and ten months of residence. The E-9 visa is specifically designed to allow people to stay and work in the country but not to settle permanently, as a minimum of five years of residence is required to apply for South Korean citizenship. Therefore, it is relatively easy to get into South Korea as a migrant worker, but difficult to successfully and stably settle. For many, once their visa is expired, they can still make visits to South Korea but cannot live permanently, as the E-9 is specifically designed to prevent visa holders from gaining permanent residency or citizenship. This type of visa plays an interesting part in refugee application in Korea. First, many people who are near to the expiration of their E-9 visa apply for refugee status. They usually gain information from older applicants of their own nationalities, and the process is done quite generically, since cities like Gimpo and Ansan have large ethnic communities and commercial industries where the refugee applicants can find a good amount of information. This certainly adds to the institutional burden of the Ministry of Justice in adjudicating these applications, as about 60-70% of Southeast Asian refugee applicants are former E-9 visa holders. These populations do not depend solely upon their status determination as refugees for staying in Korea. They have a plethora of social networks and resources which they have built over the years, allowing them to find both formal and informal work, while enjoying life within the ethnic communities.

The Bangladeshis living in Gimpo are usually long-term residents of the city and part of the Bangladeshi communities there. From the very beginning of the Industrial Training Recruitment System (the previous form of EPS program) in the early 1990s, Bangladeshis made up a significant portion of the city's labour force. While working, they created their own communities. Their presence revived the city's economy and local Koreans have gradually learned how to live with them. Gimpo, being a less-developed and less-wealthy area compared to other "new towns" in the Seoul-metropolitan area, was especially suited for foreign workers to formulate their own communities (Oh 2005; Seol 2009).

Starting in the early 2000s, some Bangladeshis, particularly those of Jumma descent, began to apply for refugee status, and with a relatively larger number than many other groups being awarded the status, totaling 119 people as of 2019. This comprises some 12% of all the refugee status grantees. The first refugee status was given to a Buddhist Jumma person in 2002, and the early refugee status grantees started to bring their families and relatives from Bangladesh, and for the most part they were successfully granted refugee status (Lee 2019). Their religion, Buddhism, and their similar phenotypic aspects and cultural affinities made it easier for them to settle, than those people coming from the Middle East or Africa (Lee 2019). One government official hinted to me that the Refugee Law was made possible because a congressional representative who was a Buddhist and came to know of Jumma people promoted the establishment of the law that could then better provide for refugee applicants.

Since then, Bangladeshis have been able to garner support from politicians and legislators, and they have shared the benefits of the recognition of refugee status within the ethnic community. This aspect was affirmed by other news reports on the active involvement of Korean Buddhist outreach activities collaborating with some Jumma (Chakma) people (Cho 2014; Lee 2019). Some of Bangladeshis have been actively engaged with local and ethnic matters, whether it be labour or marriage or asylum-seeking matters, in a form of NGO whose workforce comprises both South Koreans and Bangladeshis

(Lee 2019)[3]. Their Korean language skills are known to be competent, thanks to support from the local community and also attributable to the people's individual efforts to learn the language in order to get more opportunities in work and social life in general. Due to the high percentage of residents who are either refugees or refugee claimants, the city council once advocated for a citywide refugee decree to set up its own refugee integration program and establish a refugee support centre (KBS 2015), but this movement did not pass provincial government's approval as it violated higher provisions of a relevant law. Even though the council's refugee decree did not pass, it still indicates that the national refugee regime could have diverse figures, and a successful local integration of a refugee group can affect changes in refugee regime. Bangladeshi refugee/migrant community's voices and grassroots efforts were influential enough to propose such a motion.

The community also continues to make an effort to maintain ties with Korean Buddhist groups, which at times emerges as some practical gains to the community, such as provision of scholarships, donations and invitations to Buddhist events and gatherings. Even to this day, Bangladeshis, whether they are Jumma refugees or migrant workers, are known to support each other in economic, civil and social matters and try to live harmoniously with their local communities. The Bangladeshi case shows a prominent example of political empowerment of a refugee group which utilized its long-term experiences of residence in South Korea as a strategy towards gaining a meaningful political voice. The initial settlement of Bangladeshi labour migrants provided the ethnic community with an ethos of hard-working and an achievement-focused attitude which prepared a good soil for refugee applicants to not be solely dependent upon the status itself. The ethnic and religious affinities also played favourable roles in their local integration into South Korean society.

On the other hand, African communities in Ansan have followed a different trajectory. Within the African communities of Ansan, Ethiopians are still in too small a number to formulate their own community. Since Ethiopians are in a better position to gain statuses other than as refugees – such as through student and business visas – they tend to reside in different parts of the country, forming a small circle of ethnic community. The Ethiopians in Ansan live and interact with other nationals from the same continent, but

3    They have created the NGO "Jaehan Jummain Yeondae (Jumma People's Network in South Korea)"in 2002, and the person who actively involved in the creation of the NGO was a recognized refugee.

they enjoy distinctive benefits compared to the other nationals. Ethiopians are also more likely to receive refugee status than other nationals from the continent owing to the historical ties between South Korea and Ethiopia, as well as the former's econo-political interests in the latter – that is, South Korean government's efforts to invest in the African continent through an amiable diplomatic relationship with Ethiopia (Office of the President 2011; SBS 2011). The first African refugee recognition was made to an Ethiopian in 2001 (Lee 2019). Apart from Ethiopians, other Africans have generally not successfully obtained refugee status or humanitarian status. There are also the nationalities that are not included in the E-9 (long-term employment) program, which is more targeted toward attracting Southeast Asian populations. Because of this predicament in visa status/opportunities, many Africans enter the country with short-term tourist visas (Han 2014). Ethiopians, whose applications benefit from their ancestors' involvement in the Korean War, are not only granted refugee status more easily, but various other types of visa as well. Many Ethiopians come with student visas, or work, visiting and cultural exchange visas. During the Lee administration (2007-2012) in particular, South Korean companies began to look towards Africa as an up-and-coming region worthy of investment. Consequently, the Lee administration encouraged economic exchanges with African countries. The president himself once visited Ethiopia for diplomatic purposes and expressed interest in pursuing economic partnerships with other African countries – especially the Republic of South Africa, Cameroon, Angola, and the Republic of Congo – due to their natural resources. Within this context of increasing Korean-African econo-political activity, there are a relatively higher number of Ethiopians arriving in South Korea. Because of the higher chance for them to be recognized and to legally stay in Korea, Ethiopians are in relatively good standing compared to other African communities in Ansan. Even though they share some social and cultural affinities, Ethiopians do not appear to engage with matters of different ethnic/national groups as much as Bangladeshis do to their own national/ethnic community. Still, the ethnic and cultural differences are felt deep by South Koreans, and Africans confess that they generally feel discriminated against by South Koreans and do not feel welcomed. Since there are not many visa options available to Africans in general, many apply for refugee status in their early residence period (Han 2014). These applicants attempt to find ways to reside in South Korea, but those attempts usually end up being negative. Among African refugee applicants, three or four times applicants are common, as refugee status can be the only viable option for them to stay.

As multiple refugee applications come with disadvantages such as no work permit or education rights, they are left out of the legal system and their off-spring usually go undocumented. These precarious life conditions generate many problems in the community. Some of the support NGOs workers I met witnessed growing domestic violence by frustrated husbands and a growing percentage of depression and other mental problems due to the precarious institutional limbo state of their lives. Some African refugee applicants have been vocal about the South Korean public's indifference and even negative treatment to them (Yombi Tona and Park 2013, Lee 2019). The overall image of Africans in South Korea can further isolate the African applicants, as South Koreans started to witness their less than perfect living conditions and build negative stereotypes as 'undocumented' and 'poor.'

## Future Questions of South Korean Refugee Regime

In this chapter, I have examined the development of the Korean refugee regime since 2012, the post-Yemeni Incident atmosphere surrounding refugee issues since 2018, and the current situation of refugee communities in Gimpo and Ansan. My analysis shows that the South Korean refugee regime has changed according to external humanitarian situations, international relations and the local integration of refugees. It also shows that the refugee policy needs to consider refugee integration and existing dynamics within local communities where refugee resettlement occurs. Without taking these various dimensions of refugee regime and integration into account, Korea's refugee regime will be limited to strictly legal measures that cannot fully address the lived situation of these communities and the realistic practices in relation to migrant integration which in turn affect the overall operations of the refugee regime. The expansion of a discussion beyond specialists, more realistic proposals by civil society, and wider social consensus could start from a deeper and more accurate understanding of the lived situation of refugees in Korea. In addition, as refugee migration cannot be considered in isolation, the refugee regime, overall institutions and policies have to come up with tangible and realistic directions in accepting refugees who are also - broadly speaking - migrants. Potentially, policy makers can start to consider the ramifications of refugee applications to different ethnic/national communities in the larger refugee-migrant nexus. In the cases I illustrated in this paper, the contrast between the communities that are solely dependent upon refugee application for staying in South Korea and the communities that have various options for stay show distinctive trajectories of refugee integration and outlook of overall migrant integration within urban areas. The institutional gaps that contribute to the South Korean general public's negativity toward refugees and to specific ethnic/national groups should be mended through careful and broader policy considerations. The directions taken in developing the refugee regime have to be more actively discussed among the different stakeholders – namely, refugee/migrant communities, scholars, civil society organizations, government officials, and legislators. I suggest that refugee regime officials consult outside voices, including but not limited to: grassroots activists, shelter workers, lawyers, and scholars to discuss ways that will benefit both the refugee communities' immediate needs as well as the longer-term goals of the country as a whole. Determining the status of refugees is a legal matter that entails interpreting relevant law, examining each claim, and granting rights and benefits accordingly. However, refugee issues cannot remain a legal matter alone. In order to more effectively develop South Korea's refugee regime, we must also consider the arenas of international relations, national interests, domestic politics, and the social capacity of local communities to accept and integrate various newcomers.

## References

Abbas, Madeline-Sophie. 2019. "Conflating the Muslim refugee and the terror suspect: responses to the Syrian refugee 'crisis' in Brexit Britain." *Ethnic and Racial Studies*, 42, no. 14: 2450-2469.

Appadurai, Arjun. 1990. "Disjuncture and difference in the global cultural economy." *Theory, culture & society* 7, no. 2-3: 295-310.

Asylum in Europe 2020: Francehttps://www.asylumineurope.org/reports/country/france/statistics (accessed Oct. 9th, 2020).

BBC News. 2020. "Syria conflict: UN says Idlib displacement 'overwhelming' relief effort." 2020. 2.17.https://www.bbc.com/news/world-middle-east-51537145 (accessed Oct. 1st 2020)

Betts, Alexander. 2009. "Institutional proliferation and the global refugee regime." *Perspectives on politics* 7, no. 1: 53-58.

Betts, Alexander. 2015. "The normative terrain of the global refugee regime." *Ethics & International Affairs* 29, no. 4: 363.

Buchowski, Michał. 2016. "Význam antropologie v době vzestupu islamofobie a 'uprchlické krize': případ Polska" [Making Anthropology Matter in the Heyday of Islamophobia and the 'Refugee Crisis': The Case of Poland]. *Český lid* 103, no. 1: 51-84

Cho, Chul Ho. 2010. "Korean Wave in Malaysia and Changes of the Korea-Malaysia Relations." *Malaysian Journal of Media Studies* 12, no. 1: 1-14.

Cho, Hyun Sung. "5 70  " [50 million won brings new hope to 700,000 people]. *Bulkyo21*. 2014.10.23. http://www.bulkyo21.com/news/articleView.html?idxno=26388

Esses, Victoria M., Hamilton, Leah K., and Danielle Gaucher. 2017. "The Global Refugee Crisis: Empirical Evidence and Policy Implications for Improving Public Attitudes and Facilitating Refugee Resettlement." *Social Issues and Policy Reviews* 11, no.1: 78-123.

Greussing, Esther, and Hajo G. Boomgaarden. 2017. "Shifting the Refugee Narrative? An Automated Frame Analysis of Europe's 2015 Refugee Crisis." *Journal of Ethnic and Migration Studies* 43, no. 11: 1749-74.

Guild, Elspeth, and Madeline Garlick.2010. "Refugee protection, counter-terrorism, and exclusion in the European Union." *Refugee Survey Quarterly* 29, no. 4: 63-82.

Heo, Ho-Jun. 2018. "Jeju Yemenin 2myeong nanmin injeongtn 484myeongjung injeongnyul 0.4%" [2 Yemenis recognized as Refugees in Jeju...... Recognition Rate Is 0.4% among 484]. *The Hankyoreh*, December 14. http://www.hani.co.kr/arti/area/area_general/874426.html (accessed March 20, 2020).

Lee, Jae Ho. 2019. 5. 28 "Geudeuli Gimpoe Ppurinaerin wondongryekeun" [How did they settle stably in Gimpo?] *Hangyerehe21*. http://h21.hani.co.kr/arti.cover/cover_general/47117.html (accessed November 25, 2020)

Hong, Hyun Gi 2019. 12. 2. "Hanguk on Miyanma Nanmindeul Eodie Salka? [Where do the Burmese refugees settle in Korea?] *Yeonhap News*. https://www.yna.co.kr/view/AKR20191129061900065 (accessed September 10, 2021)

Jeju Immigration Service Office. 2019. *Jeju Yemen nanmin baekseo* [2018 White Paper about Yemen Refugees]. Ministry of Justice. http://www.immigration.go.kr/bbs/immigration/226/520085/artclView.do (accessed April 27, 2020).

Jung, Won Yeop 2016. 4. 5. "Siria nanmin campeureul gada." [We went to the Syrian refugee camps]. *JoongAngIlbo*.https://news.joins.com/article/19839337 (accessed Oct. 9th, 2020)

Lee Jae Ho 2019. "Jummajokeul Asinayo" [Do you know about Jumma people?] *Hangyereh21*. https://h21.hani.co.kr/arti/cover/cover_general/47111.h
tml (accessed September 20, 2021)

Lee, Ji-heon. 2018. 7. 5. "Jeongbu, Jeju nanminsimsaillyeog jeung-
won..Yemenin simsa 10wolkkajin kkeunna" [Government, More Staff
Members to be Assigned for Refugee Assessment in Jeju.. The Process
Will Be Done by October]. *Yeonghap News*. http://www.index.go.kr/potal/
main/EachDtlPageDetail.do?idx_cd=2820 (accessed September 20, 2021)

Mandal, Sumit K. 2014. "Arabs in the Urban Social Landscapes of Malaysia:
Historical Connections and Belonging." *Citizenship Studies* 18, no. 8: 807-
22.

McConnachie, Kirsten. 2019. "Securitization and Community-based Protection among Chin Refugees in Kuala Lumpur." *Social & Legal Studies* 28, no.
2: 158-78.

Miller, DeMond, and Sotiris Chtouris. 2018. "The Differing Perceptions of
Zones of Exclusion: The Redefinition of the Modern European Protectionist State in an Era of Unprecedented Irregular Migration." In *Migration
and the Crisis of the Modern Nation State* edited by Jacob Frank and Adam
Luedtke, 211-234. Wilmington: Vernon.

Ministry of Justice. 2018. 7. 24. "Jeju Yemen nanmingwanryeon seolmyung-
jaryo" [Explanatory Brief on Yemenis in Jeju]. *News/Notice Board. Korean
Immigration Service*, Ministry of Justice.

—— 2019. 9. 27. "Nanminsimsareul deo sinsokago jeonghwakage jinhaeng-
haget-seumnida" [We Promise Speedier and More Accurate Refugee
Screening]. *News/Notice Board. Korean Immigration Service*, Ministry of Justice.

—- 2021. 7. 2. "2020 Chulipguk Oegukin Jungchaek Tonggye Yeonbo" [2020
Statistics on Immigration Policy]. *News/Notice Board. Korean Immigration
Service*, Ministry of Justice.

—- 2021. 8. 26. "Beopmubu janggwan Apgan tekbyulipgukja beuripingjaryo"
[Press Briefing on Afghan Special Contributors]. *News/Notice Board. Korean
Immigration Service*, Ministry of Justice.

Ministry of Justice. 2020. "Nanmin tonggye hyeonhwang" [Current Statistics
on Refugees]. http://www.index.go.kr/potal/main/EachDtlPageDetail.do
?idx_cd=2820 (accessed March 2, 2020).

Mountz, Alison. 2010. *Seeking Asylum: Human Smuggling and Bureaucracy at the
Border*. Minneapolis: University of Minnesota Press.

Mountz, Alison, and Nancy Hiemstra. 2014. "Chaos and Crisis: Disecting the Spatiotemporal Logics of Contemporary Migrations and State Practices." *Annals of the Association of American Geographers* 104, no. 2: 382-90.

Nagel, Caroline R. 2002. "Geopolitics by Another Name: Immigration and the Politics of Assimilation." *Political Geography* 21, no. 8: 971-87.

Nancen 2016. 5. 27. "Parkgeunhye daetongryeongeui Etiopia bangmungwa ingwonoegyo" [The president's visit to Ethiopia and Humanitarian diplomacy]. *Data on Refugees.* Nancen (Refugee Rights Center). https://nancen.org/1534

Newman, David. 2006. "The Lines that Continue to Separate Us: Borders in Our 'Borderless' World." *Progress in Human Geography* 30, no. 2: 143-61.

Noll, Gregor. 2018. "Security in a liberal union: EU asylum and migration control policies." In *The European Union: Facing the Challenge of Multiple Security Threats,* edited by Bakardjieva-Engelbrekt, A., A. Michalski, N. Nilsson, L. Oxelheim 191–211. Cheltenham, Northampton: Edward Elgar Publishing

Office of the President. 2011. 7. 10. "Daetongryong, Han etiopia Gaebalgyeongheom gongyu wokeushap chamseok" [President, attending at a workshop to share experiences of development of South Korea and Ethiopia]. http://17cwd.pa.go.kr/kr/president/news/news_view.php?uno=1500&board_no=P01

Oh, Seung-jin. 2012. "Nanminbeob jejeongui uiuiwa munjejeom" [Several Issues on the New Refugee Law of Korea]. *Kookjebobhakwhoenonchong* [Korean Journal of International Law] 57 (2): 91-112.

Peichi, Chung. 2013. "Co-Creating the Korean Wave in Southeast Asia: Digital Convergence and Asia's Media Regionalization." *Journal of Creative Communications* 8, no. 2-3: 193–208

SBS, 2011.7.9. "Etiopia gan Yee daetongryong 'Hangukjeon Chamjeon itji ana'" [President, having gone to Ethiopia, "We won't forget your participating in the Korean War"] https://news.sbs.co.kr/news/endPage.do?news_id=N1000945523 (accessed November 25, 2020)

Seol, Dong-hoon. 2018. "Nanmingwallyeon sahoegaldeung haesowa sahoejeong habui dochureul wihan gongnonhwa gwajewa banghyang" [A Direction toward Social Consensus and Resolution on Refugees and Related Social Struggles]. July 19, A Proceeding at the National Assembly Policy Discussion.

UNHCR (United Nations High Commissioner for Refugees). 2018. *UNHCR Statistical Yearbook 2016,* 16th Edition. https://www.unhcr.org/statistics/co

untry/5a8ee0387/unhcr-statistical-yearbook-2016-16th-edition.html  (accessed April 16, 2020).

Yombi, Tona, and Jinsook Park. 2013. "Naeireumeun Yombi- Hangukeseo nanmineuro salagagi"[My name is Yombi – living as a refugee in Korea]. Ihoo

World Vision. 2020. *Syrian refugee crisis: Facts, FAQs, and how to help.* https://www.worldvision.org/refugees-news-stories/syrian-refugee-crisis-facts (accessed October 1st, 2020)

Zetter, Roger. 2007. "More labels, fewer refugees: Remaking the refugee label in an era of globalization." *Journal of Refugee Studies* 20, no. 2: 172-192.

# The Struggle for Agency of Older Refugees of the Syrian Conflict in Vienna

*Sabine Bauer-Amin*

## Introduction

*February 18th 2018, Vienna. (fieldnote)*
*I visit an Arabic speaking church in the 19th district Vienna; after the service, the priest invites me to have a small get together with the community members to introduce our research project on first experiences and expectations of refugees in Vienna. While I am chatting with different community members, a very elegantly dressed man in his late 50s comes to sit next to me. For a while, he stays silent. Then Abou Younis, as he introduces himself to me, apologizes and says that he did not want to interrupt my conversation, but he wanted to talk to me. He explains that he felt lost in Austria because he felt "as if I had left my dignity behind in Syria." Before he had left for Austria, he had worked as an accountant and had enjoyed a good social status. One of his children had studied dentistry and another was a general doctor. Now, all of them are in Vienna, but there is no possibility for them to regain their previous status. Abou Younis underlines his wish to return to his profession but there was no possibility. The labour market service had also told him that there are no job prospects for him on the Austrian market and that his children should do a vocational training (Ausbildung) instead of trying to re-enter into their previous professions. Abou Younis expresses that he was suffering mostly from this loss of status, identity and perspectives and that he did not see any future for him. For a moment, there is silence between us. The man begins to cry and cannot speak any more. Knowing about the lack of state sponsored programs for his age group, I also run out of words. After he regains his posture, he explains that he feels he is wasting his life in Austria now and that there was no possibility for him to use his time in a good way. He repeatedly addresses that he had no possibility of changing his current situation since he has no chances on the labour market, yet, he is continuously told by the Austrian authorities how important it is to find gainful work in order to become a useful member of society. Without being seen as such, and without being able to*

*create connections with other German speakers, he asks me how he would ever be able to master the German language. Trying to shift the attention to a less exhausting topic for Abou Younis, I ask him about his daily routine. He explains he has only been sitting at his house alone. I then ask if the church helped. He answers that without the church, life would be much harder. He underlines how important it was to have these meetings to talk to people in the same situation. He then refers to several other elderly men in the room. "Look, this is Abou Youssef, an architect. Next to him is Dr Girgis, a cardiologist and in the corner are Mr. Revan and Mr. Imad, two engineers. All of us are useless now. We are nobody here."*

The conversation with Abou Younis made me think about the situation of older[1] forced migrants in the Austrian refugee regime's current equation of "integration" with employment that overshadows their legal obligation to provide protection ("Responsibility to Protect", or short R2P, see United Nations n.d.) to people threatened by war and human rights violations. Why is the labour market focus so strong in Austria's dealing with refugees? What does that do to those who cannot enter the labour market (anymore)? What roles in society are left for those excluded from the Austrian "integration path" (Federal Ministry of Austria, European and International Affairs, 2015)?

The current understanding of "integration" in Austria is based on lessons learned throughout the Austrian *Gastarbeiter*[2] migration. While the current Austrian integration debate centres on the rapid acquisition of the German language and inclusion in the Austrian labour market, elderly refugees are often unable to fulfil these integration criteria, which may in turn leave them with only limited options for improving their current situation in Austria.

In this chapter, I want to shed light on the issues and challenges that elderly refugees from Syria face in Vienna. Their situation and their prospects are often overlooked, as they are seemingly considered unemployable due to the age restrictions and hence are not appealing for the Austrian government programs. Moreover, the private initiatives are not particularly interested in the elderly refugees either. This contribution discusses the challenging situation that many elderly Syrian refugees face in Austria as well as the scope for agency for the group in question, based on interviews and fieldnotes with elderly people from Syria conducted within a broader research project on

---

1    A discussion of what "older" means in this context will follow in the following chapter.
2    Transl. as guest workers; concept will be explained in detail later in the text.

refugees in Austria.[3] It aims to show the situation and perspectives, as well as the scope for agency for the group in question.

I first want to take a closer look at the pathway that the Austrian government envisions for refugees to integrate them into Austrian society. I then want to change the perspective and shed a light on a group, who cannot fulfil these requirements that the government foresees. Finally, this contribution wants to shift the focus on labour market integration as the main path towards being seen as a valuable member of society to the roles and agency of older refugees for communities. In doing so, I aim to highlight the consequences of the current refugee regime's reduced understanding of "integration".[4]

## Older refugees and refugee regimes

Elderly refugees had not been in the focus of humanitarian agencies or national refugee regimes for too long. Only from the 2000s onwards, has the UN recognised older refugees as a vulnerable group with specific needs (UNHCR Standing Committee 2020). The UN introduced a special category for people aged 60 plus for their statistical data (UNHCR 2000, 21).[5] This was partly due to the rising percentage of elderly people among refugees. According to the UNHCR statistical data, in 2011 elderly refugees (aged 60 plus) accounted for 5% (UNHCR 2011, 8), however, in 2018 the percentage of refugees aged 60 plus increased to 8.5% (UNHCR 2011, 8). On the one hand, refugees who fled their homes as younger adults are now aging in exile while on the other

---

3     The study Leaving – Persevering – Arriving (LODA): A transdisciplinary survey of the recent situation of refugees in Austria was conducted from 2017 to 2019 by the Austrian Academy of Science Institutes for Social Anthropology and Urban and Regional Studies.

4     Rather than using "integration" as a concept for analysis, I examine it as an element within the current discourse of Austrian politics on facilitating refugees' lives in Austria; It is important to note that the term is highly contested in social sciences; Therefore, instead of using it to analyse a situation, I rather want to analyse the usage of the term itself and the effect it has on refugees' lives and agency

5     Paragraph 9 states: "The recent introduction of the age category of 60 and over in UNHCR statistics is not only a reflection of increased global attention to ageing populations, but also of UNHCR activities. … The age limit of 60 applied in UNHCR's global statistics is consistent with the definition of elderly persons by the World Health Organization".

hand, many refugees were already elderly at the time of displacement. Yet, their needs are still often overlooked in the design and implementation of relief programs on an international level, but even more so at national levels (Burton and Breen 2002, 47). While international programs are usually centred on the responsibility to protect (R2P), national ones, are more concerned with "refugee integration" (UNHCR 2012, 11) and usually have to develop their own strategies for building refugees' future lives and roles in their new host society.

However, the percentage of the elderly amongst refugee populations is not reflected in the actual age distributions per their countries of origin. This is partly because the elderly are often not as mobile as younger ones (Bryceson and Vuorela 2007) and, as a result, they stay back or find refuge as internally displaced persons (IDP). In migration research the phenomenon of misrepresentation of actual refugee statistics is referred to as the "healthy migrant effect" (Wolff 2016, 45). This can be understood as the ramifications arising from the preselection of those who manage to leave and survive a conflict situation (see Kohls 2008). Elderly who are not healthy enough to leave simply stay back or else do not survive the malnutrition, atrocities and destruction of infrastructure due to war.

Contrary to this effect of preselection at the point of *leaving* a country, the "exhausted migrant effect" as coined by Paola Bollini and Harald Siem (1995) shows that migrants often suffer poorer health *after having arrived* in the countries of exile when compared to similar aged people who did not migrate (Guidi and Petretto 2019, 157). Like older migrants, older refugees are often exposed to a lower quality of life, as well as having poorer mental and physical health (Bolzman 2014, 414).

Hence, rather than being a fixed statistical entity, social age is based on the respective functions of and experiences in life-passages. Who would be defined as an elderly refugee depends as much on the life circumstances and abilities of the individual, as on the definitions of age in the respective cultural and regional context. In fact, the UNHCR acknowledges that human age is shaped though general life expectancy and aging processes, such as physical and psychological health, family and social support, cultural background, life circumstances and economic situations (UNCHR 1997, 194). This definition reflects the claim of many scholars and practitioners – in particular those of forced migration – to view age as a flexible social category (Bolzman 2014, 409; ECRE Asylkoordination Österreich 2002).

The definition of age and aging is also based on cultural interpretations. While in Austria, and in most Western European societies, age is often related to the capacity to join or leave the workforce, in other regions family status and the presence of grandchildren can play a much bigger role in defining who is "old". If one follows a definition of age according to the Austrian focus on the labour market availability, which is up till the age of 64, then only 890 Syrian "elderly" refugees applied for asylum in Austrian first instance between 2014 and 2019 (EUROSTAT 2020). This does not include those individuals who came into Austria with family reunion or resettlement programs, who are counted in different categories within the statistics,[6] nor those who have reached retirement age after having successfully completed their asylum application process.

Within the Austrian refugee regime, elderly refugees are often made to be invisible. In 2002 the NGO *Asylkoordination Österreich* had previously criticised the insufficient attention towards older refugees. Furthermore, most refugee relief organisations often lack the knowledge required for fulfilling the needs of elderly refugees and, in turn, are unable to adequately accommodate them compared to other vulnerable groups (ECRE Asylkoordination Österreich 2002, 2).

Even less is known about those who have not yet reached legal retirement age but are already highly unlikely to ever join the workforce due to their age. In Austria, all individuals between 18 and 64 are considered *"erwerbsfähig"* (fit for work) and are treated equally in the statistics. According to official reports regarding the labour market service, however, even Austrian nationals encounter difficulties finding new employment opportunities once they reached the age of 50 (see Arbeitsmarktservice Österreich 2015/2). Given the early aging of many refugees, often coupled with poorer outlook on educational and professional integration, other studies use an age limit of 30+ (ECRE Asylkoordination Österreich 2002, 9) to indicate when refugees are "older". Hence, even when only following an Austrian societal convention of seeing people who are not able to (find) work (anymore) as old, a much larger number of refugees would also fall into this critical group.

Neither the Asylum statistics of the Federal Office for Immigration and Asylum, nor the Austrian statistical agency however, provide any data on the

---

6    Resettlement cases are decided prior to arrival in Austria. Here the number of Syrian citizens over 65 years of age at the time of resettlement decision is 1730 people according to EUROSTAT.

number of refugees within this critical age group for employment (which is of 50 plus, even for Austrian nationals). While this group is officially invisiblised, the Austrian Labour Market Service (AMS) is not encouraged, in practice, to help people like Abou Youssef in finding employment. This is however in complete contradiction with the government's idea on integration, which is based on the labour market, as will be discussed later in this chapter. This approach effectively denies vulnerable groups, such as elderly refugees, societal worth, as a consequence of the equation of integration with employment.

## The Austrian Gastarbeitermodel

The Austrian refugee regime from the 1960s onwards is strongly influenced by the so-called *Gastarbeitermodel* (guestworker model). Rather than a focus on the humanitarian care-obligation, the possibilities of receiving asylum or protection in Austria are strongly bound to criteria deriving from their usability for the workforce. Hence, forced migrants, who receive some sort of asylum status, are required to "integrate" into society and sustain themselves as soon as possible. Integration here follows the primacy of gainful employment. One of the reasons why employment is seen as fundamental to integration into society, and not for example developing a sense of belonging, developing neighbourhood ties or engagement in societal clubs and associations, comes to light by a look into the historical roots of Austria's handling of foreigners.

Austria's, model is based on the previously mentioned *Gastarbeitermodel* stemming from the early 1960s (Castles and Miller 2009, 97). Its aim was to cover the need for a labour force which was understood to be cyclical rather than structural. According to Gudrun Biffl, after WWII Austria was considered to be the "alms-house of Europe" and was unable to attract highly qualified workers (Biffl 2011, 19). Salaries in Austria were considerably lower compared to other countries in Western Europe and, consequently, Austria lost many of its own highly qualified workers to neighbouring countries such as Germany and Switzerland, as well as to Canada, the US and Australia. Subsequently, Austria suffered a dire shortage in the workforce. As the country was unable to attract highly skilled migrants, the organisation of labour within companies and the technologies of production had to be restructured and adapted (Biffl 2011, 19).

During the economic upswing in the 1960s and 70s, Austria reached full employment while demand for further labour force was still not exhausted.

Therefore, foreign labourers were needed to respond to the economic developments. Austria agreed to various recruitment agreements with Spain (1962), Turkey (1964) and Yugoslavia (1966), following a similar strategy adopted by Germany, and the Benelux and Scandinavian countries. The chamber of commerce in particular focused on the regulation of *Gastarbeiter*-migration, in which workers were allowed to reside in Austria on a rotational basis and only for work reasons. Therefore, state politics followed an idea of a rotational principle as Monika Mokre explains:

> the beginning of the system of guest workers was, rather naively, based on the idea that such an import of labour was possible without any further reverberations or changes: The labour force would be imported as long as needed and would be sent back when no longer necessary. The first guest workers had consistent plans for their lives: They would stay just long enough to earn money for a good life at home (2018, 34).

Required contingents of guest workers were specified yearly, based on the needs of the market, but without any legal basis for the first 10 years. At that point, neither side had thought about a permanent settlement in Austria. With the economic crises in 1973, the demand for workers from abroad dropped. While other countries, like Germany or the Netherlands, stopped inwards migration through much more drastic measures, in 1974 Austria decided instead that the income of labour migrants would not be increased in the coming year. The main focus of the Austrian migration regimes having been on labour market rationales, it was only after the drop of labour force demands that political and public debates broadened to include questions of "family reunification, integration, asylum and the control of territory access" (Jandl 2008, 28). These debates coincided with the end of full employment and economic recession and culminated with the issuing of a new foreign employment law in 1975. With the introduction of new restrictions into migration regimes, 45,000 guest-workers lost their jobs and hence their rights to remain in Austria (Berkirchner 2013, 76). The right to remain in the country was now legally and tightly connected to strictly regulated forms of employment. Yet, those, who had already been working in Austria for more than eight years at that point, received the right to freely access the Austrian labour market.

The new law, therefore, resulted in a much higher competition in the labour market. The first years saw a 40% decrease in labour migration; however, those who were already employed, were pushed to remain in Austria longer than intended, due to the high competition in the labour market alongside the lack of return prospects (Bauer 2008, 6). As a result, many people who had migrated for temporary, rotary work then became permanent residents, followed with chain migration and family reunions in Austria (Demokratiezentrum Wien n.d.). This changed labour migration from demand-driven into supply-driven. At the same time, a much higher percentage of migrant children were now obliged to attend Austrian schools, resulting in questions of integration and German language acquisition.

With the fall of the Iron Curtain, rhetoric regarding a feared inflow of migrants started. However, the economic boom of the 1990s caused a liberalisation of access to the labour market (Jandl 2008, 28). In 1990, Austria started a campaign permitting foreign workers to legalise their status after only a very short period of time, which quickly allowed a legal residency status for 30,000 individuals (Jandl 2008, 28). Moreover, a constantly rising number of refugees and asylum seekers[7] and de-facto refugees were added to the potential labour force towards the end of the 1980s (König 1990, 24); 95,000 alone came from the then war-driven Bosnia-Herzegovina, between 1992 and 1995.

The Austrian government responded to these demographic developments with the introduction of several laws that subsequently tightened opportunities for migration, residence and employment, but also for asylum (Jandl 2008, 28). In 1990, an amendment to the asylum law was already enforced that accelerated procedures for those without valid entry permits. For others seeking employment, employment quota for foreign workers were introduced. The 1992 Alien's Act then further tightened the possibilities for entry and residence, while possibilities for asylum were limited by the introduction of the concept of "safe third countries/ countries of Origin" as a reflection of the Dublin Agreement. Many migrants were rendered hyper-exploitable, through their exclusion from most of the political and social rights that Austrian nationals have, yet being demanded to join work force, and with the possibility of staying in Austria being based on their employability in the Austrian job market (Mokre 2018, 34f). This resulted in racial capitalism, which usually describes a situation in which social and economic value is extracted from a

---

7    In 1985 there were 6,725 asylum applications, rising to 11,406 in 1987, 15,790 in 1988, 21,882 in 1989 and 27,306 in 1991. Bauböck and Perching even call these an "asylum crises". The numbers between 2004 and 2013 were once again below 20,000 (Austrian Asylum Statistics, Bauböck and Perchinig 2003, 13)

person who differs racially or ethnically from the majority population.[8] In the Austrian case, (forced) migrants were integrated into the Austrian labour market mainly to cover otherwise unpopular jobs and working conditions, such as harvest work, cleaning, building, newspaper distribution or factory work. Hence the situation in which labour market integration of (forced) migrants is based on racial capitalism, as Elizabeth Dunn ascertains for the US-American context, can also be identified within the Austrian context, where (forced) migrants "are both indispensable and stigmatized". Dunn further argues that this resulting paradox "is used to racialize and devalue their labour, creating ethnic enclaves in the labour market that simultaneously permit them to work and trap them in dangerous, underpaid jobs" (Dunn 2020).[9] These dynamics are hence also guiding the economic development of Austria after WWII.

Through the introduction of the free movement agreement within the EU, Austria limited immigration from third countries, especially for pecuniary reward. Only family members within family reunions and highly qualified key individuals were allowed to immigrate. The 1997 Alien Law connected the previous 1992 Alien's Act with the Residence Act of 1993 to create further provisions for foreign residents following a principle of "Integration before Immigration" (Jandl 2008, 29). In addition, the asylum law was further modified in response to the new Dublin Agreement. Following these changes, net migration dropped rapidly and then only rose slightly after Austria became a member of the EU. Since 2004 Austria saw a new wave of immigration, following the inclusion of Eastern countries into the EU.

In 2008, the government decided to make additional legal changes, similarly to those in the UK in 2005. Within these, they planned to consider the need for highly skilled labourers from third countries (Biffl 2011, 19). Hence, Austria's immigration history was fundamentally shaped by labour-market demands, and the supply of the resulting required workers. On economic

---

8    The term "Racial Capitalism" stems from Black Marxist engagement with slavery in the US: It generally refers to the accumulation of capital in tandem with the production of difference mainly through practices of coercion and explouptation (c.f. Ralph and Singhal 2019) In recent years, the concept of racialised labour exploitation to uphold capitalism has been used in many different contexts that create hierarchies highlighting the relation between coercion and productivity (Bhattacharyya 2018).

9    In reference to the worker's chamber's annual report of 1974, Christof Berkirchner explains that foreign workers were not seen as competitors for Austrian job seekers, since they were mainly hired for jobs which were unable to attract Austrian workers (2013, 85).

grounds, Austria is currently still in need of additional workforce, but not of non-employable or retired people (Biffl 2011, 22). This seems to be very much the intention of the current legal definition of "integration", and the legally prescribed path for all newcomers into Austria.

### Integrationsgesetz as instrument for the current refugee regime

While Austria has been a host to a huge number of refugees from former Habsburg countries like Hungary (1956), Czechoslovakia (1968) and Poland (1980s), it was the significant numbers of guest workers from Turkey and the former Yugoslavia that influenced public opinion, coupled with rising racism and xenophobia (Merhaut and Stern 2018, 29). From the 1990s onwards, the Austrian right-wing Freedom Party (FPÖ) launched anti-immigration campaigns, such as their "Austria first" campaign signed by more than 400,000 Austrians (Gottweis 2000, 8). Following this trend, asylum and migration laws in Austria have become considerably stricter. With growing moral panic over so-called "parallel societies" and disintegrated sectors amongst migrants in Austria, demands for state-supervised adaption into Austrian society became louder. Following the arrival of a relatively high number of refugees in 2015 compared to the previous years, then chancellor, Sebastian Kurz, introduced a number of laws regulating the lives of refugees in the public sphere in Austria, such as the face veil ban and, finally, the integration law, which became effective 2017.

The new integration law from 31 December 2017 defines in § 2 (1) integration as the process in which all immigrants actively participate in the measures of integration offered to them by the state. In § 2 (2) it further defines the goal of these measures as such: "Of key importance in this regard is participation through gainful work, access to and acceptance of education offers, equal treatment of the sexes, and the rapid achievement of the ability to earn one's living." (IntG § 2(1) – (2)). Integration therefore seems only to be possible through one's quick entrance into labour force and, in turn, through the acquisition of the German language. Again, through the concept of integration, the Austrian refugee regime prioritizes economic usability in the labour force above its legal duty to protect or humanitarian reasons for supporting vulnerable groups, since by definition, those who cannot join labour force are not regarded at all and are thus excluded from Austria's "integration path".

What about those people, then, who cannot work anymore due to age restrictions or due to the difficulty of joining labour force arising from their age, such as Abou Younis? Are they unable to integrate? What prospects are available to them?

## The short-comings of equating integration with gainful work

### Institutional Ageism

In order to address the shortcomings of the current legal definition of "integration", I need to come back to the previously described equation of integration with employment in Austrian law. The corollary of this is that those who do not or cannot find employment in gainful labour are not on the path of integration and are hence not in the focus of state measures, as many of my respondents have painfully remarked.

In the week following our conversation in the church, I met Abou Younis on the bus. I asked him about how life was going. He told me that he just had an appointment at the labour market service some days ago and had hoped he would finally be able to get a state-funded German class. Yet, the employee had told him that at 56 years of age, he would not be able to find work anymore and hence would not need a German class either. I asked him what he intended to do now. "I will not give up and keep on applying for jobs. Who would have thought that we would leave the war in Syria to join the war for work in Austria?"

While Abou Younis had been waiting for state-funded classes for some years at that point, he had organized some possibilities for study within the church community. And while he and others (in particular males) of his age group were out of the focus for state programs, those who seemed more valuable for the job market, received a different treatment by officials. In order to support those who are on the labour path, Austria offers several programs, like language classes, training and internships to facilitate entrance into workforce. These are predominantly (co-)funded by the labour market service. For those who are not part of the target group, significantly less support programs are offered. Hence, integration through the state is selective (Wolff 2016, 46). This selective choice was, in some cases, highly computerized until recently, and predicted one's future and the effort the state would put into support measures based on various variables.[10] The Austrian labour Market Service,

---

10    This measurement was cancelled by the court in August 2020.

for example, introduced such a system for a short time in 2020. It calculated automatically the chances of a job seeker on the labour market according to variables such as education, citizenship and gender. Those in category A were usually people who would find employment fast. Category B were individuals who had a mediocre chance of finding employment, and were those in which the service would invest. Category C, however, was comprising those with the lowest chances. The system also listed several criteria for this group, one of which was having a migration background, another being age (Alhutter 2020, 7). While for people aged 50+, special programs for (re)entering the labour market were available, the additional criteria of not having Austrian citizenship also served as a further barrier for many older refugees. As a category C applicant, Abou Younis did not feel that he was given much support in his efforts to fulfil the integration requirements and feel like a valuable member of society. Such a selective effort in integration, however, contradicts the previously mentioned humanitarian principles.

Excluding elderly refugees based on their national background and/or migration history and age in the state's integration efforts by denying their value for the economy and society of Austria serves as a basis for discrimination. Hence, efforts to support refugees are built on neoliberal calculations that are, again, based on deficient concepts of age and aging and with negative cultural ascriptions (Wolff 2016, 47). Such discrimination practices by institutions are influenced by what Robert Butler coined "ageism". Ageism is a process in which society ignores the potential contributions of the elderly and diminishes their collective worth (Bazzi und Chemali 2016, 55). Such discriminatory practices perpetuate stereotypes and indirectly justify institutional negligence of care through an unequal distribution of resources.

### Haunting of the past in the present

While many of the forced migrants that I spoke to expressed a strong desire to start working – better now than tomorrow – their actual chances on the labour market looked very different. Despite their desires to work and the inherent labour migration-logic in Austria's integration plan (BMEiA 2015), not all refugees were healthy young men fit and able to start work immediately.

As she was under the age of 50, 48-year-old Oumayma had to go through a German class for women. While the class would not necessarily translate into any future employment, she was nevertheless required to participate. Oumayma, though, unlike Abou Younis, was not very happy about this obligation as she had been suffering from hearing difficulties since her flight from East-Ghouta, and would have preferred to receive a working permit immediately without having to go through lengthy language classes.[11] Asking her about her difficulties in the class, she answered,

> Of course it is hard for those who are older. The young ones learn fast. They learn in the schools and in the courses. It is hard for those who are older than 40. Those above 40, they cannot learn. They can try to talk maybe. But beyond that, no, not for those who are 40 and older. I don't want to say that it is not possible at all. There are some who manage and some who do not. These are different capacities.

When I asked her what she meant exactly by capacities, she went more into detail, describing her own hardship of having lost her oldest son in Syria's war machinery, as well as most of her siblings and her elderly parents, along with all their belongings, the results of many years of hard work, in the rubbles of Ghouta. Oumayma explained,

> We Syrians, three quarters have psychological pressures [or stress]. They have psychological conditions. For sure, everyone who has left Syria has something. They have many psychological problems, problems, problems. I am also psychologically stressed myself. *Wallahi*,[12] I have psychological pressures. It is true, I am here with my children, but the rest of my family are still under bombing. They were bombed yesterday and they were picked up from under the rubble. I can show you the picture when they were picked up from under the rubble [*shows the pictures*] This is one thing. And also my son, my son, I don't know if he passed away or if he is good. Therefore, I have psychological stress. Do you know how? I am not able to focus. There is something distracting me. Something is occupying my mind here. I have things working in my brain at the same time. I cannot focus. I forget very fast. No, not like this. I cannot forget my family! No! I cannot forget my first-born. [...] I swear, we are suffering from this a lot. We came here, it is safe,

---

11    Austria has redesigned its previous refugee integration program. This new integration program provides and offers structured support for the first phase after having received asylum. This phase includes obligatory language acquisition as well as participation in value and orientation courses before further measures for labour market integration are taken. The program is free but also obligatory for the participant, as stated in the integration agreement (Expertenrat für Integration 2018, 78).

12    Transl. "By God", expression of emphasising a statement.

there is no bombing, but we are still under psychological pressure. There is a war in our country.

Similar to Oumayma, mental health and trauma were also critical issues for many older refugees. While there are studies connecting professional dequalification or long-term unemployment with low self-esteem and depression (Bolzman 2012), these are often also side effects of forced migration in general. Bolzman argues that "[f]or the majority, the reality is that forced migration remains dominant in their memories, and continues to be as complex in its political content as it is in terms of that person's response to it" (Bolzman 2014, 414). In particular, many of these memories of forced migration can return in older age and create mental conditions like anxiety, depression or paranoia (Bolzman 2014, 414). For many, the reasons for flight were already traumatic, yet the flight itself and the difficulties encountered after arriving in Austria are also traumatic. With the emphasis by which integration and meaningful contribution to society are framed as being merely a result of employment, long-term unemployment and dequalification become painful reminders of one's position in the new society and one's attributed value there. Hence, the current emphasis creates a mood among many elderly refugees that Abou Younis had best expressed, when he said, "All of us are useless now. We are nobody here." (see fieldnotes above).

Elderly refugees often feel difficulties in re-establishing their lives in exile and adapting to their new surroundings. In many cases, after having lived most of their lives in their homes, their sense of loss through displacement can be very strong. This is also explained through an often-greater attachment to home, land and social ties. In particular, 67-year-old Elise made this point very clear. Having lived for almost 70 years in an aristocratic family in Damascus, the move to Austria had disrupted not only her former social relations but also inverted her societal position. She narrated,

If you had been well known in all neighbourhoods and entertained social relations and you come here and no one wants to get to meet with you. Why? What is the matter with us? There is terrorism in our area [...] our level in Syria was not quite good, it was *really* good. I don't want to live on the same level as a dog. If I have to live on the level of a dog, I will return to my country. Despite the circumstances, despite the war, I will go back to my country. [...] In Syria I live in a house, our house is right behind the house of the president. The president of the republic. If here is the presidential palace, then here is our house *[indicates a small difference with her hands]*. [...]

So, in our area there is nothing. But my children, what can I do without my children? [*still in tears*] hard, hard. When we were in Syria, we were happy. We were at ease. The war and these things, but despite we were content. Happy, we lived happily. All was good. Had we just known this.

What became apparent was that mainly elderly people – who had built their life elsewhere and had left their lifetime achievements behind to move to a new country – suffered from the transformation in public status that they had gone through. Dequalification, the rupture of social relations and public recognition seemed unbearable for many, such as Elise or Abou Younis. Through the erosion and the destruction of older support networks, established rituals and habits as well as community values, elderly refugees often experience a greater feeling of emptiness from which they often cannot recover as fast as younger refugees since their prospects to build up a new life are less promising, as Burton and Breen describe (2002, 47). Oumayma also addresses this emptiness resulting from a lack of meaningful occupation.

Yes, there is a lot of time for memories. There is empty time, empty time. When we were in Syria, there was never empty time. We, as housemakers, we work in the house. We do not have free time. No, there is so much free time. Emptiness, emptiness, emptiness. And this emptiness makes the head bigger. The hardest thing in the world is emptiness. When one is alone one thinks about the memories, the past. When one has work, one is busy. If you work, you get distracted. If you are working, you are not free to cause problems. But if you have time you start causing problems. They do not have time to argue over this or cry over that, no. May God make it easy on us, ya rab.

In particular, when it becomes clear that a fast return is no longer possible, elderly refugees often express feelings of emptiness and despair (Bolzman 2014, 415). Similar studies on elderly refugees in Lebanon have shown that elderly refugees report anxiety, depression, guilt and the feeling of being a burden to their family (Bazzi and Chemali 2016, 55). This is a feeling that 65-year-old Nadhim, who was still in his asylum procedure during the time of our first meeting, also knows well. Nadhim had fled Iraq in 2002 for political reasons and sought shelter in Syria. Nadhim, whose son had already come to Austria in 2012 and whom he only joined five years later, describes his living situation as,

> I am alone. Also my son lives alone. For a while, I have lived with him [...].
> But then I returned to the camp because he needs his own private live... I
> appeared out of a sudden in his life, because I am his father and he is my
> son. I don't like that. This is why I thought I had to go back to the Camp.

Others, like 59-year old Maha, still hope for a return to Syria and see their
asylum in Austria as being only a transitory phase in their lives. Despite her
having actually had the chance to embark on the Austrian path of integration
by finding work through her sewing skills, she never really saw her future in
Austria. When I asked her about her expectations for the coming years, she
answered,

> To be honest with you, I have a little bit [mixed feelings]. Anyone of us tries
> to settle. But there is always a challenge inside every one of us. See, this
> is not my country. I do not know what the future holds, if I will survive or
> not. But I do not feel at home here. I know that this is not my country but
> maybe in the future I can go back. Maybe once the war is over, I can return.
> Or maybe I will not see the war ending. But, all what I wish for is more
> stability. But we know deep inside, that this is not our country. We are just
> here temporarily. [...] Still, there is always this little feeling inside that this
> is not our country. I am trying. I am trying really, but I cannot. And believe
> me, Austria is a very enjoyable country.

Following Elise, Oumayma, Maha and Nadhim in their descriptions of home-
sickness, the loss of status and social ties, and their bemoaning of their fate,
it becomes clear that their current situation in Austria holds few prospects for
helping them to cope. Many forced migrants of the Syrian conflict suffer from
health or psychological problems and need time to adapt to the new living
circumstances. Others have care responsibilities not just towards children,
grandchildren or the elderly but also towards others who they have grown
close with due to their shared fates of life in exile. They have grown into a
community, connected by destiny rather than by kinship, religion or ethnic
boundaries. Again, others do not plan to settle in Austria and only sought
temporary safety while waiting to return or move on. Hence, next to age,
the legal definition of integration also excludes many other people of different age who cannot enter the labour market and completely ignores the real-
life attachments, identifications and sensitivities of people. What about Abou
Younis, Nadhim and Elise? The governmental programs were not able to as-
sist them in actively shaping their situation in Austria. They were simply not

employable anymore and, therefore, were not able to "integrate" into society according to the state's definition.

## Civil Society's age blindness

Austria does have certain offers and service structures available for the elderly, to which refugees also have access. Yet, most of these services comprise part of the care structures for the elderly. In fact, intercultural restructuring processes and the inclusion and training of diversity sensitive staff have opened care concepts. For pensioner's clubs, however, German is often, but not always, the only language offered.[13] This language homogeneity makes it difficult for those without sufficient language skills, in particular since the elderly who are excluded from the job market, do not have access to paid language classes. In addition, most of these clubs are rather attractive to people beyond retirement age, while for the group of refugees in particular, who are still in their 50s or early 60s, these clubs are not accessible.

While there is a plethora of private initiatives by volunteers for refugees, most of these programs focus either on children, young adults or women. Not only do these groups receive more attention from volunteers, but also from the media; this relationship may be mutually dependent. Cynthia Enloe has coined the term "womanandchildren" to depict the "passive masse of 'womanandchildren' in need for protection" in armed conflicts (1990, 13). This need for protection of these "masses" is often translated into volunteer activities in refugee relief work, in Austria as elsewhere. Middle aged men, as well as the elderly, however, are not in the centre of empathy and need for protection. Yet, in particular, the elderly might very much need assistance, yet for exactly this group, several difficulties appear in volunteer actions.

Volunteerism is often based on power asymmetries in which no reciprocal relationship can arise. For refugees, who often need assistance in acquiring knowledge and/or language skills, relationships with volunteers are often difficult to establish. In fact, volunteers themselves are often not searching for reciprocal relations with forced migrants but rather are driven by an urge to

---

13    I thank Maria Six-Hohenbalken for pointing out pensioners clubs to me who also offer services in other languages, such as Turkish, Polish or Kurdish. While many clubs do have multilingual staff who can also offer multilingual services, this is not usually officially announced, and moreover, the website that summarizes all the possible offers is only available in German (https://kwp.at/pensionistenklubs/clubs).

help "the refugees" as a collective. 51-year-old Kurdish-Syrian Radwa, former school principal in a Northern Syrian city, described her difficulties in building sustainable friendships with Austrians the following: "I really developed a complex in this subject. I don't have any contacts with Austrians. When I first arrived to Austria, I met an Austrian woman, then we became friends, and she helped me with the language, but she doesn't have time. I saw her two months ago. She is busy helping other refugees now. So, she left me." For Radwa, it became clear that her assumed Austrian friend was not interested in building up a sustainable friendship because of mutual sympathy but had spent time with Radwa simply for humanitarian reasons. As such, Radwa was not considered as an equal potential friend but rather as a suffering object, one that could be easily replaced by other people who fell into the same category. This reduction of any personal traits, stories of affects to her refugee identity was a painful insight for Radwa and many others. In particular, for older people, who often look back on a certain social status based on their lifetime achievements (and family heirlooms), the reduction to their role as a "refugee" detached from their life stories often poses a major difficulty.

This reduction on a social level is also perpetuated on a professional level, where forced migrants are also ripped of their professional education and expertise due to diplomas, job experience and certificates not being acknowledged by authorities or potential employers. Oumayma's 53-year-old husband Radi, who started working as a carpenter at the age of ten, struggled to have his expertise acknowledged on the Austrian labour market.

> I started working at age 10. [...] And also now, I want to work here. But wherever I apply here, they tell me that I need to learn German. [...] I know there is work in Vienna. I have seen a lot of workshops here. And I have seen people who work in there without knowing the language. So it is possible. The Eastern Europeans all work without language [competencies]. And there are others, like Turks, who have been here for 15 or 20 years. They have been working and they cannot form a single sentence right in German. And they work. And they build a house. And they socialize. All of this without knowing the [German] language. The Austrian government tells us we have to learn the language. Well, I am 53 years old and we have been through very hard conditions. A war! And I have lost a young son! I do not know where he is. I do not know if he is dead or alive. Very hard social conditions! My kids! My family comes from Ghouta. Have you heard about Ghouta? It is all under bombing, attacks, killings. You have heard about the problems

there? When somebody has a background like this and a family under such conditions, do you think I would have the peace of mind to study when I have to keep up with the news about my family? That is a huge problem. It is problematic for someone like me, in my age specifically. [...] But here you need *Ausbildung*.[14] All of us want to work, but the government does not accommodate that. There are carpenters; there are blacksmiths, electricians, plumbers, lawyers, doctors, engineers. They would already be working without these minimum language requirements. Instead of spending money on these as refugees, you should allow them to work. [...] But you do not allow them to work because of the *Ausbildung* thing. They would be adding to the Austrian economy and not costing it.

For many of the elderly, who are disillusioned by the actual prospects of dequalification and the loss of societal status and reputation, the envisioned future might not always be in Austria. Very often, certificates are not accredited in Austria and job experience is not acknowledged, neither by authorities nor by potential employers. In particular, older refugees with middle or higher qualifications describe this devaluation of their education and experience as very frustrating (Brücker et al. 2016, 14).

With it being impossibile to regain former societal status, probable difficulties in acquiring language fluency, little job perspectives and difficulties in establishing social relations, for the elderly the wish to return is often strong. Elise's 72-year-old husband Ilyas, a former news reporter, made his wishes very clear, when he explained,

I came here to Austria and you cannot deny it, there I have difficulties personally. These difficulties concern my social status. The social conditions: The social conditions here: No one has time, everybody has a job to do. There is no one who has time to sit down with you and talk to you. [...] I am old, you know I do not have the capacity to learn a new language. I don't have the capacity to learn something new, especially the German language. [...] There are difficulties to integrate into the society here. There is a problem with that. [...] Trust me, if I had planned to stay in Austria, I would have learned the language. I would study, study well. It would have taken me a year, two or three, but I would have studied. But I have known since coming here that I will go back to Syria. Because I do not want to die anywhere else except for Syria.

---

14    He used the Austrian term for vocational training.

## Paths towards the future

For many older forced migrants, letting go of the past is difficult. Often, they have a feeling of loss and grief not only over what they had owned and built but also over who they used to be. Remembering the past, therefore, becomes a painful exercise on account of its stark distinction from the actual reality. With reference to Casado-Diasz, Kaiser and Warnes (2004), Bolzman explains that older refugees are often less flexible than younger ones in adapting to their changing social situations. He observes that they often try to "reproduce their former way of life in the new environment" (Bolzman 2014, 410). Hence, the move into either a previously unknown urban or rural setting, in particular, with different social rules, languages and demographic compositions causes particular difficulties for older refugees. The move itself is often synonymous with a radical loss of social and economic resources and hence everyday life and its routines (Bolzman 1994; Bolzman 2014, 410).

In terms of future orientation, many older refugees are disillusioned and frustrated about their loss and their limited chances in Austria. Many older refugees do not consider the value of investing in their own future in Austria, since they do not see any realistic chance of this improving their situation. This includes education, German classes or other professional training. Brücker et al. (2016), who came to a similar result in their study on older refugees, explain this mainly with regard to older refugees' estimation of how much time they have left, as previously mentioned by Ilyas. Also, in the previously mentioned LODA study (see note 2), participants above a certain age were often no longer optimistic about their own futures, but were more so about their children's. Radi illustrated this point in the following way,

> I am more optimistic for my children here. I hope that they work here and succeed with their life. I am hopeful for them, not for myself. I am already old. In a bit, I will die. Everyone dies at a point. We all go under the earth at a point. I just want that my children succeed. I am positive, because my children can find work here and they are in safety.

In contrast to the lack of investment in one's own future, many older refugees invest mainly in their children and demand good education and job prospects for the following generation. Often, they place all hopes for an improvement of their own situation in their children, which often puts them under enormous pressure. Radi continued by pointing at his daughter's future,

I want my daughter to succeed and continue studying. She is a good nurse. She can take care of people. I want her to have her own practice to help others. For example, she could also help elderly people. If she had a practice, I would want it to develop and become great. I want her to have a car.

His wife Oumayma, in another conversation, added even higher expectations for their youngest son,

We really did not think that we, the grownups, would have to study a new language. For our future, we thought only the children should learn it. We really thought this would be enough. You know? [17 year old son] studied anyway at the school and with the school he would study the language. And our daughter was working as a nurse. So we thought she needs the language, too. But she could not find something here, until now. And our son wants to study business administration after his school. He wants to study in an Austrian university. He will go to a university and then he will earn a lot of money. We [she and her husband] can never earn much money here. Maybe he will earn 4 or 5.000 Euros. Of course, we cannot. But at the moment he has only B2 German. He first also has to do the *Matura*. He is already studying a lot. And then we need to see how to pay the student fees. It is also around 400 Euros. This will be very hard. That is also why we think maybe he should make the Matura and then *Ausbildung*, so he can earn some money first.

For both, then, it was clear that their future depended detrimentally on the success of their children. Yet, in particular, imagining the future often causes dilemmas for older refugees, especially when the period of refuge takes longer. While for many older refugees, there is still hope of returning to Syria and to their old lives one day, they often understand the efforts that their children and grandchildren have invested in their own future in the country of residence. This is the case with Oumayma, who declared,

*Wallahi*, my girl Sabine, we are here now. I stopped thinking about my future. My future is that my children study well. I think about the future a lot. The future is for our children to learn and to become educated and succeed at the jobs that they are in. This is my future: only my children.

Yet, in the next sentence, she added her dilemma,

[*in low voice*] and that I go back to my country. Yes, that I go back to the country. I hope I will be able to, one day. I wish, I wish, by God, to go to my country. As much as you like the country that you are in, your country of origin remains very special. I am longing for my country. Do you know this feeling? I am homesick. This is very hard. It is like the longing of a child for his mother. You miss, you miss your country. I really wish.

A return to Syria would in many cases mean having to give up the cumbersome achievements of children and grandchildren in Austria. With the passage of time, however, returning to Syria becomes less and less realistic and feasible, which in turn causes feelings of resignation and emptiness for many older refugees who had hoped that their current hopelessness would only have been temporary. "These feelings of loss are particularly intense when refugees perceive their situation in the country of exile to be permanent—knowing that they may never see their country or region of origin again" (Bolzman 2014, 410).

The present situation is, therefore shaped both by feelings of nostalgia, loss and grief over the past and by hopelessness towards the future; this evokes feelings of stagnation, emptiness and being forgotten. For the generation who had lost their own previous life achievements and the heirloom of their families and past generations, starting from scratch in Austria is often difficult, in particular with the lack of state or NGO support. This generation often expressed that it is not worth investing in their own future of their own volition. Also, they do not seem to be an interesting group for the state to invest in, and for many volunteers they are not vulnerable and hence attractive enough to spend time and resources on. For Abou Younis, this was a very difficult situation, which he expresses, as "We are a lost generation. May the next one have more luck."

This situation has clear effects on their social networks. In particular, family members and the following generations are affected, but so also are ethnic networks. Yet, it is important that older refugees are not only seen as a burden, but also to underline their scope for agency and their importance in safeguarding heritage.

### Effects on families

Flight and exile have transgenerational effects on families in many ways. Forced migration affects the composition of households and causes the fragmentation of family networks (see also Bauer-Amin and Six-Hohenbalken 2020). While some members are not mobile enough to leave – or do not want to – others might find exile elsewhere in the country or neighbouring countries. Other family members might stay back in other locations along the flight route. Often, older refugees do not wish to leave or only do so to stay with their (adult) children (Bolzman 2014, 412). Yet, they often suffer greatly from their physical separation from other (adult) children and further family members, in particular when they are left back in danger. Oumayma, for example, was pained greatly by the fragmentation and physical disconnection to her family:

> So, I am here and my family is there and my sister is there and my brother is there. We are not used to the distance. We Arabs always immediately get together. We want to stay in the same neighbourhood, the same street, you know? […] All the relatives are staying together. My family is here, my in-laws next to me, my uncles and aunts and their children, we all live in the same neighbourhood. Not that everyone lives in a different neighbourhood. I wish that now it would be at least like this. But now, we are in different countries. A part in Germany, a part in Britain, wallahi al-'azim in all countries. A part in Libya, and we are here and they are in Syria. It had us dispersed in all different countries. This is what makes it very very hard for us.

Through physical separation, family life needs to be reframed in transnational ties. This leads to the development of what Coenen-Hutter, Kellerhals, and Von Allmen (1994) call "long-distance closeness." Yet, this closeness is translated into differing roles and responsibilities, since older family hierarchies and care relations are often affected by war and fragmentation. Older refugees, who had been affluent business owners or other higher social status, are often no longer able to support other family members after going through the transformation of flight (also Bauer-Amin and Six-Hohenbalken 2020, 87 ff).

Older refugees suffer particularly from such separation. The fragmentation of the family network also means a transformation and possible disruption in the passing on of family heirlooms, traditions and legacies to the following generation. For many, this feels like a failure in preserving the achievements and values of past generations and causes a sense of guilt for not being able to provide the coming generation with the material, social, capital and symbolic foundations they would have were they not lost to the war.

The lack of external support for older refugees, in particular, for acquiring language skills, often results practically in older refugees having little leverage in navigating through their Austrian everyday life and its complications without the assistance of younger ones. Often, they depend fully on their children for communication with authorities, doctors or even neighbours. When not knowing how to access the Austrian care system, in specific, this can cause an even greater burden to be placed on the shoulders of the younger ones. In addition to these missing system and language skills, the absence of prospects on the labour market and of any other financial means, often causes many older refugees to be trapped in a cycle of poverty.[15] For Elise and Ilyas, it was impossible to improve their income level and move to a better flat since they were fully dependant on the state for support, having lost all their resources in the Syrian war, which made them dependant, not only financially, but also practically, on their sons.

These dependencies of older refugees change their roles within families. Similar to the Chilean forced migrants in Switzerland in Bolzman's study, Elise and Illyas, Nadhim and many others, experience these changing roles as a decrease in self-esteem. As Bolzman notes, "Loneliness was a reality for these older people, and even when the family was trying to be supportive, life in exile is often associated with social and economic difficulties, which burdens the younger members of the family" (Bolzman 2014, 413).

### Importance of solidarity and ethnic networks for elderlies

Returning to the initial conversation with Abou Younis at the beginning of this chapter, he had pointed out how important the church community was for him. In this community, he found people with similar destinies, like Dr. Girgis, Emad and Rewan. Meeting with people who understood his situation and shared his experience of loss, emptiness and devaluation in Austria was

---

15    Up until the age of 64, refugees in Vienna who cannot find employment, receive financial assistance of 917.35 Euro for a single person household or 1,376.02 Euro for couples. Once they reach retirement age, they are entitled to a minimum pension of 966.65 Euro for single headed households and 1,524.99 Euro for couples. In 2019, the poverty line for a single person households in Austria was 1,286 Euro (EU-Silk 2019, 10). The numbers and support systems differ from one federal state to another. Asylum seekers and persons with subsidiary protection have access to different forms of support, such as allocations in organised shelters, health insurance and a smaller amount of pocket money of 40 Euros per month if living in shelters to a maximum of 200 Euros per month if accommodation is organized by the recipients themselves.

an empowering feeling for Abou Younis. This shared burden made the current situation bearable for him. In fact, many other studies have noted the importance of ethnic minority communities in providing essential support to forced migrants, particularly during the early stages of their flight (Bolzman 2014, 416). In these moments of mobility, new solidarity relations emerge as a result of the redefinition of social roles. Such networks can therefore be an unexpected but useful resource for grouping under a common destiny beyond ethnical or religious lines.

While previous studies have underlined the role of kin or ethnic networks in providing material support and practical help after arriving in the new country (Levitt and Jaworsky 2007; Olwig 2003), often communities of a shared destiny evolve that can be much different from solidarity lines that existed before the war, or are even independent from ethnic or kin networks (Griffiths, Sigona and Zetter 2005). Abou Younis' church group consisted of Arabic speakers, mostly Christians, but drawn from far beyond the usual denominational lines and, rather, being united by the shared experience of being forced migrants within exile in Austria.

Such networks can serve as bridges between the past lives and the present situation. They serve as self-help groups that allow space to exchange experiences and information about the home countries, places along the route, and Austria. In addition, these networks can become important providers of resources during exile. When financial state or (N)GO support is not sufficient or available, the establishments of jam'iyāt (saving communities)[16] serve as material support. However, they are also a support for social and cultural needs. For example, celebrations that used to be family celebrations, turned out to become important community celebrations in the absence of extended families with whom to celebrate. Before the Corona pandemics, Oumayma and Radi celebrated 'Id al-fiṭr in Vienna in the Islamic Centre alongside thousands of visitors. Abou Younis and others celebrate Christmas together in a huge Turkish restaurant, instead of their family homes. The community became a substitute extended family.

The elderly here play a particularly important role in such social and cultural resources/events. Often, they are consulted on such occasions to make

---

16    A group of people who join into a collective rotational saving and loaning effort. All members of the jam'iyāt pay into the fund, which on a monthly bases then goes to a different community member.

sure that these are celebrated according to "how things used to be done back home," as Oumayma's daughter explained.

## Resourcefulness of elderlies in preserving heritage

Almost a year after our initial meeting, I was invited to a baby party on the 40th day after birth. Unfamiliar with this kind of celebration, I was curious to go. The celebration was a female-only celebration. In the midst of the younger women, I found Oumayma with the baby on her arms. I soon approached her and sat down next to her. It turned out, she and her daughter had planned the whole event, which was based on an old tradition, which she had still celebrated in her village. Oumayma, who kept on holding the child for the whole evening, without letting it out of her arms, continuously gave advices to the mother of the child on upbringing and to two younger women who had just gotten married how to improve fertility. She became an active part in consultancy for young Syrian women in her network and a valuable resource for many on topics, in which the NGOs and Austrian state initiatives could not help much.

Older refugees, like Oumayma, can play important roles in passing on cultural knowledge and immaterial heritage. This is important, in particular, for younger ones who would otherwise grow up without any or only poor knowledge on how Syria used to be before the war. Hence, older refugees are important for passing on knowledge and skills and keeping them in the community. On the other hand, they are living testimonies of the cultural and historic richness of the now war-driven county. As such, they create stability and trust and become invaluable repertoires of resources.

Moreover, in Abou Younis' church community, the role of elderlies only became clear after a certain time of settlement and, in particular, during specific occasions, such as weddings or funerals, where they made sure that the celebration was done in the "right" way. Yet, the community also had another occasion, where the role of older refugees, in particular women, became obvious. Every three months, the youth group of the church had to prepare food for the community. It was important that it was Levantine food, especially dishes that are difficult or time-consuming to prepare. The older ladies, who soon took on leading parts in the design of the church celebrations, by choosing the songs, teaching them to others and organising the props, then gave advice on how to improve the recipes and make them taste "authentic". The interesting part here was that elderly women explained to the younger ones how they could replace certain ingredients or where in Vienna they would find the specific ingredients for the recipe. The more experienced the younger ones became in creating dishes according to the older one's tastes – within the parameters of living in Vienna – the more positively the older ones evaluated the younger one's arrival and stability in Austria. Only someone, who knew their way around the city in order to find everything needed to produce "authentic" food, had really managed to make the new city home.

Hence, older refugees, by providing the necessary knowledge on cultural and social practices can serve as important bridges for finding the space for pre-flight practices in a post-flight everyday life. This helps to see "integration" not as a rupture but as a process of becoming home. Therefore, older refugees can deliver substantial contributions "in maintaining cultural traditions and in passing on folklore, customs, and traditional practices to younger members of the community" (Burton and Breen 2002, 47). As such, they can help others to overcome the cultural loss and create links across their biographical gaps.

## Conclusion

In Austria, many organizations, governmental and non-governmental, try to lay out a path to facilitate the transition into Austrian society for refugees. However, the focus often lies on the acquisition of language and integration into the labour-market. These, therefore, are tailored for people who are instantly ready to work and to adapt to a new environment and language. These measures are built on a model of work-migration and do not take into consideration the specific circumstances of refugees, such as psychological pressures or simply the demographic difference. It is even less up to date with regards to the new demographic forms of refuge that Austria has witnessed over the last few years, when the people arriving were not only healthy and young men, but people who need time to cope with their past and present, whole families, children and the elderly. Within this neoliberal refugee regime, forced migrants who are not able to integrate fast into the labour market, are excluded and marginalized.

Alongside the neoliberal outlook, a humanitarian discourse on "womenandchildren" is also present, motivating volunteers and civil society to engage in initiatives for children and women. Yet, older refugees, who are not yet as advanced in age but still not easily employed into the labour market anymore, are not attractive to civil society initiatives either. However, their agency should not be reduced to measures of how much they can follow the guest worker model or be attractive to civil society organizations. They play major roles in supporting their adult children and preserving cultural and symbolic resources. The overt focus on effective labour market integration often causes enormous pressure, so that these important functions are often forgotten not only by governmental agents but also by forced migrants themselves. What Abou Younis' testimony brings to the forefront is the discrepancy between the ideas of "integration" focused on mainly the job market and the devaluation of elderly refugees who did not only loose their homes and previous life achievements but also their social status and possibilities to upward social mobility. On the contrary, their exclusion from most support options turns them into dependants of their children and grandchildren, which, in turn, enlarges the social loss experienced already. These enormous pressures and the devaluation of elderly refugees by society are often unbearable. Bolzman observes, "for some older refugees the best solution is to return to their home country. Generally this solution is preferred by those who have kept strong symbolic and cultural ties with their home society [...] they will try to go back and rebuild their life as it was before their forced migration" (2014, 416).

Bolzman's observation is also true for some of my interlocutors. For Ilyas, these feelings were so pressing and the loss of status so terrifying that he went back to Syria, alone, while his wife Elise remained in Vienna. When I asked him about the plans for his future, he had already alluded to the plan, that he would complete shortly after our interview:

> What is my future at my age? What I want is to live with a peaceful mind and a little bit of good health. I just need some friends with whom to get along and whom to talk to. What is my future? I need to go to my home. I really wish to go back to my country to see my friends, my people. This is my future.

# References

Alhutter, Doris, Florian Cech, Fabina Fischer, Gabriel Grill, and Astrid Mager. 2020. "Algorithmic Profiling of Job Seekers in Austria: How Austerity Politics Are Made Effective." *Front. Big Data* 3, no.5. Available online: https://www.frontiersin.org/articles/10.3389/fdata.2020.000 05/full [accessed10.12.2021].

Arbeitsmarktservice Österreich. 2015. *Ältere am Arbeitsmarkt: Bedeutung der Generation 50+ steigt.* Spezialthema no. 2.

Bauböck, Rainer, and Bernhard Perchinig. 2003. "Migrations- Und Integrationspolitik in Österreich". https://www.okay-line.at/file/656/osterr-migr-integr-politik.pdf.

Bazzi, Lama, and Zeina Chemali. 2016. "A Conceptual Framework of Displaced Elderly Syrian Refugees in Lebanon: Challenges and Opportunities." *Global Journal of Health Science* 8, no. 11: 54–61.

Bergkirchner, Christof. 2013. *Zur Genese des Ausländerbeschäftigungsgesetzes 1975,* Diploma Thesis, University of Vienna.

Bhattacharyya, Gargi 2018. *Rethinking racial capitalism.* Lanham, MD: Rowman & Littlefield.

Biffl, Gudrun. 2011. "Deckung des Arbeitskräftebedarfs durch Migration in Österreich Studie des Nationalen Kontaktpunkts Österreich im Europäischen Migrationsnetzwerk." *Bamf.* http://www.forschungsnetzwerk.at/downloadpub/2011_biffl_labour_study_DE_01.pdf.

Bollini, Paola, and Harald Siem. 1995. "No real progress towards equity: health of migrants and ethnic minorities on the eve of the year 2000." *Social Science & Medicine* 41, no. 6: 819-828.

Bolzman, Claudio, Élisabeth Hirsch Durret, Simon Anderfuhren, Marilène Vuille, and Monique Jaggi. 2008. "Migration of parents under family reunification policies. A national approach to a transnational problem: the case of Switzerland." *Retraite et société*: 93-121.

Bolzman, Claudio. 2012. "Democratization of ageing: also a reality for elderly immigrants?" *European Journal of Social Work* 15, no. 1, 97-113.

Bolzman, Claudio. 2014. "Older refugees." In *The Oxford handbook of refugee and forced migration studies*, edited by Elena Fiddian-Qasmiyeh, Gil Loescher, Katy Long und Nando Sigona, 409–419. Oxford: Oxford University Press.

Bowling, Ben. 1990. *The Development, Co-ordination and Provision of Services to Elderly People from the Ethnic Minorities: A Report on Four Innovatory projects.* London: Age Concern Institute of Gerontology, King's college.

Brücker, Herbert, Kunert, Astrid, Mangold, Ulrike, Kalusche, Barbara, Siegert, Manuel, and Jürgen Schupp. 2016. *Geflüchtete Menschen in Deutschland: eine Qualitative Befragung*. IAB-Forschungsbericht, no 9, Nürnberg: Institut für Arbeitsmarkt- und Berufsforschung (IAB).

Bryceson, Deborah Fahy, and Ulla Vuorela eds. 2007. *The transnational family: New European frontiers and global networks*. Oxford: Berg.

Burton, Ann, and Catherine Breen. 2002. "Older refugees in humanitarian emergencies." *The Lancet* 360: 47–48.

Butler, Robert .N. 1978. "Age-ism: Another form of bigotry," In *Social problems of the aging*, edited by Mildred M. Seltzer, Sherry L. Corbett and Robert C. Atchley, 243 – 346. Belmont, CA: Wadsworth.

Casado-Díaz, María, Kaiser, Claudia, and Anthony N. Warnes. 2004. "Northern European retired residents in nine southern European areas: characteristics, motivations and adjustment." *Ageing and Society* 24, no. 3: 353 – 381.

Castles, Stephen, and Mike Miller. 2009. *The age of migration. International population movements in the modern world*. New York: The Guilford Press.

Coenen-Huther, Josette, Kellerhals, Jens, von Allmen, Malik, Hagman, Hermann-Michel, Jeannerat, Fabienne Colette, and Eric Widmer. 1994. *Les réseaux de solidarité dans la famille*. Réalités sociales: Lausanne.

Demokratiezentrum Wien. *Gastarbeiter*. Accessed 23 September 2020. http://www.demokratiezentrum.org/ausstellungen/migration-on-tour/station en/07-gastarbeiter.html?index=2024

Dunn, Elizabeth. 2020. *Refugees and Racial Capitalism: What 'Integration' In the Labour Market Means*. Oxford Refugee Studies Center Public Seminar Series, December 2, 2020. https://talks.ox.ac.uk/talks/id/d3866d41-0d42-40 87-8f31-5b4afffe7c6a/

ECRE Asylkoordination Österreich. 2002. *Ältere Flüchtlinge in Europa. Untersuchungsergebnisse und Praxismodelle*, 2002. http://archiv.asyl.at/projekte/en dbericht_ecre.pdf.

Enloe, Cynthia. 1990. "Womenandchildren: Making Feminist Sense of the Persian Gulf Crisis." *The Village Voice*, Sept, 25.1990.

EUROSTAT. 2020. "First instance decisionson applications by citizenship, age and sex – annual aggregated data (rounded)," 2020. http://appsso.eurost at.ec.europa.eu/nui/submitViewTableAction.do.

Expterenrat für Integration. 2018. "Integrationsbericht 2018," https://www.b meia.gv.at/fileadmin/user_upload/Zentrale/Integration/Integrationsber

icht_2018/Integrationsbericht_2018_Zahlen__Trends_und_Analysen_-_I
ntegration_von_Frauen_im_Fokus_stand_14_11.pdf.

Federal Act for the Integration of Persons without Austrian Nationality Legally
Resident in Austria (Integration Act) 2017. https://www.ris.bka.gv.at/Do
kumente/Erv/ERV_2017_1_68_a/ERV_2017_1_68_a.pdf

Federal Ministry of Austria, European and International Affairs. 2015. "50
Punkte – Plan zur Integration von Asylberechtigten und subsidiär
Schutzberechtigten in Österreich." https://www.bmeia.gv.at/fileadmin/u
ser_upload/Zentrale/Integration/Nationale_Integrationsfoerderung/50_
Punkte-Plan.pdf.

Guidi Caterina, and Alessandro Petretto. 2019. "Health care and migration:
what data can tell us of the hard-to-measure impact of migrants on the
European health systems." *Development in Turbulent Times* 2019: 153-170.

Gottweis, Herbert. 2000. "Politische Mobilisierung BürgerInnenbewegungen
und Ansätze zur Ausbildung neuer Organisationsformen von Politik in
Österreich," http://www.demokratiezentrum.org/fileadmin/media/pdf/g
ottweis.pdf

Griffiths, David, Nando Sigona, and Roger Zetter. 2005. *Refugee community
organisations and dispersal: networks, resources and social capital*. Bristol: Policy
Press.

Kohls, Martin. 2018. *Healthy-Migrant-Effect, Erfassungsfehler Und Andere Schwie-
rigkeiten Bei Der Analyse Der Mortalität Von Migranten. Eine Bestandsaufnahme.*
Bamf. https://www.bamf.de/SharedDocs/Anlagen/DE/Forschung/Worki
ngPapers/wp15-healthy-migrant-effekt.pdf?__blob=publicationFile&v=1
0.

Levitt, Peggy, and B. Nadya Jaworsky. 2007. "Transnational migration studies: Past developments and fu-ture trends." *Annual Review of Sociology* 33:
129–56.

Merhaut, Nina, and Verena Stern. 2008. "Asylum Policies and Protests in Austria," In *Protest Movements in Asylum and Deportation*, IMISCOE Research
Series, edited by Sieglinde Rosenberger, Verena Stern and Nina Merhaut,
29– 47. Cham: Springer Nature.

Mokre, Monika. 2018. "On the Intersections of Globalized Capitalism and Na-
tional Polities Gastarbeiters, refugees, Irregular Migrants." In *They'll Never
Walk Alone. The Life and Afterlife of Gastarbeiters*, edited by Boris Buden and
Lina Dokuzović, 29– 40, Vienna et al: transversal.

Olwig, Karen Fog. 2003: "'Transnational' Socio-Cultural Systems and Ethno-graphic Research: Views from an Extended Field Site." *International Migration Review* 37, no. 3: 787–811.

Ralph, Michael, and Maya Singhal. 2019. "Racial capitalism." *Theory and Society* 48, no. 6: 851-881.

UNHCR (United Nations High Commissioner for Refugees). "UNHCR Resettlement Handbook. Division Of International Protection." Geneva, 1997. https://studylib.net/doc/18616329/unhcr-resettlement-handbook

UNHCR Standing Committee. 2000. "UNHCR's Policy On Older Refugees, (Annex II Of The Draft Report Of The Seventeenth Meeting Of The Standing Committee [29 February – 2 March 2000])." April 19, 2000. https://www.unhcr.org/uk/excom/standcom/4e857c279/unhcrs-policy-older-refugees-19-april-2000-annex-ii-draft-report-seventeenth.html.

UNHCR. 2011. "Statistical Yearbook 2011." Accessed 23 September 2020. https:// www.unhcr.org/516282cf5.html.

UNHCR. 2012. "A New Beginning: Refugee Integration in Europe." Last modified 2012. https://www.unhcr.org/protection/operations/52403d389/new-beginning-refugee-integration-europe.html.

UNHCR. Last modified 2018. "Older People." https://webarchive.archive.unhcr.org/20180621065325/http://www.unhcr.org/older-people.html.

United Nations. n.d. "Responsibility to Protect." Accessed 19 November 2020. https://www.un.org/en/genocideprevention/about-responsibility-to-protect.shtml.

Wolff, Felix. 2006. "Integration von älteren Geflüchteten." *Sozial Extra* 40, no. 6: 45–49.

# Reassessing Civil Society
# Refugee NGOS and the Role of Informal Networks in Turkey

*Denise Tan*

## Introduction

International and local NGOs are central actors within the context of refugee regimes, as many states rely on their services for the implementation of national migration and integration policies (Spencer and Delvino 2018, 4). This seems also to be true for Turkey, which is still the largest host of Syrian refugees worldwide. Many Turkish NGOs and initiatives were founded in recent years to exclusively work on refugee issues; and the "refugee crisis" became one of civil society's largest challenges (Tocci 2017, 5). Even though civil society, in the form of formalised and legally recognized associations, has received some scholarly attention within recent years (as e.g. Sunata and Tosun 2018, Danış and Nazlı 2019), little is known about how NGOs and other networks actually shape refugees' daily lives. Who are these NGOs and what kind of support are they offering refugees? Furthermore, looking at civil society as a theoretical concept, it can be understood in a much broader sense including not only formal associations but also in non-formalised ways like informal networks, social media groups, neighbourhood networks, churches or kinship groups (Demirovic 2003, 220; Layton 2004, 3). The role of these non-formalised civil society actors is even less researched. How are refugees, as active members of civil society, interacting with these civil society groups? And how is civil society linked to refugee agency and last but not least, how is it embedded within the larger context of the refugee regime? With this paper I aim to tackle these questions by referring to my ethnographic material from a case study on civil society actors in the context of "non-camp" Syrian refugees[1] in Izmir, Turkey's third largest city and in comparison with two other recent case studies from Ulaş Sunata and Salih Tosun (2018) and Didem Danış and Dilara Nazlı (2019). Therefore, I will first look at the general situation of refugees in Turkey and its refugee regime. Secondly, I will give a brief overview over civil society and its theoretical background; and present my understanding of civil society inspired by Robert Layton's approach (Layton 2004). Thirdly, the case study on Izmir will shed light on how formalised and non-formalised civil society is operating within the context of refugees. Finally, I will discuss these findings in regard to the popular concepts of refugee agency and the refugee regime. The analysis will show, that reassessing civil society within that context helps to understand how refugee agency is transforming and shaping collective actions, which help refugees, especially "non-camp refugees" who are lacking basic support from the state, to cope and organise their new life situations and life projects. At the same time the suggested focus on civil society enables the creation of a linkage between the refugee regime and refugee agency through its focus on activities and dynamics lying between the sphere of the state and the individual.

## Turkey and it's refugee regime

Since 2014, Turkey hosts the largest number of refugees, including about 3.7 million Syrians and 400,000 non-Syrian forced migrants in 2020 (UNHCR Global Focus Turkey 2020). The vast majority of forced migrants live in urban or rural areas within the local communities and nearly half of all Syrian refugees are children (meaning under the age of 18). Less than 2% of Syrian refugees live in Temporary Accomodation Centers (3RP[2] Turkey 2019-2020, 5). Thus, the large majority of Syrian refugees are "non-camp refugees", who tend to be more vulnerable (Lubkemann 2019, 206). Turkey was urged to develop a new legal framework for foreigners and asylum seekers, which the

---

1    "Non-camp" refugees is used to describe the situation of those refugees living among local communities in contrast to refugees staying in camps, as outlined for example by Ayselin Yıldız and Elif Uzgören (2016).
2    3RP is the abbreviation for the platform Regional Refugee and Resilience Plan, which is explained in the next paragraph.

government was already working on before 2011 (İçduygu 2015, 5). The Turkish government implemented the Geneva Convention in 1961, though with the geographical limitation to European citizens (an option which was offered to signatory states). Until now only refugees, who are fleeing from specific events in Europe, can gain the status as a "refugee" within the country, as Turkey never changed this geographical limitation. All other people, who are seeking asylum, are treated as "guests" with temporary protection (ibid). As a response to the specific situation of Syrian refugees, the Turkish government developed a new Temporary Protection (TP) regulation in 2014.

In 2019 around 2,7 million Syrians were registered under the Temporary Protection Regulation, which legally guarantees access to services in national systems, such as health, education and social services (3RP Turkey 2019-2020, 5). At the end of 2019 more than 680,000 Syrian children were enrolled in formal education and 33,000 students had access to tertiary education. Since 2016 the Temporary Protection Regulation also opened up the possibility of gaining access to the labour market through official working permits. Until the end of 2019 more than 130,000 working permits were issued to Syrian refugees. In addition to the working permits, refugees are also able to work officially in seasonal agriculture or animal husbandry, as those areas are exceptions. However, the large majority of refugees is still working within the informal sector without any security. Together with increasing unemployment this remains one of the key challenges. As regular incomes are missing, basic needs are uncovered, as for example adequate housing and food. Around 42% of registered refugees live under the poverty line. The state is hardly providing services for those refugees. These current numbers, developments and challenges are reported by the UNHCR and the platform Regional Refugee and Resilience Plan, abbr. 3RP (UNHCR Global Focus Turkey 2020; 3RP Turkey 2019-2020 n.d., 6ff). Interestingly, refugees face the same challenges in 2020 as in 2015, when I collected the ethnographic material for the case study in Izmir. During that time, finding jobs, a regular income, adequate houses and access to health care were the most urgent needs of refugees.

The UNHCR as well as the platform 3RP are core players within Turkey's refugee regime. The 3RP platform is co-lead by UNHCR and UNDP together with international, national and local partners to strategically address and coordinate activities to support Syrian refugees themselves and also the governments of the top five host countries Turkey, Lebanon, Iraq, Egypt and Jordan (3RP n.d.). In Turkey, the 3RP works together with the governmental organisation Directorate General of Migration Management (DGMM). The DGMM is

> ...the main entity in charge of the implementation of policies and processes for all foreigners in Turkey. It is the sole responsible authority in Turkey for procedures regarding temporary protection beneficiaries and international protection applicants (including registration, documentation and refugee status determination), stateless persons and other foreigners. (3RP Turkey 2019-2020 n.d., 13).

As mentioned by the 3RP, the DGMM has also a coordinating role, which should connect local authorities, international organisations, EU institutions, civil society and other stake holders. The UNHCR furthermore states that "Civil society[3] actors will remain key to the response and defining their role as complementary to the government service provision a priority for the coming years." (UNHCR Global Focus Turkey 2020). Thus, similar to many other European countries, Turkey's refugee regime is strongly relying on civil society services, which act complementary to state services. But what or who is civil society in that context and what are NGOs working on refugees doing on the ground to support refugees within their current situations?

## Reassessing civil society conceptions

The concept of civil society in its modern meaning originated in the late 18th century when the development of private and economic interests initiated the differentiation between civil society and the state. Georg W.F. Hegel, Karl Marx and Alexis de Tocqueville are well known for their conceptions of civil society, which influenced current approaches (Abdelrahman 2004, 18). In the social sciences, civil society became relevant during the 1980s in relation to East European and Latin American state transformations (Hemment 2004, 219f). At that time the social movements, which lead to those democratic revolutions, were recognised and described as part of civil society. This led to the current dominating liberal political approaches, which define civil society

---

3    UNHCR does not offer a definition of civil society per se. However, on their partnership platform, the UN partner portal, they refer to civil society organisations, as either NGOs, community-based organisations or academic institutions (UN partner portal n.d.).

as voluntary and self-organising associations that contribute to democratisation and boost liberal values (see e.g. Keane 2013, Edwards 2011). Thus, within public discourse but also within academia civil society is mostly understood as NGOs or other recognized associations or initiatives. This is also the case for forced migration studies and relevant stake holders within the refugee regime.

Anthropologists and other scholars have elaborated different perspectives on the concept of civil society and challenged the "NGOization" and ethnocentric biased dimension of civil society (Hann and Dunn 1996; Comaroff and Comaroff 1999). Informal associations based on kinship, village, religious or ethnical affiliations are, in a narrow sense, coercively organized and would be excluded from this perspective. However, anthropologists have argued that these groups play an important role within social organization, strengthening community cohesion, and act as a sphere lying between the individual/core family and the modern state (Hann 1996, 5).

Another approach to civil society was developed by scholars, who picked up Gramsci's perspective, within which civil society is understood as an integral part of the state and not something outside or in opposition to it (Demirovic 2003; Abdelrahman 2004; Al-Rebholz 2014). Beside the political society, which describes the government and its institutions, civil society is the state's most resilient constitutive element. It is a non-violent sphere built on consent. This includes all socio-cultural institutions, in which values and meanings are established, such as private organizations, the publishing industry, schools, associations, clubs and churches (Kumar 1993, 383). This approach is used to observe and analyse power struggles within the state and its different social groups or classes.

However, "...whether in liberal or neo-Marxist guise the Western concept of civil society continues to exert a powerful fascination in political anthropology" (Hann 2018, 3). Therefore, I am sticking closely to the definition of civil society given by anthropologist Layton, who tries to avoid those ethnocentric, Western dimensions and which allows me to reflect in a more inclusive and encompassing way on the role of associations and collective actions within the context of refugees. Layton understands civil society in a broader non-normative sense as social organisations which occupy the space between the household and the state (Layton 2004, 3). These social organisations enable people to coordinate and manage resources and activities. Although he emphasizes the economic component, Layton also includes non-economic activities. According to him socio-cultural organisations like ethnic or kinship groups, churches, mosques, clubs and, as I would add, informal networks belong to civil society (ibid). Thus, not only do voluntary groups belong to civil society but also networks which are "coersive", such as kinship groups. Furthermore, civil society is detached from a normative dimension, which is relevant within dominating liberal political approaches for which NGOs as civil society actors par excellence contribute to democracy, social cohesion and the "good society" (Fewer 2013). Additionally, this understanding of civil society does not differentiate between members of a society. It does not matter if a person is a Turkish citizen, a refugee or an asylum seeker; as everyone is equally part of civil society while being involved within collective activities.

## Civil society and NGOs in Turkey

The term civil society, called *civil toplum* in Turkish, gained importance in Turkey during the 1980s, similar to other parts of the world. As political activities from parties and trade unions were forbidden at that time, civil society groups were the only possibility for expressing discontent (Ergun 2010, 509). Since the 1990s, NGOs are booming, especially in the three largest cities: Istanbul, Ankara and Izmir, where one-third of all NGOs operate. When Turkey was approaching the EU, civil society in Turkey received another boost (Dereci 2015, 19). The EU as well as other international organisations represent a liberal understanding of civil society, which sees civil society and especially NGOs as a condition for democratic institutionalization. Thus, civil society actors were strengthened and new NGOs emerged. These new NGOs, which were mostly funded by the EU, spread Western European-oriented social, cultural and political ideas around Turkey (Ergun 2010, 507). In addition the funding of international organisations and local refugee NGOs became an essential part of the EU-Turkey Statement in 2016 (Anatolitis 2020), with the aim to hinder further refugee influx.

Still, similar to Turkey's political landscape, Turkish civil society is strongly divided along different ethnic, religious and ideological lines (Şimşek 2004, 63). Associations can be recognized as Turkish, Kurdish, Alevi, Sunni, Islamist, Kemalist, politically right or left. There are also cross-cuttings between these groups. In addition, it should be mentioned that Islamic associations played and continue to play a relevant and strategic role for the AKP and its retention of power (Yilmaz and Bashirov 2018). Charity organisations became substitutes for the state's welfare services. I will pick up this issue later on in the context of service provision for refugees.

While in 2004 61,000 NGOs were registered (Şimşek 2004, 48) the number has grown to 130,000 in 2017 (Tocci 2017, 10). This boost of formally recognised associations strengthened the "NGOization" of civil society, which describes the narrow understanding of civil society as NGOs. Therefore, I will first of all take a closer look at NGOs as formalized civil society actors, dealing with refugees (refugee NGOs as I call them) building up on my case study of refugee NGOs in Izmir. In a second step I will focus on non-formalized civil society actors, which came up as relevant actors within the refugee context in Izmir.

### Refugee NGOs in Izmir

A large number of those NGOs, which were established during the last decade, were founded in response to the high influx of refugees. This is also the case in Izmir, Turkey's bottleneck to Europe. Located next to several Greek islands on Turkey's West coast, hundreds of thousands of refugees entered Izmir in search of smugglers, who would organise their refuge across the Mediterranean Sea. I conducted ethnographic fieldwork among refugee NGOs and "non-camp" Syrian refugees during autumn 2015. That was the year with the highest number of refugees arriving in Turkey (UNHCR Dataviz n.d.). According to UNHCR, over 350,000 refugees have arrived at Greek islands next to Izmir's coast during September and October 2015 (UNHCR n.d.). Thus, over three hundred thousand people must have transited the city within these two months alone. Refugee NGOs estimated the number of refugees staying in Izmir at that time from 67,000 to 100,000. At the beginning of 2019 over 200,000 Syrian refugees were officially registered in Izmir. Still the number might be higher as not all refugees are registered yet. Refugees, who are settling in Izmir, are staying in specific areas near Basmane like in Kadifekale or in areas at the outskirts of the city as, for example, Torbalı or Foça.

Izmir counts over four million inhabitants, and Syrian refugees mingled into the city's population without attracting too much attention. Refugees came to Izmir long before the Syrian crisis started in 2011. The Association A[4] founded in 2008, was the first NGO working on refugee issues in Izmir. People from Somalia, Sudan, Afghanistan and Iraq were searching for smugglers who would help them to find ways to get to Greece. Besides Association A, I interviewed representatives of five other associations during my fieldwork

---

4     The names of the interviewed associations are anonymised throughout the paper for
      safety reasons.

(B, C, D, E and F). Besides those interviews, I carried out an in-depth analysis at the association E and conducted problem centred interviews with eleven households of refugees covering 56 persons of different age, gender, ethnicities and social classes. The six associations were all legally recognized by state authorities at the time of the fieldwork. While three of these six organisations exclusively worked on refugee issues (A, B, F), the other three had a broader range of topics and address other groups as well (E, C, D).

**Association A** is a professional NGO based on a legal and human rights-based approach. Association A's work is project-driven and their financial situation is dependent on project funding from the EU and other institutions. The employees are women, though the rest of the voluntary team is gender-mixed. They offer legal support to refugees, asylum seekers and migrants. Additionally, Association A monitors the situation of refugees in Izmir as well as in other places, and supports refugees who have been locked up in detention centres. Based on interviews and encounters with their clients, they also try to inform the public about illegal treatments of refugees, as for example through push-backs, forced "voluntary returns" or for example, the handling of those refugees, who gathered at the Turkish-Greek border in spring 2021.

**Association B** is a nationwide organisation in Turkey, which was founded in 1995 during the Iraqi war. It is the oldest national organisation working on refugees and partner organisation of the UNHCR and is responsible for registering asylum seekers for the UN. The local branch in Izmir was opened in December 2014, as the situation of refugees in Izmir became an urgent issue. The employees are mostly social workers, translators and further employees who have experience with marginalised groups. Association B offers psychological assistance, health care, educational activities like language courses, but also music or painting courses for children within these centres. Refugees can address Association B with any kind of problem and the organisation tries to follow up on each refugee's case. They especially focus on vulnerable people, like families with missing male members, disabled people, orphans and unattended minors. They also deal with legal questions such as, for example, deportation decisions or push-back cases as well as relocation programs in relation to UNHCR programs.

**Association C** is an Islamic organisation, which belongs to the Hatuniye mosque in Basmane and is located directly inside the mosque's building.

It is typical for bigger mosques to maintain their own charity associations. Employees are mostly men. Referring to its ideological background, the association can be positioned near the AKP. As the Hatuniye mosque is located directly in the centre of Basmane, refugees have always been among their regular beneficiaries. Before the Syrian war started, mainly Afghans, Somalis and refugees from other African countries came there to get something to eat. Since the Syrian crisis, refugees have occupied the place in front of the mosque, where they laid out their mattresses and build up provisional homes using cords, sheets and cartons. The organisation regularly distributes food and material packages.

**Association D** Is the second association with an Islamic background, and it is a national charity organisation with branches all over Turkey. It has similar goals as Association C. They do typical charity work and are funded by donations of private actors. Their only activity related to refugees happens in cooperation with Association C. They sponsor the food for meal distributions at the Hatuniye mosque.

**Association E** was founded in November 2014 and is affiliated with the "Peoples' Democratic Congress" (HDK), which is a union of left-wing organisations and parties in Turkey. The organisation is based on volunteers and funded through private donations. Many of the volunteers are doctors or medical staff. Therefore, they provide free medical check-ups for refugees in the area of Basmane, but also in Foça and Torbali. Additionally, they collect information on refugees' needs and call out for donations in order to prepare food and hygienic packages, especially focussing on women and children. Detailed reports are published and events organised in order to inform both the public and also state institutions on refugees' conditions and to improve their situation on a long-term basis. As the organisation is known to be affiliated with HDK, the police watch them closely. Especially after the *coup* attempt in 2016[5] and the ongoing repression against NGOs, activists, journalists and academics, the organisation had to adapt their work, for example by focussing solely on organising cultural events.

---

5    In June 2016 parts of the military started a *coup d'etat* which failed and led to mass arrests within the military and police forces, but also of prosecutors, judges, civil servants and journalists.

**Association F** is an organisation founded for Syrians by Syrians. A small group of friends, Syrians who came to Izmir before the war began, started to help out Syrian refugees with translations at hospitals. They were teachers, businessmen and medical students. Out of this small group the idea of an official organisation arose and was finally established in September 2013. Their main aim is to support Syrian refugees in all different kinds of ways: mostly they are translating for them, passing information, gathering donations, giving out food and non-food packages for families and helping refugees to find homes or jobs. The association is based on volunteers. Their main work happens via phone, over Facebook or direct contact. As Association F had strong contacts with Syrian refugees, who are spread around Izmir, they became attractive partners for international organisations (IOs). Over the years they started several cooperations with IOs, like *Women and Health Alliance* (WAHA) and *Mercy Corps*. However, *Mercy Corps* similar to hundreds of other NGOs, was closed in 2017 by the Turkish government. Only a few days later Association F's own Facebook page was hacked by a Turkish right-wing group and since then the association has stopped its social media presence, though they continued with their work.

Not only Association F became an important broker for international organisations. My observations showed that also E, B and A were functioning as key intermediaries for international organisations as well as for journalists, researchers and other international institutions. They were depending on local NGOs in order to obtain access to the field, get in contact with refugees and receive information on the current situation.

Thus, one half of the interviewed organisations, especially the professional NGOs, had employees who carried out their work; the other half was based on volunteer work. Most people who got involved with organisations belonged to the higher-educated, middle class. Employees and volunteers were gender-mixed in most NGOs. All NGOs, except Association F, had to work with translators, in order to be able to communicate with refugees in Kurdish or Arabic. The beneficiaries of NGOs often didn't know from whom they received help. Instead, the translators became the persons whom they could trust. The translators were remembered and recognized by refugees, and therefore held key positions within the associations as they were the ones, who were in touch with them. All of them had some sort of office, and three of them received refugees in their offices. The other three were out-reaching and thus connected with refugees at the places where they stayed or where they were otherwise needed. Two of those with employees were project-based, thus they were financed by institutions like the EU or UN. These two organizations were also the only ones, which were following a rights-based approach trying to maintain a politically neutral position. Consequently, they could be recognized as classical Western NGOs. The other organisations were dependent on private donations. Two associations were based on Islamic ideology and one could be positioned as left and pro-Kurdish. The last one of the six associations was led by Syrian immigrants and had no clear ideological connotation.

The case study revealed a strong division between Islamic and non-Islamic organisations. Those organisations which could be defined as rights-based and left-wing oriented cooperated with each other on specific occasions or at least knew about each other's work. Also, the Islamic associations cooperated with each other at certain points. And even though these two larger ideological groups often carried out similar activities to address refugees and shared similar goals or claimed the same demands, cooperation over cross-cuttings were inconceivable.

Concerning the activities of refugee NGOs, it can be said that three of the associations (E, A and F) tried to inform the public about refugees' conditions in Izmir in order to achieve positive changes on a broader and structural level. However, most of the activities directed to refugees themselves were some sort of material help, in the form of food and non-food packages for families, and serving hot meals (E, C, D, B, F), or the provision of health services (E, B). These activities can be subsumed under the term of humanitarian aid, as they are necessary for covering the basic needs of refugees. Only a few organisations offered activities directed at empowering refugees in rebuilding their new lives in the city such as language courses (B, E) or helping to find jobs (F).

However, that NGOs had to fill in to cover those basic needs, reveals the lack of support and resources provided by the state. But considering the huge number of more than 100,000 refugees living in Izmir, it is obvious that refugee NGOs were only able to address a small amount of them. Still refugees managed to organise their own lives. The findings, presented below, will show the crucial role that non-formalized civil society, in the form of neighborhood or kinship networks as well as social media groups, plays in regard to coping and managing refugees' life situations in Izmir.

## Refugees and non-formalized civil society in Izmir

As I have outlined, civil society can be understood as being much more than just formally organised or institutionalized associations. Civil society summarizes all collective economic and non-economic activities of a community. Kinship or neighbourhood networks, churches, mosques or informal networks are part of civil society. Similar to many other researchers I started my fieldwork in Izmir with formal organisations and NGOs. Through observations in the field and especially in relation to how NGOs work within the refugee context, the relevance of other informal networks became obvious. Last but not least, the interviews with refugees revealed how different forms of civil society play essential roles within refugees' daily lives and struggles.

My ethnographic findings showed that refugee NGOs actually depend on informal networks as they are operating as prerequisites which enable them to reach refugees in the first place and implement their activities successfully. Local NGOs that are office-based somehow need to reach out to refugees who are spread around the city with four million inhabitants. For example, an employee of Association B explained, that when they first started to build up their local branch in Izmir, they had to go out on the streets in districts, where refugees were supposed to live in order to find them. They conducted interviews with over hundred households in order to learn about refugees' needs and to inform them about their activities. This procedure took a lot of resources from the organisation. After some time, they learnt that the information is passed mouth-to-mouth by refugees through kinship and neighbourhood networks. Now the employees knew that they just had to call a few families and the information concerning their activities would be spread through those networks. Similar to Association B, Association A and Association C were also relying on such informal networks, which led refugees to their offices. Without them, local NGOs would constantly need to put resources into finding and getting in touch with the refugees directly. Similarly, those NGOs who were not operating within offices, but reaching out to their target group also focused on specific areas, where refugees were known to stay. These areas in Izmir mostly included Basmane and Kadifekale. Consequently, refugees who were staying in other areas or who might not be well connected to informal networks were less likely to be informed about NGOs' work or to receive direct help.

Hence, while local NGOs are brokers between refugees and the media and the international community; informal civil society actors are intermediaries between refugees and local NGOs. However, this also means that many refugees might never hear about those offers and support from NGOs. Taking the large number of refugees into account, it is also clear that the majority of them never got in contact with any organisation, nor could they be handled by the local NGOs.

Thus, informal networks among refugees function as information providers and help in connecting them with NGOs. Finding and receiving information on how things work within the country of residence are crucial for refugees to organise their current life situation, especially when they do not understand the language. Besides these mouth-to-mouth networks, social media groups are highly relevant for information as well. A few Syrian migrants, who have been living in Turkey for some time and saw the need to help other Syrian refugees newly arriving in the city, founded the Facebook group "Syrians in Izmir" in 2015. This group of friends was also part of the same group that initiated the foundation of the formal association, Association F, as described above.

Today the Facebook group counts over 3,800 members. Information shared within the group ranges from postings on banks, which offer bank accounts to Syrians, hospitals and medical support, useful phone numbers, NGOs' offers, and job offers. It is also used for selling or buying things like vehicles or electronic devices; and it is a platform to ask questions and for exchange with others. The language used within the group is mainly Arabic. One of the founders of the group explained that the Facebook group is very important, as it enables them to spread reliable information as many rumours are passed among refugees. The importance of social media for refugees was also examined, for example, by Alencar (2017) and, connected to this, smartphones are essential devices, as outlined by Kaufmann (2020).

Drawing on examples from the interviews conducted with refugee households throughout the fieldwork I will now illustrate further how refugees were organising their resources and getting support within informal networks from their neighbourhoods or through Syrian solidarity groups. Thus, the next paragraph will show that non-formalised civil society is strongly driven by refugee agency and additionally reveal solidarity actions of the local community. A small part of the families I interviewed had relatives or neighbours living in Turkey before they had arrived there. They were the first anchor points in their new country of residence. For example, when Hasan[6],

---

6    The names of the interlocutors have been changed for privacy reasons.

arrived in Turkey, he directly went to stay with his relatives in Mersin. They helped him to find a job and he worked in the fields for some time. After a few months, Hasan moved to Istanbul, where he tried to leave for Europe. Since he couldn't gain enough money, he became stranded in Izmir, similar to a large number of other refugees. He started to work at a phone shop and to help refugees with transportation and translations, which means that he actually got involved with the smuggling of migrants from Turkey to Greece. Hasan sent the money he earned to his family in Syria, who were then able to leave for Turkey themselves.

In another interview, Ahmed told me that his relatives were already living in Izmir and they helped him and his family to find a house in Kadifekale, a district in Izmir with a high percentage of Kurdish population. Similar to Hasan's and Ahmed's cases, another family knew that their neighbours in Syria were fleeing to Turkey and they stayed in contact with them. They followed them directly to the same place, where the men of the family were able to acquire jobs within agriculture. Thus, these (transnational) kinship and neighbourhood networks helped refugees during their flight and led them to specific places in Turkey, where they knew they would meet people they already know and who, furthermore, would be able to help them to start organising their new lives within their new country of residence. Relatives or neighbours from Syria supported them to find houses and jobs; two essential elements and basic needs for starting a new life.

Not only former neighbourhood networks are relevant, but also newly established informal networks within the districts in which refugees are staying. One of the main districts, where refugees were finding houses in Izmir, is Kadifekale. Flats were cheap but very simple and often sub-standard. They merely consisted of one or two rooms for each family. For example, one family with three children, lived in the back of one house on the ground floor. The flat consisted of one room of about ten square metres and a little kitchenette. For the interview, we were sitting in the main room, which was laid out with carpets. On one side was a small, low table with a little TV on it. Some pillows were positioned next to the walls. There were no windows in the room; the walls weren't rendered and the actual doors were missing in all door frames. Consequently, the front entrance remained open the entire time. The whole family, consisting of five persons, was living and also sleeping in the single living room. As described earlier, most families are composed of at least five family members and often extended family members belong to the household as well. In one case eleven people and one new-born child were living together in one small flat.

All of those families, who were living in flats at the time of my fieldwork, experienced support from their neighbours in the district. Most of them received material support like carpets, a small TV or kitchen materials for their flats. These neighbours were Turkish and Kurdish people, but especially also other refugees. Esat, father of a family, explained that he didn't receive money from his employer last month, so he wasn't able to pay the rent for the house. Another Syrian refugee, who was not a direct neighbour, but who lived near his house, gave him money for the rent. The man was very grateful for that, although he continued to have the same problem in the following month. In addition to the material help, information concerning associations and NGOs was also passed on through those informal neighbourhood networks, as mentioned before. These examples from Hasan, Ahmed and Esat show how Syrian families were managing their own livelyhoods using old and new neigbouhood networks and ties, while the Turkish state and its institutions weren't present and didn't play an active role within organising their new lives. Also NGOs who received the role of complementing the state's lack of support, weren't reaching them. Instead Ahmed, Hasan and Esat were acting on their own using connections and building up other forms of support mechanisms. Thus they were relying on their own agency, which enabled them to take a foothold within their new country of residence.

## Civil society – between the refugee regime and agency

Civil society refers to the space between the state (governmental institutions), and the household (the family and the individual). This means that focussing on civil society within forced migration studies offers an additional possibility to analyse activities and happenings between the dynamics of the refugee regime and refugee agency. In relation to Layton's definition of civil society, all kinds of collective actions, which aim to manage and coordinate resources and activities, can be understood as civil society. Throughout my case study I highlighted formalized civil society organisations, like NGOs, on the one side and non-formalized civil society organisations, like neighbourhood, kinship or social media groups on the other.

Besides international organisations, national and local NGOs need to be recognised as central social actors within refugee regimes, as governments strongly rely on these NGOs to provide services to refugees and fill the gaps in order to cover basic needs. Additionally, local NGOs are relevant stake holders as they function as intermediaries linking refugees with international organisations, the media and also researchers. As a reaction to the high influx of Syrian refugees, Turkey's refugee NGOs landscape increased immensely and the Turkish government strategically shifted responsibilities to civil society organisations (Danış and Nazlı 2019, 153). The majority of those refugee NGOs are service-oriented and provide humanitarian aid. Since Barbara Harrell-Bond's ground-breaking work on refugee camps and her criticism on humanitarian aid, several anthropological studies have exemplified the ambiguity of humanitarianism (Harrell-Bond 1986; Verdirame, Harrel-Bond and Lomo 2005). Thus, NGOs' activities need to be closely analysed in order to see in which ways they are interacting with refugees. Some NGOs might contribute to refugees' empowerment, others might create and/or recreate dependencies. The case study from Izmir has shown that only a few NGOs help refugees to gain more self-empowerment for example through language courses. Furthermore, there was only one addressing refugees' needs to find jobs and houses, which are elementary for building up a new life in the country of residence. This was done by the association, which was led by Syrian migrants. Sunata and Tosun's case study shows similar outcomes by highlighting that organisations led by Syrians seem to be more successful in empowering refugees (2018, 13). They also add that community centres, which provide spaces for refugees to socialize and organise themselves are similarly relevant for refugee integration (ibid).

However, the reason why so many refugee NGOs remain limited to humanitarian aid is connected to Turkey's refugee regime and its political climate. There is an ongoing tension or competition between the regime's duty to provide those in need with the right to asylum, show compassion and hospitality on the one side; and the securitization of refugees, creation of fear and repression through national policies on the other (Fassin 2019, 5050). As Turkey traditionally has a "strong" state, authorities are highly suspicious concerning civic participation in general (Çarkoğlu and Cenker 2011, 755). These strong state institutions impede the creation of horizontal ties between different civil society groups and try to keep civil society apolitical. In 2017 only 23,000 of the 130,000 associations were dedicated to research or advocacy on political and social issues like gender rights, education, climate or refugees. Thus, politically charged issues are avoided (Tocci 2017, 10). In particular, the coup d'état attempt in 2016, and subsequent state of emergency, increased the repressive atmosphere and led to the reduction of civic space. Over a thousand associations were closed and NGO staff members imprisoned. Also, international NGOs, such as the already mentioned Mercy Corps, an humanitarian organisation working on Syrian refugees, were affected by the crackdown (Tocci 2017, 10ff). Thus, refugee NGOs are similarly affected by those state restrictions. As mentioned above, Association E had to limit their activities addressing refugees in Izmir to cultural events, as they were under strict observation by the police.

Danış and Nazlı's case study on refugee NGOs has shown that specific organisations, which share the same ideological religious grounds and are loyal to the state, are in a "faithful" alliance with the government (Danış and Nazlı 2019). They conclude that Turkey is using

> ... a new approach in refugee policy where the AKP government promotes certain non-governmental actors such as municipalities and civil society organizations (...) to fulfil the requirements of the state's responsibilities. This new approach is a selective governance model where the state delegates some of its functions of refugee reception to NGOs that it considers to be ideologically and politically akin (Danış and Nazlı 2019, 153).

This new form of refugee governance strategically prioritizes social assistance and ignores or even hinders advocacy of refugee rights initiatives (ibid, 153). Moreover, Sunata and Tosun's fieldwork highlight that NGOs showing religious references and proximity to AKP's ideology gain positive effects for their projects and activities (2018, 17). However, this means that if an organisation is not in line with the government's views, as the example of Association E shows, the organisation is in danger of being threatened, under surveillance or even closed. In order to survive, organisations have developed strategies to remain outside of mainstream and official channels and keep a low profile (Sunata and Tosun 2018, 17).

Thus, formal civil society, in the form of legally recognized NGOs, is strongly connected to and overseen by the Turkish government and the refugee regime. The existing tension described above has direct effects on NGOs' daily work. In contrast to that, non-formalized civil society remains mostly outside of the governments' reach or control. Kinship, neighbourhood networks as well as social media groups, or Syrian solidarity groups are untouched by policies, restrictions and the political circumstances. Although the Turkish government tries to take control over the internet and social media from time to time by blocking platforms like Facebook and YouTube.

This also happened during my fieldwork when bomb attacks directed at a peace rally in Ankara caused over a hundred people's deaths. But people already know a lot of ways to overcome these barriers and the restrictions never hold on for long.

Non-formalized civil society is strongly connected to refugee agency. Agency is "closely linked to performance as it underlines the individual's capacity to engage actively with their social and cultural context" (Bauer-Amin 2017, 139). The term agency is also connected to the individual's capability to receive and manage material and non-material resources as well as to engage within organising practices as the stories from Hasan or Ahmed have examplified (Essed, Schrijvers, and Frerks 2005, 2). Refugee agency is therefore used to highlight refugees' own decisions and choices, and their strategies to counter-balance victimisation as imposed by humanitarianism. As the analysis of refugee NGOs in Izmir has shown, most of them carried out humanitarian aid addressing basic needs, while only few of them offered sustainable support through language courses or a platform to find jobs. This lack of empowerment and ongoing focus on humanitarianism might explain, why the conditions and needs of refugees have not changed within the last five years.

Non-formalised civil society is characterized by the collective actions of refugees themselves as well as the local community. The analysis of activities of these civil society networks shows that their objectives are to some extent similar to those of humanitarian aid. Informal neighbourhood networks help to cover basic needs and get material support. But the difference is that these networks are based on refugee's agency, as refugees organise themselves within those networks in order to manage their resources. As my fieldwork has shown, these informal networks are highly relevant in regard to activities around passing information on how things are working, where to get further help, and especially the possibilities to finding jobs and houses. These issues are necessary to organise a new life within the current county of residence. The informal networks are at the same time relevant intermediaries between refugees and formalized civil society, as NGOs rely on those networks to get in touch with their beneficiaries. The state and its institutions, on the other side, are hardly present within this daily struggle. Though as a consequence, the refugee regime itself is dependent on those informal networks as it is strongly relying on civil society organisations to provide services to refugees.

Donny Meertens' case study from Columbia has shown similar outcomes concerning internally displaced migrants fleeing to urban settings (Meertens

2004). Refugees who engage in informal networks get rooted sooner within the city and are able to rebuild new "life projects" as Meertens calls it (2004, 76). Women, in contrast to men, are stronger at engaging within informal networks, and therefore they are able to cope with their new situations more quickly than men, who rely more often on political networks and institutions of the refugee regime. Although Meertens does not refer to these networks as civil society throughout her paper, all of these collective activities and networks she highlights can be summarized under civil society. Furthermore, her study shows that these informal networks, hence civil society, are spaces where new directions, gender relations and forms of social inclusion, which are not built on former relationships, are created.

## Conclusion

The case study from Izmir shows that refugee NGOs' work mainly focuses on humanitarian aid, in the form of material help or health services in order to cover basic needs. This exposes the lack of systematically organised and sustainable support for refugees from state authorities, who are shifting the responsibility of care and refugee support to civil society organisations. As other case studies have shown (Danış and Nazlı 2019; Sunata and Tosun 2019), one of the reasons why NGOs are limited to humanitarian aid, is linked to the political climate and the refugee regime. The case studies reveal the constant tension of the national refugee regime, created by the urgency to support refugees within the country of residence and the desire to control them. Turkish refugee NGOs, who are not in line with the government's perspectives, face repression, are under surveillance and in danger of being shut down; while (especially religious) organisations, which are ideologically near to the leading party, are supported. Keeping the field of activities of NGOs limited to humanitarian aid is furthermore a fruitful strategy by the state to hinder refugee agency and empowerment.

However, the focus on non-formalised civil society shows how refugees are managing their new life situations by relying on their own agency without interference or support from the refugee regime or NGOs. This is helpful for shedding light on the coping mechanisms of "non-camp" refugees, classified as especially vulnerable and still less studied by academics (Lubkemann 2019, 206). Syrian refugees in Izmir organise and manage their resources within informal neighbourhood, kinship or social media groups. Those are the spaces, where they find material help, job offers and useful information on how to organise their life situations. These informal networks also function as prerequisites for refugee NGOs. Syrian refugees learn about the NGOs' offers through their neighbours or social media groups of Syrians. This means that non-formalised civil society is largely driven by refugee agency, which in turn shows how refugee agency is converted into collective activities and social structures. Additionally, changes in gender and social relations can become visible through the focus on non-formalised civil society, as Meertens study on informal networks among Colombian refugees exemplified (2004). As civil society understands refugees as an inclusive part of the local community, encounters between different social groups and individuals become visible as well.

Last but not least, studies on civil society, as forms of social organisations, show power relations that emerge around social actors, and the ties that bind them to different levels of the state and international agencies (Hann 2018, 2). This allows us to strategically connect different social actors within the refugee regime, including not only NGOs or international organisations, but also all other social organisations, which become relevant for refugees' daily lives within their country of residence. Non-formalized civil society actors link refugees and their needs and objectives with local NGOs, which are for their part embedded within the refugee regime. Thus, focussing on civil society as formalized and non-formalized actors, helps in analysing different aspects of refugee agency and the refugee regime and, furthermore, would allow researchers to problematise the complex relationship between those two concepts.

## References

Abdelrahman, Maha M. 2004. *Civil Society Exposed: The Politics of NGOs in Egypt*. Library of the Middle East Studies 40. London, New York: Tauris.

Alencar, Amanda. 2017. "Refugee integration and social media: a local and experiential perspective". *Information, Communication and Society* 21, no.11: 1588–1603. https://doi.org/10.1080/1369118X.2017.1340500

Al-Rebholz, Anil. 2014. Das Ringen um die Zivilgesellschaft in der Türkei: Intellektuelle Diskurse, oppositionelle Gruppen und Soziale Bewegungen seit 1980. Transcript Verlag.

Anatolitis, Konstantinos. 2020. 'EU Signs Final Contracts under the €6 Billion Budget of the Facility for Refugees in Turkey'. Text. European

Neighbourhood Policy And Enlargement Negotiations – European Commission. 17 December 2020. https://ec.europa.eu/neighbourhood-e nlargement/news_corner/news/eu-signs-final-contracts-under-%E2%82 %AC6-billion-budget-facility-refugees-turkey_en.

Bauer-Amin, Sabine. 2017. "Resisting the current Refugee Discourse: Between Victimization and Reclaiming Agency". In *From Destination to Integration – Afghan, Syrian and Iraqi refugees in Vienna*, edited by Josef Kohlbacher and Leonardo Schiocchet, 09–35. Vienna: Austrian Academy of Sciences Press.

Çarkoğlu, Ali, and Cerem I. Cenker. 2011."On the Relationship between Democratic Institutionalization and Civil Society Involvement: New Evidence from Turkey." *Democratization* 18, no. 3: 751–773.

Comaroff, John L., and Jean Comaroff, eds.1999. *Civil Society and the Political Imagination in Africa: Critical Perspectives.* Chicago: University of Chicago Press.

Danış, Didem, and Nazlı, Dilara. 2019. "A Faithful Alliance Between the Civil Society and the State: Actors and Mechanisms of Accommodating Syrian Refugees in Istanbul". *International Migration,* 57, no 2: 143–157.

Dereci, Sezin. 2015. "Promoting the Enabling Environment for Functioning Civil Society: Analysis of Civil Society Environment in Turkey." *Revista de Estudios Internacionales Mediterráneos* 17. https://revistas.uam.es/index.php /reim/article/view/940, accessed March 14, 2016.

Demirovic, Alex. 2003. "NGOs, the State, and Civil Society: The Transformation of Hegemony. Rethinking Marxism". *A Journal of Economics, Culture and Society* 15, no 2: 213–235

Edwards, Michael. 2011. "Introduction: Civil Society and the Geometry of Human Relations." In *The Oxford Handbook of Civil Society*, edited by Michael Edwards. 3–14. Oxford: Oxford University Press.

Ergun, Ayça. 2010. Civil Society in Turkey and Local Dimensions of Europeanization. *Journal of European Integration* 32, no. 5: 507–522.

Essed, Philmena, Frerks, Georg, and Joke Schrijvers. 2004. "Introduction: Refugees, Agency and Social Transformation". In: *Refugees and the Transformation of Societies: Agency, Policies, Ethics and Politics*, edited by Philomena Essed, Gerog Frerks, and Joke Schrijvers, 1-16. New York/Oxford: Berghahn.

Fassin, Didier. 2019. "Refugees, Anthropology, and Law". In *The International Encyclopedia of Anthropology*, edited by Hillary Callan. 5050-5059. Oxford: Wiley & Sons.

Fewer, Tim. 2013. "Doing NGO Work – The Politics of Being "Civil Society" and "Good Governance" in Cambodia" *Australian Geographer* 44, no. 1:97–114.

Hann, Chris. 1996. "Introduction. Political Society and Civil Anthropology." In: Civil Society -Challenging Western Models edited by Chris Hann and Elisabeth Dunn. 1–25. London: Routledge.

Hann, Chris. 2018. "Civil Society". In *The International Encyclopedia of Anthropology*, 1–3. https://doi.org/10.1002/9781118924396.wbiea1499.

Hann, Chris, and Elisabeth Dunn, eds. 1996. *Civil Society – Challenging Western Models.* London: Routledge.

Harrell-Bond, Barbara. 1986. *Imposing Aid: Emergency Assistance to Refugees.* Oxford: Oxford University Press.

Hemment, Julie. 2004. "The Riddle of the Third Sector: Civil Society, International Aid and NGOs in Russia." *Anthropological Quarterly* 77, no. 2: 215–241.

İçduygu, Ahmet. 2015. Syrian Refugees in Turkey: The Long Road Ahead. Washington DC: Migration Policy Institute. http://labs.ozyegin.edu.tr /ozumigs/files/2015/05/TCM-Protection-Syria.compressed.pdf, accessed February 16, 2016

Kaufmann, Katja. 2020. "Understanding why smartphones are so essential to refugees." In: *Agency and Tutelage in Forced Migration* edited by Schiocchet, Leonardo; Nölle-Karimi, Christine; Mokre, Monika. ROR-n Plattform 2, no.1: 39-42. Vienna: ROR-n, Austrian Academy of Sciences. https://doi.or g/10.1553/RoR-n_Plattform_Vol_02(1).

Keane, John. 2013. Civil Society Old Images, New Visions. Hoboken: Wiley. h ttp://public.eblib.com/choice/publicfullrecord.aspx?p=1272686

Kumar, Krishan.1993. "Civil Society: An Inquiry into the Usefulness of an Historical Term." *The British Journal of Sociology* 44, no. 3: 375–395.

Layton, Robert. 2004. Civil Society and Social Cohesion – A Reassessment. Working papers/Max Planck Institute for Social Anthropology 63.

Lubkeman, Stephen C. 2019. "The Anthropology of Forced Migration in Africa." In *A Companion to the Anthropology of Africa*, edited by Roy Richard Grinker, Stephen C. Lubkemann, Christopher B.Libkemann, Christopher Steiner and Euclides Gonçales, 199 –227. Hoboken: Wiley

Meertens, Donny. 2004. "Life Project out of Turmoil: Displacement and Gender in Colombia." In *Refugees and the Transformation of Societies: Agency, Policies, Ethics and Politics*, edited by Philomena Essed, Gerog Frerks and Joke Schrijvers, 69-80. New York/Oxford: Berghahn.

3RP Turkey 2019-2020. n.D. Accessed September 15, 2020. http://www.3rpsy riacrisis.org/wp-content/uploads/2020/02/Turkey_english.pdf

3RP n.D. "In Response to the Syria Crisis", Accessed September 15, 2020. htt p://www.3rpsyriacrisis.org/

Şimşek, Doğuş. 2019. 'Transnational Activities of Syrian Refugees in Turkey: Hindering or Supporting Integration'. *International Migration* 57, no.2: 268–282. https://doi.org/10.1111/imig.12489.

Şimşek, Sefa. 2004. "The Transformation of Civil Society in Turkey: From Quantity to Quality." *Turkish Studies* 5, no.3: 46–74.

Spencer, Sarah, and Delvino, Nicola. 2018. Cooperation between government and civil society in the management of migration: Trends, opportunities and challenges in Europe and North America. COMPAS.https://www.co mpas.ox.ac.uk/2018/cooperation-between-government-and-civil-society -in-the-management-of-migration-trends-opportunities-and-challenge s-in-europe-and-north-america/

Sunata, Ulaş, and Salih Tosun. 2018. 'Assessing the Civil Society's Role in Refugee Integration in Turkey: NGO-R as a New Typology'. *Journal of Refugee Studies*. https://doi.org/10.1093/jrs/fey047.

Tocci, Nathalie. 2017. Trends in Turkish Civil Society. Center for American Progress.Washington, Istanbul Policy Center, and Istituto Affari Internazionali. https://www.academia.edu/36769967/Trends_in_Turkish_Civil _Society

UNHCR Dataviz n.d. "Turkey Inter-Sector Dashboard". Accessed 15, September 2020. https://data2.unhcr.org/en/dataviz/38

UNHCR Global Focus Turkey. 2020. Accessed 15, September 2020. https://reporting.unhcr.org/node/2544?y=2020#year

UNHCR n.d. "UNHCR Refugees/Migrants Emergency Response – Mediterranean." Accessed August 8, 2016, from http://data.unhcr.org/mediterran ean/country.php?id=83

UN Partner Portal n.d. Accessed 15, September 2020 https://www.unpartner portal.org/landing/

Verdirame, Guglielmo, Barbara E. Harrell-Bond, Zachary Lomo, and Hannah Garry. 2005. *Rights in Exile: Janus-Faced Humanitarianism*. Studies in Forced Migration, 17. New York: Berghahn Books.

Yilmaz, Ihsan, and Bashirov, Galib. 2018. "The AKP after 15 years: Emergence of Erdoğanism in Turkey". *Third World Quarterly*, 39, no. 9: 1812-1830

Yıldız, Ayselin, and Elif Uzgören. 2016. "Limits to Temporary Protection: Non-Camp Syrian Refugees in İzmir, Turkey." *Journal of Southeast European & Black Sea Studies* 16 (2): 195–211. doi:10.1080/14683857.2016.1165492.

# PART 3: Ambiguity and (Un)settlement in Agency

# "Young Strong Men Should Be Fighting" – The Vulnerability of Young Male Refugees

*Monika Mokre*

## Introduction

European discourse on refugees has changed dramatically since 2015 – from a discourse on the vulnerability of refugees to a discourse on security, i.e. from refugees *in* danger to refugees *as* danger (Gray and Franck 2019). This discursive shift mirrors and enhances ever more restrictive refugee regimes – protection *against* refugees instead of protection *of* refugees. However, neither of these two discourses does justice to the individual and often complex situations of refugees and neither of these discourses perceives refugees as acting persons with political and social rights. Both discourses can be read as postcolonial forms of desubjectivation (Lorence 2018). At the same time, these two discourses do not appear separately, but complement each other in a form of biopolitics in which the body of the refugees is represented and perceived either as a suffering or a threatening one (Fassin 2001). In this way, understandings of refugee agency are framed in a specific way fundamentally excluding the possibility for refugees to find and develop their own way into receiving countries and societies: Either they are seen as helpless victims or as problematic perpetrators. This representation corresponds to a differentiation according to gender and age, which largely excludes young male refugees from the narrative of vulnerability and thus makes them vulnerable in a specific form.

## Vulnerability as a postcolonial construct

"All refugees are vulnerable", is the title of an article by Lorenz (2018) in which he deconstructs this seemingly self-evident statement from a postcolonial perspective. The attribution of vulnerability represents a form of epistemic violence that by definition renders refugees powerless and speechless. In this sense, humanitarian aid also always means the denial of subjectivity and of possibilities for action. "There is no care without control" (Agier 2008, 4). Humanitarian protection of refugees is the "left hand of empire" (ibid., 200): Cultural and/or individual inadequacies are paternalistically compensated for instead of imperialist mechanisms of oppression and exploitation being epistemically analyzed and politically fought. The vulnerability paradigm clearly shows the origin of this term from disaster research, even though, throughout its development, vulnerability research has repeatedly turned against the idea of vulnerability being natural and inevitable (Lorenz 2018, 64-66). The vulnerability of refugees is attributed to causes in political systems and human behavior – but these causes are supposedly beyond the sphere of influence of those who provide humanitarian aid. They can only combat the consequences and symptoms.

This not only obscures the post-colonial, imperialist structure of the globalized world order. At the same time, the right of refugees to assistance becomes a consequence of an individual's need for help rather than a legal right. This ambivalence is already present in the Geneva Convention, whose preamble refers to the "social and humanitarian character of the refugee problem" as well as the "deep responsibility for refugees" (UNHCR n.d.). And, of course, the term "well-founded fear" in the definition of refugees also represents an at least partial psychological characterization of refugees that can be translated into vulnerability. On the other hand, however, specific individual rights of refugees arise from the Geneva Convention in combination with the Declaration of Human Rights, which are not only humanitarian but can also be read as empowerment.

According to Pupavac (2008, 273), this concept of refugees as particularly needy persons was not prominent during the Cold War, when refugees were depicted as political heroes and served as an argument for the moral superiority of capitalism over real existing socialism (cf. also Chimni 1998). While a political-legal approach to refugees was dominant during this time, since the fall of the Soviet Union, claims by refugees have primarily been argued on a humanitarian basis. The rights of refugees have increasingly receded into the background; the "suffering" of these people, not the danger of political persecution, is in the foreground. This leads to a form of biopolitics in which the "suffering body" of refugees is the justification for protection and support. Embodiment (in the literal sense) of suffering becomes a condition for being considered an "authentic fugitive" (Fassin 2001). This representation goes hand in hand with a "feminization" of the image of refugees along classical gender roles of helpless women and strong men. This deprives female refugees of the possibility of self-determined action and tends to exclude male refugees from the status of refugees (Judge 2010).

## Refugees in danger versus refugees as danger

For some EU countries, the short summer of "Willkommenskultur" (Welcome Culture) in 2015 represented a highlight of this humanitarian access to refugees in all its ambivalence. The need for help and protection of (especially Syrian) refugees was out of question for a short time and was widely supported by the population, especially in Germany and Austria. At the same time, however, these characteristics of refugee status were directly linked to other characteristics that cannot be derived from the Geneva Convention, in particular a willingness to integrate and gratitude towards the receiving state. Thus, in mainstream discourse, the one-sided right of refugees to protection and life opportunities has been used to construct an exchange relationship in which any "non-good behavior" of the refugees leads and should lead to the loss of rights. A legal relationship thus became a mutual moral relationship, the termination of which seems justified if one of the two sides does not fulfill its obligations. Other discourses focus with similar consequences on particularly talented refugees and the services they can provide for their country of residence. Here it is obviously implied that non-talented or less talented refugees are less worthy of protection. Overall, discourses that demand special capacities from refugees lead to similar criteria being applied to refugees as to voluntary migrants, thereby contradicting the legal situation (Judge 2010, 13).

In the German-speaking countries, this understanding of duties and neglect of duty of refugees reached a discursive climax after it became known that "migrants" (among them, incidentally, only very few refugees) had sexually harassed women in Cologne to a very considerable extent on New Year's Eve 2015/16. These incidents confirmed the prejudices against refugees and migrants by an increasingly nationalistic and xenophobic mainstream. And those who continued to support refugees (in some cases with considerable personal effort) had nothing to counter these prejudices but the (quite implausible) assertion that refugees were not capable of such acts.

Problematischer erscheint hingegen eine antirassistische Politik, die mitt-
lerweile in einer paternalistischen Identitätspolitik verstrickt ist, in der ihr
Gegenüber – die Geflüchteten – stets nur Opfer sein können, darin also Un-
schuldige (...) In dieser Reaktion steckt indes eine Entmündigung [...]. Diese
Reaktion spricht von einer Moral der Schuld, in der die anderen immer nur
Getriebene ihres Schicksals sind, niemals aber verantwortliche Menschen
sein können. [An anti-racist policy appears problematic, which is meanwhile
entangled in a paternalistic identity policy, in which its counterpart – the
refugees – can only ever be victims, i.e. innocent people. This reaction, however, contains an incapacitation [...]. This reaction speaks of a morality of
guilt in which the others are always only driven by their fate, but can never
be responsible people.] [Monika Mokre's translation] (Perinelli 2016).

After the short period of general good will towards refugees in 2015, the discourse and the political handling of refugees have become harder and harder
by leaps and bounds, so that in retrospect the paternalism of 2015 appears
rather as a golden age even in a critical view of the "Willkommenskultur". An
image of the general helplessness of refugees has given way to a mainstream
discourse according to which refugees are usually "economic refugees", if not
criminals or even terrorists who do not deserve "our" protection. The humanitarian discourse has increasingly been overlaid and thwarted by a security
discourse – from "refugees *at* risk" to "refugees *as* risk" (Gray / Franck 2019).
Moral condemnations of refugees now already begin with the (inevitable) illegal border crossing into the EU (Ingvars and Gíslason 2018).

This approach to flight as guilt and danger is exemplified in the program that the Austrian coalition government has set itself in January 2020.[1]
This can already be seen in the slogan advertising this program – obviously
expressing a compromise between the neoliberal-conservative Austrian People's Party with its focus on migration control and the Greens: "Let's protect
climate and borders". Consequently, the chapter on "Migration and Asylum"
(190-200) is primarily concerned with border protection, repatriation to countries of origin and transit, compliance with the Dublin Agreement, readmission agreements – in other words, measures that prevent an asylum application and/or remaining in Austria. Positive measures concern the protection

---

1    See: https://www.wienerzeitung.at/_em_daten/_wzo/2020/01/02/200102-1510_regieru
     ngsprogramm_2020_gesamt.pdf

and legal status of minors (197) and the empowerment of women (199). Measures for women and young girls are also listed separately in the chapter on integration, which primarily mentions the duties of migrants (205, 207).[2]

The vulnerable refugee has become an exception, the recognition of which makes it possible not to completely abandon the claim of humanitarian commitment. "Recognizing the intersectional formulation of oppressions based on race and gender (as well as sexuality, class and other axes of social identity) that has been identified by black feminist and feminist postcolonial scholars [...], we trace the gendered and racialized images of threat and vulnerability through which refugees come to be read as risk or as at risk" (Gray and Franck 2019, 278).

Thus, the definition of vulnerability is transformed from a general figure of disempowerment and desubjectivation to an individual question of survival. In his own, almost admirably naive clarity, Donald Trump has put the answer to this question in a nutshell: "Look at what's happening all over Europe. It's a mess and we don't need it. [...] When you look at this migration, you see so many young, strong men. [...] And you're almost like, 'Why aren't they fighting? You don't see that many women and children'."[3] Critical comments on this statement – such as those in the article quoted – focused on current statistics that show that more and more women and children are fleeing to Europe – but not on considerations of whether young men should really be expected to "fight".

## Women and children first!

A content analysis of British newspaper articles published between September 2015 and March 2016 (Gray and Franck 2019) clearly shows the images associated with vulnerability: It is about "womenandchildren" (Enloe 1993, 166). Children, women, especially pregnant women, and in some cases old or disabled refugees become the symbol of the vulnerability of refugees. Even the death of women and children is seen as a greater tragedy than that of men in the articles studied. When men are described as victims, they are minors,

---

2    These measures include a ban on headscarves for girls up to the age of 14, where there
     are plausible doubts as to whether this actually serves integration.
3    See e.g.: https://www.washingtonpost.com/news/fact-checker/wp/2016/05/16/trumps-c
     laim-that-young-strong-men-dominate-the-european-migrant-crisis/?arc404=true.

elderly and/or physically disabled men, or in some cases family fathers. These images of "refugees in need" are also reproduced by those who seek to create understanding and compassion for refugees. For example, a photographer who worked for the UNHCR reports that he was told to take pictures of women and children (Turner 2016). This fulfills and reproduces the public's ideas about refugees; at the same time, these images also correspond to the helpers' own image of their task. "(F)or many humanitarian workers a young Syrian man with gelled hair and turned-up fake leather collar ... looks like a threat, not like a beneficiary." The fear of these young men cannot be reconciled with the professional ethics of humanitarian workers, so these young men become invisible: "(T)hey simply do not occupy a place in the humanitarian imaginary" (Turner 2016).

This does not mean, however, that young men do not appear in the reporting. They are described as a threat, often because of their sheer presence: "Describing the 'Jungle' camp in Calais, for instance, one article highlights how neighbouring residents speak of being 'terrified by the presence of hundreds of men living rough, just yards from their front doors'" (Mulholland 2015, quoted from Gray and Franck 2019, 281).

The analysis also makes it clear that images of refugees have shifted along the axis from humanitarian aid to securitization from August/ September 2015 to early 2016 – from the emblematic image of the drowned Alan Kurdi to "representations of the in-comers as a (racialized, masculinized) threat" (Gray and Franck 2019, 283). After the events in Cologne, not only the discourse on refugees in the German speaking countries changed dramatically but the image of vulnerable refugee women disappeared for the most part also from the British media. "(T)he idea that racialized women need to be 'saved' from their oppressive cultures and from the hardships of their refugee journeys recedes into the background in the face of the more immediate concern for the 'saving' of 'our' women. Refugee women, who were previously held apart as a particular group in need of support, are now reabsorbed into the threatening (masculinized) mass of 'refugees' written large" (ibid., 286).

Young male refugees are under general suspicion of deviant behavior, of violence – especially sexualized violence – and of the ability and will to secure their survival by illegal means. These attributions of "foreign" masculinity are part of a colonial tradition:

> According to Butler, the unclear character of racism is thus less an independent axis but rather a condition for being able to articulate gender orders.

And vice versa, the diffuse, precisely indefinable gender roles function as a resonance space for racist ideas. The one expresses itself through the other and thereby re-actualizes itself. [...] What black feminists aptly described decades ago with their view of race and gender: 'All Blacks are men, all women are white.' (Perinelli 2016).

Here, too, we can clearly see the biopolitical and gendered embedding of the discourse on refugees. If it is not about the suffering (mostly female) body, then it is about the physical threat of male refugees. The suffering body needs care, the threatening body needs control and/or exclusion (Judge 2010). At the same time, the physical threat by male refugees is updated in other contexts, for example in the fear that refugees will take jobs away from locals because of their physical strength or that they will be more sexually attractive to local women.[4]

## Gender-specific reasons and experiences for refuge

So, whoever is a vulnerable refugee – young men are not. But in war situations young men are vulnerable in a specific way, because not only Donald Trump, but also the respective belligerent parties believe that they "should fight" – for whatever or against whatever. In civil war situations, for example in Syria, the different belligerent parties try to recruit fighters by force; the same applies to the Taliban and the IS in Afghanistan (Rasuly-Paleczek 2017, 65). "(T) the most vulnerable and constantly targeted population group in situations of war is non-combatant men of battle age, since they are perceived as a threat to the forces at war" (Suerbaum 2017, 126; see also Tan 2017, 44). Thus, young men have to leave the country if they do not want to participate in acts of war. "There are a lot of young men leaving Syria because they don't want to be in the military. It's better than being Syrian and killing one another."[5] As in many other countries, desertion is punished with imprisonment in Syria. In a political-legal discourse on flight, the refusal of military service on grounds of conscience could be considered a reason for asylum; in the humanitarian

---

4    This focus on physical characteristics also plays a role in the relationship between refugees, as JUDGE (2010) shows using the example of Afghan and Syrian refugees in Athens.

5    See https://www.aljazeera.com/indepth/features/2016/05/world-afraid-young-refugee-men-160530110614219.html

discourse on individual suffering, this consideration has no place. Instead, draft resistance of refugees is interpreted as cowardice and the flight to Europe as a violent invasion – in the words of Czech President Miloš Zeman: "I am profoundly convinced we are facing an organized invasion and not a spontaneous movement of refugees."[6]

Danger for the sons is often the reason for the flight of the whole family, as Magdalena Suerbaum records in her anthropological study of Syrian refugees in Egypt. This also results in a specific sense of responsibility of these young men for their family; in the words of one of the interviewees: "Men should be strong. They are stronger than women. They should support the family. I work and study at the same time. This makes us men. We stand more than we can" (Suerbaum 2017, 125).

On the other hand, men also assume their responsibility for the families by setting off alone to Europe in the hope of being able to bring their family of origin and/or wives and children on a safe path. "They tell us, 'We do this dangerous trip on our own, we get asylum, and there is a law in the European Union that the family can come,'" says Christof Zellenberg, the chairman of the Europa Institute [...]. "You see few newcomers over 50", he adds, because "this is a grueling trip, and you need to be young and strong."[7]

But this murderous journey is often even more dangerous for young, strong men than for families, women and children. According to the UNHCR, in Libya, for example, young men are forcibly recruited by various parties to the civil war.[8] And under the very often inhumane conditions in camps and en route, the meager state care, the always inadequate resources of NGOs and even the efforts of traffickers for their clientele are primarily given to those who are considered more vulnerable. Lewis Turner (2016) reports on the situation in Jordanian refugee camps: "Men are significantly more likely than women or children to be refouled to Syria for alleged security reasons, to suffer from particular forms of police harassment, and to be forcibly encamped (or otherwise punished) by Jordanian authorities for labor market violations." Although it is generally very difficult for refugees to find paid work in Jordan, it is assumed that this possibility is open to men. In the

---

6    See https://www.aljazeera.com/indepth/features/2016/05/world-afraid-young-refugee-men-160530110614219.html.

7    See https://www.nationalreview.com/2015/10/why-europes-migrants-are-men/

8    See https://www.dpa-international.com/topic/unhcr-warring-libyan-parties-using-migrants-fighters-urn%3Anewsml%3Adpa.com%3A20090101%3A200117-99-508611

camps, families without an adult man are considered more needy than those with a family man – although this thesis is not supported by UNHCR statistics. Therefore, single women with children receive more financial support and better access to basic infrastructure, which should be open to all. The refugees often respond to this by registering women with children as families and their accompanying family fathers as single men. Additional pressure on refugee men comes from the obligation (recognized by themselves and their families) to support the family in the country of origin, even if they are not financially able to do so (Kamal 2017, 90 and 92).

Also, special psychosocial programs or spaces are more likely to be provided for women and children – partly because the financiers of NGOs are particularly interested in special services for these groups. Programs for dealing with sexualized violence that want to include male victims of sexualized violence often meet with incomprehension or even rejection by financers, since, they assume that, by definition, men cannot be victims of sexualized violence (Turner 2016).

The NGO *Médecins Sans Frontières* reports similarly about the situation on the Balkan route:

> A recent study by MSF [Médecins Sans Frontières] showed that male migrants are more likely to be subjected to violence from state authorities including the police and the military, smugglers and vigilante groups [...]. They are also more likely to be detained during their journey and be repeatedly 'pushed back', expelled and deported (Arsenijević et al. 2018, 87).

Here, too, the NGOs are focusing primarily on families, women and children. The study quotes two male refugees: "(F)or single people, guys like me, nobody cares. [...] So we, single men, are simply left on the street. [...] I went to Miksaliste [support hub for migrants] and asked if I could stay there just for one night and go in the morning. They said 'no, this place is only for minors and families, you can't stay here'" (ibid., 91). The study also cites refugees on the Balkan route who report that traffickers are more concerned with the basic needs of women and children and that male refugees have been forced to support families in difficult terrain and to carry their luggage.

This form of differentiation also finds its way into official policies towards refugees. For example, the Helsinki Committee reported in 2017 that the Hungarian government had introduced different transit zones for families, unaccompanied minors and men traveling alone. While the first two groups were given priority, only one unaccompanied man per week was allowed to apply for asylum (ibid., 87). And the Canadian Prime Minister Justin Trudeau, known as a liberal, declared his country's willingness to accept 25,000 Syrians as early as 2015, but explicitly excluded men without families from this program.[9]

## No permission for arrival

Refugees and migrants of all sexes embark on the perilous journey to Europe with high hopes – and are usually disappointed in these hopes. This situation leads to gender specific consequences, in some ways, affecting men more than women (while, in other ways, women are more negatively concerned). "Men often lose their ability to fulfil their traditional roles of protector and provider and find themselves ill-equipped for new urban or camp-based market opportunities" (Buscher 2015, 6).

In addition to the often much lower – if any – earning potential and life chances, young fugitive men in particular clearly experience rejection by the majority population. A young refugee from Eritrea realistically says: "If I always see bad things about refugees in the media, how can I make friends with them?" Of course, this also applies, and possibly to a greater extent, when it comes to contacts with women: "Over 80 percent of the young men interviewed were single and childless. Many of them also want to get in contact with women of the same age. But the negative image attributed to them when it comes to dealing with women, and in some cases racially exploited, is well-known to the refugees and makes it more difficult for them approach other people in an unbiased way."[10] Here can also be seen one explanation (of many) for the events of Cologne on New Year's Eve 2015 and similar forms of sexual assault.

> (A)ll male associations can be really dangerous for women – and also for other men [...]. This applies to the army, the prison, the mob on Father's Day, or even to soccer fan culture. But also many male refugees, especially those from North African countries, are forced by the racist Aliens Act into men's associations. [...] Forced housing [...] (becomes) a place of frustrated,

9    See. https://www.aljazeera.com/indepth/features/2016/05/world-afraid-young-refugee-men-160530110614219.html.

10   See https://www.infomigrants.net/en/post/14219/young-male-refugees-struggle-with-disappointment-and-mental-health-issues

subalternized groups of men [...], in which affective and sexual misery also prevails. For these men it is difficult to meet someone, they are not allowed to work, cannot buy anyone a beer, have no room of their own where they can take someone home with them and are therefore considered unattractive in the market of sexual or romantic possibilities (Perinelli 2016).

In many European countries, it is also apparent in asylum procedures and with regard to residence rights that young men are more likely to be deported (Bosworth et al. 2016). In this vein, until the takover of the Taliban in summer 2021, the Austrian asylum courts, regularly ruled that returning to Afghanistan were not a problem for young men who are able to work - although the German expert Friederike Stahlmann, for example, came to the opposite conclusion due to the dangerous security situation and lack of health care.

In addition, the hegemonic image of violent and potentially criminal refugees leads to a constant overestimation of the criminality of this population group on the one hand, and on the other hand to higher sentences, longer periods of imprisonment, and fewer chances of probation than for comparable offences committed by nationals. Frequently, criminal convictions result in the loss of residence permits and deportation (Mennel and Mokre 2017). Here, too, the intersectionality of gender and racial attributions is very clear: In fact, young men (regardless of their origin) are statistically more inclined to deviant social behaviour than other population groups. In reporting, however, criminal behavior is attributed almost exclusively to migrant men. Violent and sexual offences are particularly prominent, but statistically speaking, migrants are underrepresented here. Domestic and foreign perpetrators are more or less in balance when it comes to drug-related offences, while migrants are overrepresented in property offences (Pilgram et al. 2016). The over-representation of property crime can be explained without further analysis by the precarious financial situation of undocumented migrants and asylum seekers in particular, but it also correlates with income statistics that differentiate between Austrian and non-Austrian citizens.[11] Thus, even though immigrant men are over-represented in some categories, a causal relationship between criminality and country of origin is not backed up by statistics.

---

11    A relevant special evaluation from the integrated statistics of wage and income tax 2016 is available to the author.

## "Being a real man"

Hegemonic discourses about refugees make it difficult for young male refugees to find their place in society and to unite their self-image with the image imposed on them by the outside world. The victim role assigned to refugees reduces the status of refugees of any gender to an object of charity but is furthermore only open to young men to a limited extent. In the "Willkommenskultur" of summer 2015, the role of the grateful victim was often projected onto young men[12]. For many of them, this meant a considerable amount of support, but at the price of losing the opportunity for self-empowerment.[13] In the meantime, this figure of the "good fugitive" is no longer available to most young men. They are not only second-class people in their country of residence, but also second-class refugees compared to "womenandchildren". This is not only an uncomfortable position, but also one that can hardly be reconciled with traditional ideas of masculinity (not only in the Global South, but also in the Global North). "Everything used to go to men, now nothing. Back in Syria and in many other countries, men are in the first place. Because he [a man] is the pillar of the family. He is a leg of the chair, because they prefer kids, then women, then dogs and then men" (Arsenijević et al. 2018, 91). The living conditions in Europe also often make it impossible for refugees to realize their own ideas of life: "Be a real man", pursue a profession, start a family. A Nigerian migrant in Austria summarized this situation: "Under these conditions, I was no longer able to live a clean life, that is, not to get involved in anything criminal [...]. But I had other options, namely [...] to find a woman with enough money and be her boy toy. That way I could have calculated how to buy my residence permit. So, I thought, 'In order to stand my own ground and make decisions, I have to earn my own money'" (Simo and Simon 2015, 98).

The contradiction between self-perception and life hopes and the reality during as well as after the end of (the physical) flight leads to psychologi-

---

12   Different images of the "good refugee can be found in different countries of arrival. E.g., McCluskey (2017) describes at depth that, in Sweden, this image has rather been related to the "national Swedish value of gender equality than to the model of the "grateful victim.

13   See on this, albeit very undifferentiated: https://www.dasbiber.at/content/sugar-mam as-und-ihre-fluechtlinge. Critical herein: https://www.derstandard.at/story/200006209 7156/ueber-sugarmamas-und-antaenzer

cal problems that could only be meaningfully dealt with in a stable life situation. In addition, however, psychotherapeutic services are also provided primarily for women. Furthermore, many male refugees (as well as many European men) find it difficult to reconcile their self-image with the need for psychotherapeutic help as a 26-years old Syrian refugee explains:

> In our countries, it is dangerous to speak of psychotherapy. People think you must be crazy when you speak of such things. But here, it is different. A lot of people need help. We also need help. Not just us, everyone. [...] But I would never dare to openly tell the people that I stay with at my accommodation center that I need such a doctor, a psychologist. They would think I'm insane.[14]

## Summary and outlook

This paper pursued two analytical goals: On the one hand, it has been shown that discourses on the vulnerability of migrants and the threats posed by migrants do not contradict but rather complement each other. On the other hand, the aim was to show the specific genderedness of these two discourses, which in particular serve to exclude young male refugees from help and support.

Vulnerability and threat can be understood as postcolonial forms of biopolitics that reduce refugees to suffering or dangerous bodies. This understanding of refugees has been prevalent since the end of the Cold War; since 2015, the representation of refugees has shifted from an emphasis on vulnerability to one on danger, and at the same time both discourses coexist and complement each other. In particular, "womenandchildren" (Enloe 1993, 166) are understood as vulnerable and worthy of protection, while young male refugees are represented and perceived as a danger.

Gender-specific reasons for men's flight, such as compulsory military service in war zones, are ignored, as are men's physical and psychological traumas. Governments, NGOs and even traffickers provide care – if at all – to women and children (Arsenijević et al. 2018). Even after the arrival of refugees, it is particularly difficult for young men to find support and international

---

14    See: https://www.infomigrants.net/en/post/14219/young-male-refugees-struggle-with-disappointment-and-mental-health-issues.

protection is increasingly being denied on the grounds that young, healthy men can survive in their home country. Both in public opinion and through the judiciary, young migrant men are prejudiced against and punished more severely than natives (Mennel and Mokre 2017).

However, vulnerability – as well as criminality – are not an essential characteristic of certain groups of people, but are constructed in and from a specific context: "The concept of 'vulnerability context' considers the interplay between the features of these persons and their hosting communities, their interactions and experiences, and how different solutions for attention and inclusion affect them."[15] Vulnerability can therefore only be assessed on an individual level and not defined in a generalized way based on gender or age. Vulnerability also arises from government action, as the reports from different phases of flight show. In analytical terms, it would make sense here to use gender mainstreaming methods to determine the gender-specific effects of certain measures in the area of migration and asylum. For example, in 2021, Austria introduced a new paragraph in criminal law criminalizing participation in a religiously motivated extremist association "with the intent to thereby promote the commission of religiously motivated extremist acts".[16] It can be expected that punishment for political positions (formulated in a general way but clearly aimed at so-called "political Islam") will primarily affect male migrants.

At the same time, it should be noted that numerous opportunities only granted on the ground of vulnerability by governmental and non-governmental organizations should be open to every refugee at every stage of his/her flight. It is an undue limitation of humanitarian commitment if vital infrastructure is only created for the most needy.

Refugees should not be provided with food on the basis of charity, but, due to legal and political considerations, they should have equal life opportunities as the long-term resident population.

With this claim, refugees also succeed from time to time in regaining their subject status through political activity. This represented a substantial part of refugee protests that have taken place repeatedly in various European countries for many years. In this sense, the Refugee Protest Camp Vienna, for example, propagated "We demand human rights, not charity" in 2013 and gave a donation, which was to benefit the protest, to an NGO with the request that

---

15    See https://www.uni-med.net/progetti/raisd/
16    https://www.jusline.at/gesetz/stgb/paragraf/247b

it be used for people in need. "So the point is to explain to other people that it is not about money, but about a solution. We are not asking for donations or rooms that then belong to us – at this moment we are talking about human rights" (quoted after Mokre 2015, 100).

In a similar way Ingvars and Gíslason (2018) interpret a protest of Syrian refugees in Athens in 2014. 13 Syrians organized a sit-in at Syntagma Square, in front of the Greek parliament. "In this way, the young Syrians paved the way for an emergent refugee masculinity through which male refugees could gain respect locally, regionally, and globally. They also challenged the mediated narratives of migrant criminality, immorality, and greed" (ibid., 3). By articulating and embodying their claim to be part of the political community with political rights, they were able to gain this status, at least temporarily. In doing so, however, they also renegotiated their "masculinity". They found a role that was neither marked by the "feminization" of the victim role nor by the threat scenario of the criminal refugee, but rather had a self-empowering effect and opened up possibilities for action. This self-empowerment was based on the claim to the "right to have rights" (Arendt 1973, 177), with which refugees could escape the controlling care and representation by others, thus, gaining political agency by challenging refugee regimes.

Of course, these political activities are not open to all refugees – nor are they wanted by all. But they point to an approach to the problem of flight that has largely been lost in recent decades, namely rights and especially the right of inclusion in the political community. This access also offers the possibility of genuine solidarity between refugees and non refugees, without differentiation based on ascribed individual needs. This does not solve the problem of vulnerability, which is ultimately a profoundly human characteristic, very unequally distributed and dependent on numerous circumstances. But perhaps it does open up the view to individual vulnerability, which is the basic condition for dealing with it.

## References

Agier, Michel. 2008. *On the Margins of the World. The Refugee Experience Today.* Cambridge: Polity Press.

Arendt, Hannah. 1973. *The Origins of Totalitarianism.* New York, NY, Harcourt Brace Jovanovich.

Arsenijević, Jovana et al. 2018. "'I feel like I am less than other people': Health-related vulnerabilities of male migrants travelling alone on their journey to Europe". *Social Science & Medicine* 209: 86–94.

Bosworth, Mary et al. 2016. "Punishment, Citizenship and Identity: An Introduction." *Criminology & Criminal Justice* 16: 1–10.

Buscher, Dale. 2015. "Formidable Intersections: Forced Migration, Gender, and Livelihoods". *SSRN Electronic Journal* January 2015. DOI: 10.2139/ssrn.2734741.

Chimni, B. S. 1998. "The Geopolitics of Refugee Studies, A View from the South". *Journal of Refugee Studies* 11, no. 4: 350–374.

Enloe, Cynthia. 1993. *The Morning After: Sexual Politics at the End of the Cold War.* Berkeley, CA, University of California Press.

Fassin, Didier. 2001. "The Biopolitics of Otherness: Undocumented Foreigners and Racial Discrimination in French Public Debate. *Anthropology Today* 17, no. 1: 3–7.

Gray, Harriet, and Anja K. Franck. 2019. "Refugees as/at risk: The gendered and racialized underpinnings of securitization in British media narratives." *Security Dialogue* 50, no. 3: 275–291.

Ingvars, Ardis, and Ingólfur Gíslason V. 2018. "Moral Mobility: Emergent Refugee Masculinities among Young Syrians in Athens". *Men and Masculinities* 21, no. 3: 383–402.

Judge, Ruth. 2010. *Refugee advocacy and the biopolitics of asylum in Britain: the precarious position of young male asylum seekers and refugees.* Working Paper 60. Oxford, Refugee Studies Centre.

Kamal, Noura. 2017. "Journey to Europe: Memory and the Path to Tomorrow." In: *From Destination to Integration – Afghan, Syrian and Iraqi Refugees in Vienna. Edited by* Kohlbacher Josef and Leonardo Schiocchet, *ISR Forschungsbericht* Heft 45, 83-103. Wien, Verlag der Österreichischen Akademie der Wissenschaften.

Lorenz, Daniel. 2018. "'All refugees are vulnerable': Vulnerabilität, Konflikte und Katastrophen im Spiegel Postkolonialer Theorie". *Zeitschrift für Friedens- und Konfliktforschung*, Sonderband 2: 60–98.

Mc Cluskey, Emma. 2017. " 'Solidarity' and 'gender equality' as a discourse of violencein Sweden: Exclusion of refugees by the decent citizen." *Working Papers in Urban Language & Literacies.* Paper 209.

Mennel, Birgit and Monika Mokre. 2017. "Integration durch Kriminalität". *Juridikum* 4: 523–532.

Mokre, Monika. 2015. *Solidarität als Übersetzung. Überlegungen zum Refugee Protest Camp Vienna.* Wien: transversal.

Perinelli, Massimo. 2016. *Post Colonia. Feminismus, Antirassismus und die Krise der Flüchtlinge.* https://www.zeitschrift-luxemburg.de/post-colonia-feminismus-antirassismus-und-die-krise-der-fluechtlinge/.

Pilgram, Fuchs, Walter, und Christina Schwarzl. 2016. *Delinquenz ausländischer Staatsangehöriger in Wien.* Vorarbeiten für eine fortlaufende Beobachtung. Forschungsbericht. Wien: IRKS.

Pupavac, Vanessa. 2008. "Refugee Advocacy, Traumatic Representations and Political Disenchantment." *Government and Opposition* 43, no. 2: 270–292.

Rasuly-Paleczek, Gabriele. 2017. "Many Reasons for Leaving Afghanistan: Social Obligations in Times of Protracted Violence." In *From Destination to Integration – Afghan, Syrian and Iraqi Refugees in Vienna. ISR Forschungsbericht* Heft 45, 57-82. Edited by Josef Kohlbacher and Leonardo Schiocchet. Wien, Verlag der Österreichischen Akademie der Wissenschaften.

Simon, S., and Kader, Simo. 2015. "Wir nennen das Gefängnis ‚Schule'." In *Das große Gefängnis.* Edited by Birgit Mennel and Monika Mokre, 97–112. Wien, transversal.

Suerbaum, Magdalena. 2017. What Does It Mean to Be Young for Syrian Men Living as Refugees in Cairo? *Middle East – Topics and Arguments*, 9, pp. 122–131.

Tan, Denis. 2017. "Being en Route": Flight Experiences of Forced Migrants in Austria and Turkey. In *From Destination to Integration – Afghan, Syrian and Iraqi Refugees in Vienna. ISR Forschungsbericht* Heft 45, edited by Josef Kohlbacher and Leonardo Schiocchet, 37-56. Wien, Verlag der Österreichischen Akademie der Wissenschaften.

Turner, Lewis. 2016. *Are Syrian Men Vulnerable Too? Gendering the Syria Refugee Response.* https://www.mei.edu/publications/are-syrian-men-vulnerable-too-gendering-syria-refugee-response

UNHCR (ed.). n.d. *Abkommen über die Rechtsstellung der Flüchtlinge vom 28. Juli 1951* (In Kraft getreten am 22. April 1954), Protokoll über die Rechtsstellung der Flüchtlinge vom 31. Januar 1967, (in place since October 4, 1967). https://www.unhcr.org/dach/wp-content/uploads/sites/27/2017/03/Genfer_Fluechtlingskonvention_und_New_Yorker_Protokoll.pdf

# Cleavage and *Hijab* Among Women from the Syrian Conflict in Brazil

*Mirian Alves de Souza*

This chapter aims to contribute to an anthropological production on refugees, offering a critical analysis of certain speeches by humanitarian agents. It is relevant to present a critical point of view, because "the world of humanitarianism tends to elude critical analysis" (Fassin 2011, 35). This text is based on research on Syrians refugees in Brazil, focusing on the management of organizations involved in the process of refugee protection and asylum. Here I seek to present narratives that challenge the image of refugee women as eternally vulnerable or oppressed by "culture", recognizing their agency and describing other intersectional power dynamics.

The purpose of this text is to contribute to research on refugees and Middle Eastern women. There are few studies that focus on women refugees from Syria in Brazil addressing their relations with humanitarian work. This chapter engages in a dialogue with and contributes to the literature that seeks to break with the homogeneous narrative about refugees as bodies that need to be saved, problematizes certain humanitarian discourses. This chapter explores the importance of an analysis recognizing the agency of women, defying the dichotomies of tradition and modernity as well as humanitarian rhetoric about female victim refugees. The victim of this rhetoric is a helpless forced migrant who is also seen as a "conservative" woman without freedom of choice and strength. This sort of discourse reinforces reductionist images ignoring that women wearing hijabs often do so out of a conscious choice. Saba Mahmood's (2005) perspective plays an important role in this analysis, because her agency concept is built from women who do not conform to liberal and secular projects and who exhibit a high level of reflexion about their religion experience. Mahmood problematizes the universal desire to be free, situating the agency not only in terms of resistance but in terms of capacities for action, fed by concrete and specific subordination relations.

Scholars in the field of refugee studies have produced critical works seeking to describe and analyse the refuge and displacement experience in consideration of the conflict that produced forced migration and the historical and social contexts of origin, transit and destination of people, as well as their different cultural belongings (for example, Malkki 1995; Harrell-Bond 1986; 2002; Fassin 2010; 2011; Agier 2011; Schiocchet 2017; Hamid 2012; 2019; Navia 2014; Lokot 2018).

Based on research in Southern Sudan, Barbara Harrell-Bond (1986; 2002) challenges the homogeneous narrative about refugees, showing that her interlocutors were different in many ways (age, education, gender, social class and so on). In the context of a refugee camp, she articulated her research with refugees around humanitarianism, questioning humanitarian aid rationality and validity. Harrell-Bond argues that Ugandans entering Sudan required different types of humanitarian assistance, including provision of food and medicines. But she brought to the work of humanitarian agencies the same type of scrutiny that was already used for development projects. Harrell-Bond (1986) studied how good intentions gave way to irritation and even hostility when humanitarian workers experienced discomfort, failure and betrayal by people they thought were grateful. "Harrell-Bond argued that those working in such conditions were victims along with the refugees and that agencies needed to be aware of their likely responses when setting up relief programs" (Colson 2011, 160-61).

Harrell-Bond considered humanitarian agencies, their international supporters, local governments and host persons at a time when humanitarian work was seldom subjected to ethnographic assessments. Elizabeth Colson (2011, 161) thinks that *Imposing Aid* (Harrell-Bond 1986) made many people hostile to the idea of seeing their work exposed to public scrutiny. Currently, *Imposing Aid* remains relevant and reaffirms the importance of looking critically at certain humanitarian practice (for example, Agier 2011; Hamid 2012; Schiocchet 2017). As Colson considers "ethnographers who study the system of humanitarian assistance continue to corroborate Harrell-Bond's critique and further illuminate the overall deleterious impact of refugee camps" (2011, 161).

The works by Sonia Hamid (2012, 2019) are based on this critical perspective. Researching an "integration" program for resettled Palestinian refugees in the city of Mogi das Cruzes, in São Paulo State, Hamid discusses the use of the "culture" category, often mobilized by those working in program management. Hamid (2019, 115) argues that the concept of culture was treated in a totalizing way to explain assisted subjects' behaviour. It was used, in general, almost as an accusation, insofar as it pointed out undesirable elements that needed to be transformed, in spite of the difficulties. Despite the diversity of practices and behaviours among refugees, Hamid described humanitarian workers mobilizing a predefined concept of culture, ignoring cases that defied their predetermined vision and seeing those cases as exceptions (2019, 129).

Empirical research (Lokot 2018; Hamid 2019) questions emphasis on "tradition" and "culture" categories triggered by humanitarian agents that do not describe or explain the meaning of "culture" or "tradition". Michelle Lokot argues that, in humanitarian narratives, Syrian refugee families in Jordan are classified as "traditional", even though the meaning of "traditional" is not explained beyond the seemingly typical division of roles between women and men (Lokot 2018, 02). The binary – liberal or conservative, traditional or modern – framework hides many more complex nuances. Statements about refugee women must be contextualized considering historical, social, cultural and political elements that shape their identities. There is not a pre-determined visual image of the refugee, nor of the "refugee woman".

The main objective of this chapter is to contribute to gender studies and scrutinize the ambiguous images of refugee women. It seeks to exhibit how organizations working with Syrian refugees in Brazil deploy divergent images of "culture". The expectations within and the entanglement with cultural conceptions or perceptions of traditional versus modern, re-echo in the humanitarian aid work agents, fostering or impeding refugee agency. The goal is to scrutinize the humanitarians' workers expectations with regard to their clients' agency and to serve their specific imagery. In a devising agency, refugees have to muddle through various rhetoric and struggle with contradicting images and ideology-laden representations to engage with the host society which affects almost all aspects of life.

Liisa Malkki (1995, 8), based on her research with Hutu refugees in Tanzania, is very critical of narratives on refugees that ignore the conflict and persecution and oppression context that gives rise to displacement. They ignore a central dimension of refuge to privilege the refugee's body and culture. "It is striking how often the abundant literature claiming refugees as its object of study locates 'the problem' not first in the political oppression or violence that produces massive territorial displacements of people, but within the bodies and minds of people classified as refugees".

The centrality of women's bodies in academic and humanitarian discourses has been discussed from the perspective of gender studies in the Middle East (Abu-Lughod 1996; Mahmood 2005; Rabo 1996; 2008). Women and/or families were and are still used to symbolically represent the progress and cultural tradition of societies across the region (Rabo 1996, 156). Contemporary anthropological production has expanded this perspective to offer a more nuanced approach to Middle Eastern women, questioning reductionist discourses (Mahmood 2005; Chagas 2011).

Considerations on women's agency have contributed to this discussion. Saba Mahmood's (2005) ethnography in Cairo's mosques with a conservative women's movement gave way to a new concept of agency. Mahmood developed a concept of devoted agency that expands women's capacity to understand their sense of self, their aspirations, projects and desires, including the desire to submit to a recognized authority. These were configured in the context of non-liberal traditions. Mahmood defends that separation between the notion of agency and that of resistance is a fundamental step for considering will and politics' forms that do not conform to secular and liberal feminist norms, including "state feminism".

## Syrian Conflict and the Brazilian response

Since the beginning of the Syrian conflict in 2011, an estimated 6,7 million people have been internally displaced, 5,6 million have left the country, and 13,5 million need humanitarian aid. The Syrian civil war is an ongoing armed conflict waged mainly between the Syrian regime, led by President Bashar al-Assad, and many opponents' groups, as well as between these opponents' groups. Before the conflict, Syria's population was estimated at 22 million people. Currently, half of that population is displaced from their homes. Syria is the country producing the most refugees in the world (UNHCR 2018). About the war in Syria, Pinto (2017) exposes the complexities of the conflict – often approached from a sectarian perspective, and criticizes this view – showing how President Bashar al-Assad's regime used violence to forge a sectarian conflict, stemming from pre-existing tensions.

Most refugees from the conflict are in neighbouring, bordering countries, which are home to 90% of the total displaced people. Countries that received the most Syrian refugees are Turkey, Lebanon and Jordan (UNHCR 2018). In Brazil, from 2011 to 2018, 3,326 Syrian citizens were recognized as refugees, according to official data from the National Committee for Refugees (CONARE 2019), which administers refugees in Brazil. Entry of people affected by the Syrian conflict in Brazil was facilitated, for "humanitarian reasons", by easing visa requirements in Brazilian embassies and consulates. Guidance from the Ministry of Justice and Ministry of Foreign Affairs was to recognize the Syrian conflict as a civil war and a generalized framework of human rights violations. Syria was home to approximately 500,000 Palestinian refugees, of which 149,822 lived in one of nine official camps (Castellino and Cavanaugh 2013, 157). Through Normative Resolution 17 of 2013, valid for two years and renewed in 2015 and 2017, CONARE guided the issuance of visas for people affected by the Syrian conflict considering Palestinians and citizens of other nationalities residing in Syria. The inclusion of nationals from other countries in the Brazilian refugee policy enabled individuals – which, although affected by the war, are usually excluded from protection programs – to access protection.

During 2011 and 2012, at the onset of the conflict in Syria, the Syrian communities in Brazil tried to reunite with their relatives in Syria to enable them to flee violence and persecutions. At that time, the Brazilian government adopted a flexible policy as borders were opened to Syrians who were able to obtain tourist visas. This was a request advanced especially by the Christian Syrian component of Brazilian society, which has a longstanding presence in the country. Representatives of the Brazilian Arab community, with the support and intermediation of sectors of the Catholic Church, contributed to putting in place a governmental resolution to facilitate the entry of persons affected by the Syrian conflict to Brazil. Historical linkages and relationships between Syria and Brazil are fundamental, as they are meaningful about the sort of relationship between these people who arrived after the war broke out in Syria and the pre-existing communities in Brazil (Souza and Manfrinato 2020, 115).

From 2013, however, the migrant demography from Syria changed: many Syrians who are living in Brazil have no previous connections with pre-existent Arab networks. Predominantly are male and they started acquiring the young men icon who fled the military conscription in Syria. Throughout the Syrian crisis, the perspective of hosting the 2016 Olympic games and the 2014 World Cup had also created an idea of an economically thriving Brazil, where a workforce would have been needed. That counted as well as a pull factor for Syrians who came to relocate here. Syrians in Brazil can instead only access an eligibility system. That means they are self-settled refugees.

## Fieldwork

Fieldwork was conducted from October 2015 to September 2018, in Rio de Janeiro and São Paulo States, Brazil. In Rio de Janeiro, my research, which focused on the management of organizations involved in the process of refugee protection and asylum, adopted the methodology of participant observation by which I became a regular consumer of "Arab food" and studied Arabic which was taught by the language teachers who are refugees. In São Paulo, I conducted semi-structured interviews, which had more specific objectives. However, even in this context, in which I had little contact with interlocutors, the presence of small children, interviews in parks, cafes, museums and gardens created a more informal and empathic atmosphere. The notion of reciprocity, "giving something back" (Liamputtong 2007, 60), guided the research, so fieldwork included my assistance with opening a bank account, access to public health and education services, and assistance to humanitarian organizations.

I was interested in the relations of the interlocutors with the humanitarian agencies involved in their bureaucratic process of refuge and migration. The interlocutors were Syrian citizens and other nationals, such as Palestinians and Lebanese. These refugees lived in urban areas of Rio de Janeiro and São Paulo cities and presented great socioeconomic diversity. They were between 18 and 65 years old and were mostly from Damascus, Aleppo, Deir ez-Zor, Daraa, Raqqah and Homs in Syria. The Brazilian state did not provide assistance for refugees to come to Brazil and they were not welcomed by any special refugee program.

I conducted 15 interviews. Arabic classes with my interlocutors were very important because they configured regular activities. Interviews and private lessons were conducted at my home, in some interlocutors' residences, in cafes, restaurants and Casa de Rui Barbosa Foundation (FCRB). Research conducted in FCRB facilities allowed access to humanitarian workers and other relevant players in refuge management, especially those who participated in FCRB Summer Courses on Refuge editions. The narratives of two interlocutors are central to this article, which aims to give visibility to women who challenge an image of vulnerability and passivity present in certain humanitarian discourses.

## Randa's cleavage

In the 1st Summer Course on Refuge of Casa de Rui Barbosa Foundation, in December 2015, there was a visit to *Caritas*, in Rio de Janeiro, in which participants met Randa. She was young and, although only having been in Brazil for a few months, spoke Portuguese, using English just for more complex discursive formulations. She introduced herself to the audience as a Syrian citizen seeking asylum in Brazil and addressed some aspects of her life. She said that she worked as a telemarketing agent in Turkey to pay for her air ticket to Brazil. She also explored her interest in studying at a Brazilian university, her curiosity for new cultures and the Portuguese language.

Randa had lived in Damascus with her mother, where she was born in the 1990s. Her family was Syrian from Damascus, and Sunni Muslim, but, like her parents, she was not a practising Muslim. Randa's parents divorced when she was a child and, although she lived with her father for some years, she spent most of her life with her mother. Randa studied at a bilingual school in Damascus, which explained her fluent English. She used to go to painting classes at the Russian Cultural Center and attended other upper-middle-class social spaces in Syria. In the last decade, however, her family experienced a sharp economic decline, aggravated by the outbreak of the conflict in 2011. When Randa arrived in Brazil in 2015, she did not receive any financial support from relatives. With the money earned through working as a bartender in Beirut and a telemarketing agent in Istanbul, she was able to sustain herself and her mother for the first few months.

At the end of the visit to the *Caritas* office, participants formed small groups to leave the premises. In one of these groups, Maria, who had a leading and senior job position in an international humanitarian organization, openly questioned Randa's nationality, saying: "I am sure she is a Palestinian pretending to be a Syrian in order to get refuge. Now everyone is Syrian. With this cleavage, she is not Syrian" (Fieldwork, December 2015). Maria's speech has dimensions discussed by anthropological literature on the theme of refugees, such as distrust of the refugee and particular visual construction of the "victim" as bodies that need to be saved (Harrell-Bond 1986; 2002; Fassin 2010; Lokot 2018; Hamid 2019).

At the time of visit to *Caritas*, the Syrian conflict had attained high public visibility. In September 2015, photographs of a Syrian child drowned on a beach near the city of Bodrum, Turkey, reverberated globally. Turkish photojournalist Nilüfer Demir took a series of photos of the boy Alan Kurdi, who had died while trying to cross the Mediterranean Sea towards Europe with his family. Only the father survived and photographs of little Alan, dressed in a red T-shirt and blue pants, drew attention to the conflict. In a photograph, the child was lying on the beach, exactly where the water met the coast; face down, body facing the ocean. In another photograph, an adult in uniform and green beret, captured from behind, was beside the child. In a third photograph, the adult, half-turned to the camera and identifiable as a man, took the child and started to move away from the water (Adler-Nissen et al. 2019, 75).

Recognition of the Syrian conflict as a humanitarian crisis, given the repercussion of Alan Kurdi's photographs, relates to Didier Fassin's idea that the exposure of a suffering body is what remains as the last audible symbolic resource in situations of extreme social or legal exclusion (Fassin 2016, 46). Photographs of the little boy, Alan Kurdi, helped the Syrian conflict to be recognized by a large number of people in Brazil as a humanitarian crisis and not as a distant war. These photographs contributed to making the Syrian conflict and the humanitarian crisis it created widely known in Brazil, although the number of refugees at that time was already four million. In her research with Palestinian refugees from the Syrian conflict in São Paulo, Helena Manfrinato analysed mobilization and support received from civil society by refugees in face of the public commotion produced by the boy's photographs: "His lifeless body confronted against an inhospitable immensity of water, completely vulnerable, ignited people's commotion and indignation, making them wish to repair it and reverse the feeling that help was too late" (Manfrinato 2016, 428).

This comment by the humanitarian agency evokes the Syrian conflict's visibility, which is related to the public commotion produced by photographs. In this context, the transit of Syrian nationals was classified as humanitarian, allowing Syrians to be categorized as refugees. In saying that "now, everyone is Syrian", Maria assumed that Randa falsely associated herself with an identity widely recognized as that of a victim. Arguably, the boy Alan was a victim. Randa, however, with her cleavage, did not fit the image of victim, common to certain humanitarian workers. Harrell-Bond argues that external justification for financing institutional and administrative structures, which were created to distribute aid, depends on specific ways of portraying refugees as helpless and desperately in need of international assistance. This image strengthens the view that outsiders are needed to help them. It also conditions the behaviour of those who help, which are also interested in pathologizing, medicalizing and labelling refugees as helpless and vulnerable (Harrell-Bond 2002, 57). As Randa did not correspond to a certain image of victim, she was not recognized as a Syrian national. The concept of "vulnerability" is often important in defining who receives services and who does not (Agier 2011, 213) and this is particularly true in the case of Syria.

Randa became my interlocutor. When I met her, she gave interviews and spoke openly about her experience as a refugee, but, after one year in Brazil, she began to refuse successive requests for interviews from researchers and journalists. Randa said she was especially tired of the same interview dynamic, with questions that focused on the problems and sufferings of the Syrian war. She said she felt her interviewers' disappointment with the absence of certain images in her narrative:

> I almost apologized for not seeing a dead relative. The only two bodies I have seen in my life were in Malaysia and Brazil. In Malaysia, I was in the car with a friend and I saw the body of a motorcycle driver on the road and, in Brazil, I saw the body of someone who was run over in the BRT [Bus Rapid Transit and System]. I'm sorry, but no one in my family died in the conflict and I didn't cross the desert to leave Syria (Interview in June 2016).

Randa did not have a narrative of suffering that showed her as a vulnerable victim. She lost the most important source of family income due to the conflict, the rental of a property in Damascus. The area where the property was had been closed and she did not know if the building had been destroyed. Family and friends were dispersed in several countries or in Syria, facing daily problems, such as fear of violence by the Assad regime and armed groups, lack of basic items such as energy, drinking water, telephone and internet, but she did not have the story and visual image that people seem to expect from a refugee.

Representation of Syrian women, conveyed by humanitarian speeches and the media, was strongly criticized by Randa and other Syrian women, such as journalist Milia Aidamouni. Milia left Damascus for Jordan in 2013 due to political pressure. Together with her colleague Rula Asad, she founded the Syrian Female Journalists Network. Milia's work promotes a better understanding of Syrian women's role in the uprising and breaks stereotypes surrounding female journalists in the region. The network sought to expand representation of Syrian refugees and present them in more plural images and to sensitise foreign media that insisted on portraying Syrian women in a one-dimensional way:

> Foreign media tries to portray Syrian women as one dimensional – she's a victim, a mother of a detainee, a wife of a prisoner, a hostage in a hostile country waiting for humanitarian aid. But from Day One, women were part of the uprising. They took to the streets, they helped in the field hospitals, they created community centers to support each other in their local communities. Syrian women as refugees are also breaking stereotypes and changing the image of Syrian women. No one talks about the challenges they are facing [in Jordan] after four or five years of being a refugee (Nobel Women's initiative 2016).

Randa challenged the refugee woman's one-dimensional image criticized above. The view of Palestinian women as dressing in an exposing way was also questioned. For Randa, "she [Maria] has a very limited vision, everything is relative. There are the liberals and there are the conservatives, both on the Syrian and Palestinian side. But there is no such thing as a woman being liberal because she is Palestinian and traditional because she is Syrian. Or conservative because she is Palestinian and liberal because she is Syrian" (Interview in June 2017).

The binary framework – liberal or conservative and traditional or modern – hides much more complex nuances. Statements about Syrian or Palestinian women require contextualization of the historical, social, cultural and political elements that shape their identities.

## Samia's *hijab*

Samia was born in Damascus in the 1980s, in an unofficial Palestinian refugee camp. Her grandparents left Palestine in 1948 and became refugees in Golan, Syria. With the Israeli occupation of the territory in 1982, they went to Homs and then to Damascus. Samia grew up in the suburbs of the city and studied at the University of Damascus, where she met her husband. After a few years of marriage, Samia left Syria with Khaled and the couple's small son. In 2015, they arrived in Brazil, after living in Jordan and having their visa applications denied by several countries. Samia learned that members of her family and friends, who were in Lebanon, had obtained visas for Brazil. She called a cousin who lived in São Paulo. He informed her about the refuge process, local Arab communities, mosques and job opportunities offered by the city. In view of the couple's high qualifications, however, they decided to stay in Rio de Janeiro where, given the visibility of the World Cup (2014) and the Olympic Games (2016), they would have better employment opportunities. However, they only stayed for eight months in Rio de Janeiro. Through family contacts, Khaled got a job in the city of São Paulo, to where they moved.

I met Samia and her family in 2016 in Rio de Janeiro and, in 2017, we met again in São Paulo. Samia suggested that we participate in an event for refugees, promoted by several humanitarian agencies in partnership with public agencies of the city of São Paulo, private sectors, and confessional institutions. Samia attended the event in response to an invitation from friends who worked as volunteers in an Islamic association linked to the mosque. Samia said she only frequented the mosque in Damascus episodically. When she left Syria after the conflict, she and her husband began to go regularly to the mosque in Amman and, later, in São Paulo. Samia said that, unlike Khaled, she was not used to going to the mosque or praying at home daily. However, with the start of the Syrian conflict, and outside Syria, she started to feel connected to religion: "going through what the prophet Muhammad went through, connected me to Islam" (Samia, interview, June 2017). The experience of forced migration due to the Syrian conflict brought Samia closer to religion and Muslim communities in Amman and São Paulo. Samia compared her experience of forced migration with the *hijra* which can be literally translated as "departure", "emigration", "flight", "abandon" and refers primarily to Prophet Muhammad's migration from Mecca to Medina in 622 A.D. (Masud 1990, 30).

This event in São Paulo was held in a large public space and provided information on the theme of refuge and human rights. The event had volunteers and humanitarian workers from UNHCR, Caritas of São Paulo, and NGO's: *I Know My Rights* (IKMR) and Refugee Reintegration Institute (*Instituto de Reintegração de Refugiados*) ADUS, among other organizations. Humanitarian workers, placed in several tents distributed throughout the space of the event, gave information about refugees, women and children's rights. These organisations' volunteers distributed pamphlets and other informative materials. In one of these tents, I met Joana, who was formally working with one of the organizations present in the event, and two volunteers. Joana held a leadership position in her organization, had international experience in a humanitarian agency, a college degree and a postgraduate degree. Volunteers were attending the last period of their undergraduate courses and had already had previous experience in volunteering with other organisations. They all spoke English and lived-in middle-class neighbourhoods in the city of São Paulo.

In one of the event's food tents, I interviewed Joana and the volunteers. Joana started the interview explaining to me about her work and her organisation's role in the event. Then, she started talking about "Syrian women" in a more specific way, based on Samia's experience. Joana and one of the volunteers had met Samia at another event held by their organizations, which was specifically intended for refugee women and children. Joana described Samia as a "traditional" woman and stated that her "traditional culture" was a "problem" for her "integration" into Brazilian society. She repeated this several times, while the volunteers nodded in approval. Given the question, "what does 'traditional' mean?", Joana replied: "Samia looks like she is from my grandmother's time, not like my grandmother, because my grandmother worked. [...] She is very traditional" (Interview in June 2017).

Volunteers stressed that Samia was even more "conservative" and "religious" than other Muslim women attending the event, as these women wore skinny jeans and colourful *hijabs*. Unlike Samia who wore a long, loose skirt, long-sleeved turtleneck shirt, long waistcoat, cap and *hijab* in a monochromatic combination with different shades of black and grey. Joana went on to explain that "Muslim culture" and "Arab culture" would not allow women "to have freedom [...]. They are very traditional" (Interview in June 2017).

Although Joana did not know Khaled, she interpreted that it was Samia's husband who was the reason why Samia was not interested in the job opportunity that had been offered to her. When they met, Joana offered to help Samia to find a job position in the context of an employment program. They chatted in person and then exchanged messages through WhatsApp. Joana argued that, at first, Samia was interested in the job offer, as she had sent her resume. A few days later, however, she did not respond to the messages sent by the volunteer of the organization in which Joana worked and, finally, she replied that she was not interested at all. For Joana and the volunteer, Samia's husband had led her to give up running for a job. This assumption was based on the idea that Samia's family was "very traditional". Joana continued to speak, always with the gestural agreement of the volunteers, reaffirming the "traditional culture" of Samia and "Muslim women" who "wore veil and stayed at home". Joana seemed very annoyed by the fact that Samia missed the opportunity – not only of a job, which was not easy to find, but also of a way to get closer to São Paulo society.

I asked Samia about Joana's job proposal. The job as an administrative assistant involved 44 work hours per week and which paid the minimum salary for the professional category. In addition to that, she would have had to go through a selection process involving curriculum vitae analysis and an interview. Samia did not participate in the application procedure and justified her disinterest. She mentioned several elements for her decision, but the most significant one from her perspective had to do with her three-year-old son. One argument was that she would have to be long hours away from him. She explained that, accepting that job offer, she would be absent from home for almost 13 hours per day, considering workday time, nine hours, and daily commute (home-work-home) of two hours and thirty minutes. Another argument is that the salary, considering her family budget, would not allow her to pay a pre-school monthly fee. Samia already knew that she would not be able to obtain a place in a public kindergarten. As soon as she arrived in São Paulo, she was informed about that.

Samia did not find information when seeking assistance on access to kindergarten, bilingual schools and diploma revalidation. She argued that problems related to gender inequality and power relations in the family appeared to be the focus of humanitarian workers. One of the volunteers mentioned above sent to Samia, through WhatsApp, material from campaigns to combat gender violence. In a complaining tone, she showed me the history of communication with the volunteer on her cellphone, and commented:

> I already blacked out, but you can still see what she always sends me. Maybe she thinks that I suffer violence because I wear *hijab*, I don't know [...]. I had teachers in Syria and classmates who thought that my father made me wear *hijab* [...]. Now they think it's [...] [Khaled]? [...] But she [the volunteer] didn't answer me if her university could validate my diploma (Interview in October 2017).

The first messages were received without problems, such as the UN campaign "Orange Day for the end of sexual violence against women and girls". However, Samia became uncomfortable with the messages that addressed gender violence exclusively and with the absence of consistent responses to her requests. For Samia, her clothing, cultivated as a way of reaching *al-haya* – a feeling described as modesty and shyness among Muslims – could not be seen as a "problem". Samia did not relate modernity to secularization (*almana*) and questioned the modernizing project of feminism by humanitarian agents and the Syrian regime.

Samia questioned the standard of modernity in the Syrian regime, in which modern women were defined by their secular clothing. For her, the modernity of the Syrian regime was expressed through the First Lady's looking glass. Samia argued that Asma Al-Assad, the president's wife, adopted remarkably secular dress and was an international reference in style and elegance not only in Syria. In 2008, Asma Al-Assad was elected by the French magazine Elle "the best dressed first lady in the world", ahead of Carla Bruni and Michelle Obama. Ironically, Samia observed that,

> While the regime tortured and murdered children in the country's South, Vogue magazine wrote a flattering article on Asma. Is Asma an example of modernity? [...] She wears clothes from international brands, shows her legs, arms [...] and murders her own people (Interview in October 2017).

The First Lady is an educated, Sunni and secular Muslim woman whose image reinforces the modernizing principles of the Syrian regime. According to Samia, there was strong publicity surrounding the modernity of Asma, because she expressed global values of modernity. Women and/or families were and are still used to symbolically represent progress and cultural tradition of societies across the Middle East (Rabo 1996, 156). The image of Asma is used by the Ba'ath party's modernizing project, in which gender conceptions considered "traditional" (such as the use of *hijab*) are condemned as remnants of a patriarchal order that the party strives to eliminate.

## Agency and "women who wear *hijab* and stay at home"

The image of Syrian women with no cleavage, wearing *hijab* and oppressed by her "traditional culture" corresponds to a stereotype that, as this text shows, was reproduced by humanitarian workers occupying senior positions in their organizations' bureaucratic structure. As Michael Herzfeld argues, "stereotypes are produced at the top" (1992, 71). Although the use and diffusion of stereotypes are often attributed to popular discourse, Herzfeld (1992) shows how they are mobilized by states and bureaucratic actors.

The Ba'ath party's modernizing project mobilized the stereotype of Syrian women in *hijab* and oppressed by their patriarchal culture. According to Annika Rabo, initiatives such as study groups for adult women – organized by the Women's Union, organization controlled by the Ba'ath – is used as an important instrument to train women to "rid themselves of traditional attitudes" (Rabo 1996, 160). In the official speech of the Ba'ath party, society must be "modernized" and women have an important role in this process. The party promoted equality between men and women through suffrage, educational policies and employment opportunities. Official rhetoric holds that men and women, side by side, must build a new and developed nation for the good of all (Rabo 1996, 157). However, as Deniz Kandiyoti argues, nationalists in the Middle East, which created state feminism, say that women's seclusion had to be abolished because female at home were "a wasted national resource" and not because they had equal rights:

> A nationalist/feminist alliance of progressive men and women produced a new discourse on women and the family which was predominantly instrumental in tone. Women's illiteracy, seclusion and the practice of polygyny were not denounced merely because they so blatantly curtailed the individual human rights of one half of the population, but because they created ignorant mothers, shallow and scheming partners, unstable marital unions, and lazy and unproductive members of society (Kandiyoti 1991, 10).

In the speeches of state feminism and humanitarian workers, the Islamic veil is a symbol of female oppression while work, in turn, is a symbol of modernity and an indicator of women's freedom. Both speeches do not recognize the agency (Mahmood 2005; Chagas 2011) of women who "wear a veil and stay at home", to use Joana's phrase to refer to Samia.

The speeches of Maria, who does not see Randa as a refugee from Syria because of her cleavage, and that of Joana, according to which a woman wearing a *hijab* is submissive to her husband, do not recognize the agency capacity of female refugee. These speeches assume the culture as a problem and do not consider the very existence of women whose image defies a certain discursive construction about the "Syrian refugee woman". In an attempt to explain the main problems faced by refugees, reports from humanitarian organizations also treat Syrian women as a unified whole, without reference to class, education or other relevant factors. Reports (Oxfam and Abaad 2013, 14; Women's refugee commission 2014, 01; Buecherand Aniyamuzaala 2016, 04) should be questioned, for example, for emphasizing that only men are family providers. This narrative does not apply to all Syrian women and must be contextualized based on different social and cultural belonging criteria (Lokot 2018).

Social class, as well as value attributed to work (Salamandra 2004; Hijab 1988), has an important role regarding the exercising of paid activity. Randa worked as bartender, telemarketing agent, and as an English and Arabic teacher as well. With the money from her work, she supported her family in Brazil. Randa's mother, however, never worked. She was born into a wealthy family and, even in the face of family economic decline, refused to do so. For

Randa, her mother did not accept the need to work because she had an "elite mentality". Randa's mother also wore a plunging neckline, so the fact that she did not work could not be easily attributed to her "traditional culture".

Nadia Hijab (1988; 2001) shows that social class and working conditions must be considered, before attributing the reason for the low participation of Syrian women in the labour market exclusively to culture. Hijab (1988, 88-89) argues that women of very middle socioeconomic levels were privileged. They worked in the public sector, which in the Arab world is seen as offering the most valued and respectable careers for women, both in terms of job security and because the nature of the work is non-manual. In this case, women were eager to avail themselves of the opportunity to work to satisfy economic needs. This was not necessarily the case for women from lower socio-economic backgrounds.

According to Hijab, all the single respondents planned to leave their jobs when they married. However, "many women who left the factory on marriage found they had to return because of economic pressure. The married women were determined that their children would have an education so as not to end up like them. They had been forced into tiring, poorly paid jobs because of severe economic need." (Hijab 1988, 88-89).

Samia did not want to participate in the job selection process due to some factors, including low payment and lack of a nursery school for her son. The "blame Islam" approach for the situation that women are out of the labour market ignores the fact that many of the problems faced by these workers are, in general, shared around the world. In this sense, it is not possible to attribute the weight of tradition to Samia's failure to enter São Paulo's labour market.

Hijab challenges the common assumption that women in the Arab world do not work (2001, 41). She argues that the work is strongly located in areas where it is "invisible", mainly in agriculture, family businesses, domestic economy and elsewhere in the informal economy. Business concerns in the Arab world are managed by families and it is taken for granted that bosses will nominate, or help to nominate, family members into paid positions, just as civil servants will seek to advance the appointment of family members in their own departments or other departments. In rural areas, a family's livelihood depends on the work of all its members – husband, wife and children – in the field or in food processing and other activities related to agriculture. The same is true of small family businesses in urban areas (Hijab 1988, 12; Quataert 1991, 163).

The invisibility of the women's workforce also appears in family discourses. Mary Chamie observed – when quoting a survey on participation
of women in Syria's workforce – that when she initially asked men about
whether their wives worked, a large proportion answered that they did not.
When the question was rephrased to "If your wife did not help you with your
work, would you be forced to hire a replacement for her?", the overwhelming
majority answered yes (Chamie 1985, 99). This is the case of Samia, who
worked as an assistant to her husband, dividing her time between that work
and caring for her family.

Samia had professional plans and complained that, in Damascus, there
was no prospect of work. She wanted to migrate to a country in the global
north, like Canada, where she could find the conditions to build a career.
Samia said she was different from women in her husband's family, which
was part of the Damascus elite, because if they went to university or worked,
it was just for "attracting husbands". Christa Salamandra (2004) argues that
most jobs open to women in Damascus, no matter how prestigious, do not pay
enough to allow women to become economically self-sufficient. Jobs are seen
as temporary measures on the way to marriage or, later, as a supplementary
income. "For young single women, they are primarily a venue for display, the
ultimate aim of which is to secure a successful future in the private, rather
than public, sphere" (2004, 52).

In her family of Palestinian refugees, Samia mentioned a different framework. Most women wished to spend more time with their children, to develop
a deeper feeling of care and "connectivity" (Joseph 1994, 55) with their families.
However, even though prioritizing family and domestic life, they felt obliged
to work out of their homes for long hours, as they played a key role in family
economy. For her cousin, who intended to get married very soon, formal work
was conceived of as a hindrance. She was anxious to quit her low-paid job as
a kitchen assistant in a restaurant, after the wedding. This work was also very
heavy and, from her family history, she knew how exhausting it would be to
take care of the house, the family and still have a formal job. The desire to stay
at home, then, should not be ignored nor reduced to a women's segregation
issue.

This research indicates that it is a mistake to consider that women from
lower classes are more segregated than urban and elite women. For Samia,
single women were very controlled in their family, but after marriage, and
especially after children's birth, this control was almost non-existent. Her
husband's elite and secular family had a much more restricted conception

of social spaces in which women could move. Annika Rabo argues that rules on interaction between men and women may be less stringent in rural areas (2008, 134). Elite women in Damascus, however, find opportunities for interaction, albeit more limited, in semi-public spaces such as gyms (Salamandra 2006, 154-55). This literature, as well as gathered data, contrasts with the discourse stating that the biggest challenge faced by Syrian women and girls to access basic resources and specialized services is "due to their limited ability to leave home without a male family member" (Oxfam and Abaad 2013, 03). When addressing the issue of segregation, mobility and social interaction among Syrian refugee women in Jordan, Oxfam and Abaad's report makes no reference to local and global political and economic forces and their unequal impact on women's lives.

The assumption that the main challenge for refugee women relates to their own culture appears in above-mentioned humanitarian discourses. The search for cultural explanations about the behaviour of Muslim or Arab people is addressed in the research by Abu-Lughod (1996), Lokot (2018) and Hamid (2019). This way of thinking about Arab / Muslim alterity, far from being configured as something recent, refers to the very idea of Orientalism (Said 1978), produced since the 18th century. In Orientalist discourses, the condition of women, symbolized by the use of the veil, occupied a central place, being used to determine the degree of evolution / modernity of a society, justifying colonization practices. The way "women have become powerful symbols of identity and visions of society and nation" (Abu-Lughod 1996, 3) in the/a postcolonial world has been widely questioned in anthropology. Some criticisms of Orientalist views, however, refer to the idea that wearing the veil means liberating the hegemony of Western cultural codes and a way of opposing the oppressive secular state that promotes, as in the Syrian case, state feminism. Mahmood (2005) offers a remarkably different perspective to think the use of the veil.

Mahmood's ethnography in Cairo's mosques, within a conservative women's movement, showed the strength of a new conception of agency, a devout agency that escapes the dichotomy of subordination and resistance. Mahmood defends separation between the notion of agency and that of resistance as a fundamental step to think about the forms of will and politics that do not fit feminist secular and liberal norms (Mahmood 2005, 14). Mahmood's perspective expands our capacity of understanding and interrogating women whose sense of self, aspirations, projects and desires – including that of submission to a recognized authority – were configured in the context of non-liberal traditions.

The use of the veil by Samia and other interlocutors cannot be understood, as in the above-mentioned speech of the humanitarian worker, as an expression of her husband and traditional family's imposition. This view of Muslim and Arab women as passive and submissive, attached to the structures of male authority, has already been widely questioned (Mahmood 2005, 6). I do not consider it equally appropriate to think of the veil in terms of freedom of choice or as a response to Syrian state's secularization process (Rabo 1996, 167). Mahmood's perspective is constructed based on theoretical questions and, above all, on conservative religious women daily practices. They are not trying to escape tradition nor to reform the religious concept of gender. Mahmood values the point of view of her interlocutors, for whom the use of the veil (as for Samia) is an exercise in modesty and shyness (*al-haya*), one of the religious virtues for devout Muslims in general, and for women in particular. For Samia, the use of the veil, as well as the adoption of a more Islamic clothing and regular praying (*salat*), relates to a disciplinary process for the composition of a virtuous self. This process shows that religious values and practices are also of different importance in different phases of one's life.

Considering the influence of the Aristotelian conception of habitus in Islamic thought by Abu Hamid al-Ghazali (1058-1111) and Ibn Khaldun (1332-1406), Mahmood describes how habitus refers to a conscious effort to reorient will through an agreement between internal motivations, external actions and emotional states, obtained through repeated practice of virtuous acts. Mahmood conceives the veil as a disciplinary practice that constitutes devout subjectivities, recognizing the agency of women whose action is aimed at building a virtuous habitus.

## Conclusion

This chapter engages in a dialogue with and contributes to the literature that seeks to break with the homogeneous narrative about refugees as bodies that need to be saved, and problematizes certain humanitarian discourses. Samia rejects the expectations (being a suffering *hijab*-wearing victim) and instead insists on real support. Her narrative highlights the female and refugee agencies and becomes visible to the similarities between the humanitarian workers' speeches and the Syrian Baath regime discourse of secularism and rejection of Islamic clothing. Mahmood's (2005) concept of agency is important here because it was built from women who do not conform to liberal and secular projects and it criticizes the dichotomies of tradition and modernity as well as the humanitarian rhetoric about the "real" Syrian refugee.

This chapter also offers an ethnographic contribution to academic production on refugees from the Syrian conflict in Brazil, challenging the image of refugee women as eternally vulnerable or oppressed by their "traditional culture". Refugee women's narratives defy the humanitarian workers discourses that reproduce stereotypes and reduce the complexity of the refugee experience to a "cultural problem" by treating women as a unified whole with no reference to class, education, devotion or other relevant factors. The main goal is to expose and problematize tensions between the agency and "refugee regimes" based on the refugee's experiences with the humanitarian workers. This chapter sought to confront culturalist explanations, often mobilized by "refugee regimes", with the Syrian social and political context, women's social class, their desires and distinct modernity projects.

## References

Abu-Lughod, Lila. 1996. *Remaking women. Feminism and Modernity in the Middle East*. Princeton: Princeton University Press.

Adler-Nissen, Rebecca, Andersen, Katrine, and Lene Hansen. 2019. "Images, emotions, and international politics: the death of Alan Kurdi". *Review of International Studies* 10: 1-21.

Aghacy, Samira. 2004. "What about masculinity?". *Al-Raida* 21, no.11 :104–105.

Agier, Michel. 2011. *Managing the Undesirables: Refugee Camps and Humanitarian Government*. David Fernbach, Cambridge, UK: Polity.

Five Years of Conflict. 2016. Disponível em: https://insights.careinternationa l.org.uk/media/k2/attachments/CARE_Syria-women-work-and-war-rep ort_2016.pdf

Castellino, Joshua, and Kathleen Cavanaugh. 2013. *Minority Rights in the Middle East*. Oxford Press.

Chagas, Gisele Fonseca. 2011. *Sufismo, carisma e moralidade: uma etnografia do ramo feminino da tariqa Naqshbandiyya-Kuftariyya em Damasco, Síria*". PhD diss., Universidade Federal Fluminense.

Chamie, Mary. 1985. "Labour Force Participation of Lebanese Women". In *Women, Employment, and Development in the Arab World*, edited by Julinda Abu Nasr, Nabil F. Khoury and Henry T. Assam, 73 – 102. Berlin: Mouton.

Colson, Elizabeth. 2011. "Imposing Aid: The Ethnography of Displacement and its Aftermath". *Kroeber Anthropological Society*, 100, no.1: 154-167.

CONARE. Refúgio em números. 4ª. Edição. 2019. https://www.acnur.org/po rtugues/wp-content/uploads/2019/07/Refugio-em-nu%CC%81meros_ver sa%CC%83o-23-de-julho-002.pdf.

Fassin, Didier. 2010. *La Raison Humanitaire: une histoire morale du temps présent.* Hautes études, Paris, Éditions de l'EHESS (avec Le Seuil/Gallimard).

Fassin, Didier. 2011. "Noli me tangere. The moral untouchability of humanitarianism". In *Forces of compassion. Humanitarianism between ethics and politicis,* edited by E. Bornstein and P. Redfield, 35–52. Santa Fe, School for Advanced Research.

Fassin, Didier. 2016. *Didier Fassin. Entrevistado por Débora Diniz*, Rio de Janeiro: EdUERJ.

Hamid, Sonia C. 2012. *(Des) Integrando Refugiados: Os Processos do Reassentamento de Palestinos no Brasil.*. PhD diss., Universidade de Brasília, Brasília.

Hamid, Sonia C. 2019. "Integrando" refugiados: discursos e práticas de gênero na gestão de palestinos no Brasil. *In: Pessoas em movimento: práticas de gestão, categorias de direito e agências*, edited by Angela Facundo Navia, Sonia Hamid, Bahia Munem and Charles Gomes, Rio de Janeiro: FCRB/7Letras.

Harrell-Bond, Barbara. 1986. *Imposing Aid: Emergency Assistance for Refugees.* Oxford University Press.

Harrell-Bond, Barbara. 2002. "Can humanitarian work with refugees be humane?", *Human Rights Quarterly* 24, no.1: 51–85.

Herzfeld, Michael. 1992. *The Social Production of Indifference: Exploring the Symbolic Roots of Western Bureaucracy.* Chicago: University of Chicago Press.

Hijab, Nadia. 1988. *Womanpower: The Arab Debate on Women at Work.* Cambridge: Cambridge University Press.

Hijab, Nadia. 2001. "Women and work in the Arab world." In *Women and power in the Middle East*, edited by Suad Joseph and Susan Slyomovics. Philadelphia: Library of Congress.

Joseph, Suad. 1994. "Brother/sister relationships: Connectivity, love, and power in the reproduction of patriarchy in Lebanon." *American Ethnologist* 21, no. 1: 50–73.

Kandiyoti, Deniz. 1991. *Women, Islam and the State.* Basingstoke: Macmillan.

Kant de Lima, Roberto. 2010. "Sensibilidades jurídicas, saber e poder: bases culturais de alguns aspectos do direito brasileiro em uma perspectiva comparada". *Anuário Antropológico* 2: 25-51.

Keddie, Nikki R., and Beth Baron. 1991. *Women in Middle Eastern History. Shifting Boundaries in sex and gender*. New Haven: Yale University Press.

Liamputtong, Pranee. 2007. *Researching the Vulnerable: A Guide to Sensitive Research Methods*. London: SAGE Publications.

Lokot, Michelle. 2018. "'Blood doesn´t become water'? Syrian Social Relations during Displacement". *Journal of Refugee Studies*, (Dec.): 1-22.

Mahmood, Saba. 2005. *Politics of Piety: The Islamic Revival and the Feminist Subject*. New Jersey: Princeton University Press.

Malkki, Liisa. 1995. "Refugees and Exile: From 'Refugee Studies' to the National Order of Things". *Annual Review of Anthropology* 24: 495-523.

Manfrinato, Helena Morais. 2016. "'Dos quadros de guerra à participação: notas sobre a jornada do refúgio palestino em São Paulo'". *Cadernos de campo* 25: 421-436.

Masud, Muhammad Khalid. 1990. The obligation to migrate: The doctrine of hijra in Islamic law. In *Muslim Travellers: Pilgrimage, Migration and the Religious imagination*, edited by F. Eickelman and James Piscatori, 29–49. Berkeley: University of California Press.

Moghadam, Valentine. 1993. *Modernizing Women: Gender and Social Change in the Middle East*. Boulder, Colo.: Lynne Rienner.

Moghadam, Valentine. 2013. "Women, work and family in the Arab region: Toward economic citizenship, DIFI Family Research and Proceedings", Special issue on "Protecting the Arab Family from Poverty: Employment, Social Integration and Intergenerational Solidarity". http://dx.doi.org/10.5339/difi.2013.arabfamily.7. *Qsience*.

Nobel women's initiative. 2006. "Meet Milia Eidmouni, Syria". https://nobelwomensinitiative.org/meet-milia-eidmouni-syria/

Oxfam and Abaad. 2013. "Shifting Sands: Changing Gender Roles among Refugees in Lebanon". *Oxfam International*, 2013. http://policy-practice.oxfam.org.uk/publications/shifting-sands-changing-gender-roles-among-refugees-in-lebanon-300408

Pinto, Paulo G. Hilu. 2017. "The Shattered Nation: The Sectarianization of the Syrian Conflict". In *Sectarianization: Mapping the New Politics of the Middle East*, edited by N. Hashemi and D. Postel, 123–142. London: Hurst & Company.

Quataert, Donald. 1991. Ottoman Women, households, and textile manufacturing 1800-1914. In *Women in Middle Eastern History. Shifting Boundaries in sex and gender*, edited by Nikki R. Keddie and Beth Baron. 161 –176. New Haven: Yale University Press.

Rabo, Annika 1996. "Gender, State and Civil Society in Jordan and Syria". *In*: *Civil Society: Challenging Western Models*, edited by Chris Hann and Elizabeth Dun, 155–177. London: Routledge.

Rabo, Annika. 2008. "Doing Family: Two cases in contemporary Syria". *Hawwa* 6, no. 2: 129–153.

Salamandra, Christa. 2004. *A New Old Damascus: Authenticity and Distinction in Urban Syria*. Bloomington: Indiana University Press.

Salamandra, Christa. 2006. "Chastity Capital: Hierarchy and Distinction in Damascus". In *Sexuality in the Arab World*, edited by S. Khalaf and J. Gagnon. 152-162. London: Saqi Books.

Said, Edward W. 1978. *Orientalism*. New York: Pantheon.

Schiocchet, Leonardo. 2017. "Integration and Encounter in Humanitarian Tutelage". In *From Destination to Integration – Afghan, Syrian and Iraqi Refugees in Vienna*, edited by Josef Kohlbacher and Leonardo Schiocchet, 9–35. Vienna: Austrian Academy of Sciences Press.

Souza, Mirian Alves, and Manfrinato, Helena Moraes. 2020. "Refugees of the Syrian Conflict and the Struggle for Housing in Brazil." In *Agency and Tutelage in Forced Migration*. Edited by Leonardo Schiocchet, Monika Mokre, Christine Nölle-Karimi, 119–125. Vienna: ROR-n e OAW.

UNHCR. 2014. Woman Alone: Fight for survival by Syria's Refugee Women. 2014. https://www.unhcr.org/ar/53bb8d006.pdf

UNHCR. 2018. Global Trends, Forced Displacement in 2018. 2018. https://www.unhcr.org/5d08d7ee.pdf.

Women's Refugee Commission. 2014. Unpacking Gender: The Humanitarian Response to the Syrian Refugee Crisis in Jordan. 2014. https://womensrefugeecommission.org/resources/gender-issues/985-unpacking-gender-the-humanitarian-response-to-the-syrian-refugee-crisis-in-jordan.

# Reading the Routes: Exploring Experiences of Place-Making Through Refugees' Photographs, Walks, and Narratives in a Swedish Town

*Katarina Giritli Nygren, Sara Nyhlén, and Rozalie E. Böge*

## Introduction

This chapter focuses on processes of home-making in the context of temporary staying permissions. During the autumn of 2015, the number of refugees and migrants to Europe was high, causing headlines and prompting stormy political debate. This was also the case in Sweden, where initial public engagement and support was soon followed by demands for limitations on the number of refugees granted asylum and shelter; in the end, this came with great changes in migration policy. In Sweden, in 2016, a change came to residence rights, making temporary residence permits the norm (Governmental Proposition 2015/16:174) and with this change Sweden's refugee regime has moved from having one of the most generous migration policies to the minimum EU level (Hudson et al. 2020). This causes uncertainty and limited decision-making possibilities since the refugees are at the mercy of state institutions and court decisions. In the wake of these changes, we study which strategies refugees actively apply as they make a new home while having only a temporary permit of residence in Sweden. Since previous studies have revealed that asylum seekers often have embodied experiences of, and relate themselves to, the legislation of the country they are currently staying in (Kymäläinen and Nordström 2010), it is important to focus on the setting with temporal staying permits. How does one make a home when your legal status of residence is temporal? In addition, having fled from somewhere or being a refugee often also includes having lived at many places and in many countries, which means that the current place might just be one of many where the refugee will be engaged in the processes home-making.

In this context, the purpose of the current chapter is to explore the ways in which temporal migrants interact with the spatial possibilities of a city in the processes of (temporal) home-making. Drawing on critical refugee studies, using the theoretical concept of home-making, the chapter explores the processes that migrants use while inhabiting their new (possibly temporal) town of residence as 'their' space. We use a walk-along-mapping photo-elicitation method, which provides insights into the texture of spatial practices by revealing the subjects' engagement in their town environment and the way in which their new temporal place of residence is articulated in its (dis)connection to their individual stories. Inspired by Robertson et al. (2016), we use the photographs taken by the participants when out walking to train our focus on their ways of seeing, experiencing and understanding their surroundings. In what follows, we present the study's background and the theoretical concepts that guide the analysis. We then discuss the method and empirical results and conclusions of the research project.

## Refugees, place and home-making—research background and theoretical starting points

> Where is home? On the one hand, 'home' is a mythic place of desire in the diasporic imagination. In this sense, it is a place of no return, even if it is possible to visit the geographical territory that is seen as the place of 'origin'. On the other hand, home is also the lived experience of locality, its sounds and smells. (Brah 1996, 192)

Transnational processes such as migration have helped change the idea of a stable relation between people and place, which has led to the development of new understandings of individuals' connections to place and home (Butcher 2010, 24). To understand how someone who has not chosen their place of residence makes a new temporal place their home, it is necessary to problematise what home is and how it is related to place. In the quote above, Avtar Brah raises the question, "Where is home?" by arguing that home is not necessarily connected to a physical place where you live or have lived: it can also be a part of the imagination of a community or an origin from somewhere, as in diaspora contexts. Most people who move internalise their home, taking it with them, and in the new setting, they reach out to connect to their surroundings, adopting strategies that ensure each place is either "being at home" or "not at home" (Brah 1996).

Previous studies of refugees' home-making strategies have shown that the participants used strategies to integrate their past lives and places into their new settings (Risbeth and Powell 2013; Williamson 2016). Using participatory methods, one study (Robertson et al. 2016) focusing refugees' home-making practices finds that the search for the familiar in a new material setting was the usual strategy for remaking, reimagining and reconstituting places to make a home. Many of the photographs the participants generated in that study were concerned with bringing familiarities and characteristics from the participants' past into their present (Robertson et al. 2016). Indeed, people become attached to new places and make sense of them because of personal memories and past meanings. Similarly, in their study of young asylum seekers, Kymäläinen and Nordström (2010, 82) show that there is a "fluid space between the past and the future" that ensures that the familiar—the things that have been seen, heard or felt before—is significant in the construction of a daily life somewhere new. Despite calls to focus on the "politics of dislocation", the temporary aspect and "what it means to be situated in a particular place", the ways in which refugees position themselves in the "here and now as well as the far away" have not been addressed much at all (O'Neill and Hubbard 2010, 46). Following Butcher's lead (2010), we argue that living in a particular place is no guarantee of a sense of that place being your home or that it is in any way essential or a stable condition; rather, we think of it as something that has to be achieved and practised (see, e.g., Raffaeta and Duff 2013). This means that we understand efforts of making something home as a process where refugees use their own agency, experiences and strategies.

Based on their studies of the ways in which refugees build up a sense of home, O'Neill and Hubbard (2010) suggest that it is relevant to ask questions such as the following: When is a place at home? What is the difference between "feeling at home" and claiming a place as one's own? Indeed, finding home in a new city is not limited to finding a residence; it is as much about making a home because it requires strategies to make a place familiar, understandable and connected to one's self. The home-making processes that enable refugees to replace home also help generate new spaces for them. In previous studies, the ability to appropriate place has been shown to go hand in hand with spatial divisions, where power structures are reproduced and experienced in what are often contradictory ways (e.g., Giritli Nygren and Schmauch 2012).

Theoretically, we draw on the theories focusing on place and home-making from the field of critical spatial theory. We take our cue on how to understand home from writers such as bell hooks' (1990) "homeplace", Sara Ahmed's (1999) "being at homeness" and Avtar Brah's (1996) "being at or not at home". Following their thoughts, we understand home as something more than a material object: it comprises imagination, routinised everyday practices, relationship networks and a representation imbued with social meaning, cultural ideals, memories and values.

This requires us to take the meaning of making home as a relational entry point, meaning that we understand the informants' involvement in locality as not simply a question of inhabiting an existing space; rather, it is also about taking an active part in the making of that space (see Ahmed 1999). The investment of self in a locality, according to Ahmed (1999), is not limited to inhabiting a space that is already constituted by others it is a process where the refugees use their own agency. For Ahmed (1999, 341), the lived experience of "being at home" implies that subjects develop in a space that is anything but extrinsic to them; being at homeness suggests that the subject and space leak into each other, and so, they inhabit each other. Hooks (1990) uses the concept of "homeplace" to link issues of marginality and identity to the issues of space and place; she defines homeplace as a site where one can freely confront issues of humanisation and can strive to be a subject. "Homeplace" is used to describe potential sites of resistance—places where non-white, racial bodies can occupy space—and in her account, this task of making "homeplace" is all about the construction of a safe place. We use this notion of homeplace and at homeness as an analytical handle.

## Walking and talking place—walk-along photo elicitation

Earlier research has shown that photographing places where everyday activities are situated can add significantly to our understanding of how place is related to experience. According to Guillemin and Drew (2010, 177), participant-generated visual methods have benefits for researchers because they broaden the range of data that can be accessed and can act as a medium of communication between the researcher and participant (Clark-Ibanez 2004, 1512). Because we are exploring place-related experiences in an urban setting, we also find a visual ethnographic approach (Pink 2007) to be relevant. Thus, our chosen method combines participant-generated photos with the research techniques of photo-walking, mapping and interviewing, bringing us to a more meaningful, diverse understanding of each participant's sensation of space and place. As Guillemin and Drew (2010, 177) note, these methods also have an empowering function because they tease out stories about place that are rarely told otherwise.

The study took place in the city of Sundsvall, which is (in a Swedish context) a medium sized city with approximately 96,000 inhabitants. Its heritage builds on the Swedish forest industry but is now a university city. The city is located in the northern parts of Sweden, along the coast. Like almost all cities in the northern parts of Sweden the region is struggling with population decline.

To generate visual participatory and narrative data, we charted how the movement-based data related to the participants' physical experience of walking around town by combining walking and mapping. This method can find some of its origins in Kusenbach's "go-along" (2003), a hybrid form of interviewing and participant observation where "fieldworkers accompany individual informants on their 'natural' outings, and—through asking questions, listening and observing—actively explore their subjects' stream of experiences and practices as they move through, and interact with their physical and social environments" (2003, 463). Inspired by those who have found that moving around gives the researcher a better understanding of the places visited during such walks (e.g., Fink 2011; Evans and Jones 2011) one of the authors of this chapter, who was new to Sundsvall, asked in her apartment building for interested participants to the study. The apartment building was designated for students and migrants. The researcher recruited the participants by informally asking if anyone would like to participate in the study, three persons said yes. Following this up with formal, written information about the study in both Swedish and English, that is, informed consent. We asked the participants to show us "their Sundsvall" and then one researcher took individual walks with the participants through "their city" encouraging them to take photos during their walks—photos of places important to *them*. Here, walks mean that the researcher can observe the participants' physical experiences in conjunction with their place-related narratives. Therefore, the current study's material are participatory photo walks, including maps of the walks, and photo interviews in English (in one case with an interpreter present) with the three refugees that accepted our invitation to participate in the study. In total, the participants took 68 photos during the walks in Sundsvall, they then selected which photos to use during the interviews leaving us with 28 photos that were used in the photo interviews. During the walks the researcher took field notes, and the interviews were recorded and transcribed verbatim. Due to the different lengths in walks two participants took two walks with the researcher and the third only one, all of the participants did two follow up photo-interviews. The walks and interviews were conducted during late summer and early autumn, when there was still daylight and the ground was free from snow[1]. We now turn to presenting the backgrounds of the participants—two men and one woman, all anonymised.

Registered refugees in Sweden are entitled to a monthly allowance and housing paid for by the state. However, it is the authorities' decision where they are housed; those who wish to choose must make their own arrangements and will receive no housing benefits. Of the three participants, Omar was placed in Sundsvall by the Swedish Migration Agency, while Hawa and Ali chose to move there. All three have temporal staying permits; they are attending the official Swedish language course, the Swedish for Immigrants (SFI) programme, provided free to immigrants by the local authority. They also spend time at the town's 'house of culture'—a free public library and museum that charges no admission—where they can come into contact with Swedes and attend informal conversation classes with native speakers.

### Omar, 26

In 2015, Omar fled Syria for Sweden. He has been living in the accommodation in Sundsvall since 'he got his papers'; he was placed in Sundsvall by the Swedish Migration Agency, and at the time of our interviews he said that he wanted to stay in Sundsvall. Omar lives with his younger brother, but their parents are still in Syria. When he first arrived in Sweden he was placed in a refugee camp located in a small village on the Swedish countryside. During his time there, a place where he did not want to stay, he made some friends who he has been holding on to even after they left the camp. He hopes to learn Swedish as quickly as possible to fulfil his dream of becoming an art teacher. In his free time, Omar makes paintings and hangs out with his friends.

---

1    In the region where the study was conducted the winters are cold and snowy and has Nordic light, which means there is close to no daylight during the winter but almost endless daylight during the summer.

## *Hawa, 22*

Hawa was born in Eritrea, but she has no memories of her life there because her parents emigrated to Saudi Arabia when she was young, living in refugee camps. She does, however, speak her language of origin. Hawa fled to Sweden with her sister and arrived in 2016; the sisters are unified, and both live in Sundsvall after having been apart for some time. Hawa was placed by the Swedish Migration Agency at refugee centres and then in a temporary accommodation in the south of Sweden. When she was given the chance to choose where to live, she chose Sundsvall. Having grown up in refugee camps, Hawa now wants to live beyond such premises and talks a lot about feeling ready for living her life in Sweden. In her free time, she likes to hang out with her friends, go out for coffee or go clubbing.

## *Ali, 34*

Ali is from Syria, but before he came to Sweden, he was living in Jordan. He arrived in Sweden in 2015 and was placed in Sundsvall in early 2017. He has no family in Sundsvall, and his mother and brothers are still living in Syria. Ali has a university degree in business and administration, and his goal is to open his own business in Sundsvall. He is very focused on developing his Swedish language skills and finding all the help he can get with learning the language. He has an active social life and spends much of his time in central Sundsvall; however, he feels that he has no friends who can hang out with him.

Ali, Omar and Hawa took Rozalie through their day and city. All the routes are framed by the town's location between a harbour, the forest and the two hills surrounding the city. The routes started from the same location—the apartment building where the participants lived—taking them across the river to the town centre, where various locations were passed, photographed and talked about. Ali took the longest route, passing shops, night clubs, the cinema, the mosque and his school, while Hawa's and Omar's routes were shorter and did not connect to as many places as Ali's.

## Home-making in a temporal setting

Our methodological approach of walking and mapping required one of the authors to accompany the participants, listening to them and exploring how they experience the town as they moved through their physical and social environments (see Kusenbach 2003). When we asked Ali, Hawa and Omar to show us 'their Sundsvall', they highlighted numerous places to which they had already formed a connection during their time living in the city. They not only showed how they walk through their town but also 'through their day' because they had different reasons for going to the various places and for their choice of route, depending on what they had in store for their day. They have routes they take when they are going shopping, routes when they are going for a walk and routes when they are going to study. As will be shown, as Easthope (2014) explains, finding one's route is also an act of active place-making that can connect and replace former homes. Our study shows how the participants are involved in city-making as they engage in the daily life of the city, as previous shown by Çağlar and Glick Schiller (2018), but our analysis also shows how the participants are actively creating their home-making processes.

To capture the bodily dimension of walking together, we took the act of moving around to show how places are created by routes (Lee and Ingold 2006). We understand the place-making act of routes as a process that transforms space into familiar places, it is a process that entails a dialectical relation between self and place that help individuals to make sense of an unfamiliar environment (see also Castillo 2014 for a similar understanding). The connections between routes, places and stories create individual but contextual meanings that are imbued with the participants' memories of their places of origin alongside their new memories and experiences since moving to Sundsvall. Walking with the participants and listening to their stories along the way yielded a great number of places, including those they did not want to photograph or talk about. The places they choose to show us had different meanings: some were for recreation and relaxation, while others were for meeting friends or practicing Swedish. The material shows how all three participants, despite their temporal status, engage in the processes of fashioning individual ways to relate to the town, thus engaging in the act of home-making (see, e.g., Ahmed 1999). The following result is divided into three narratives: framing and narrating place, the practice of sitting on a bench and home making through place taking.

> ... I like this mountain. Because I feel better up here when I see the city, my city here in Sundsvall. When I come up, you can see the Sundsvall; you can see everything. [...] You can see my house from there; you can see the church, the centrum, everything. [...] Sometimes I feel good when I see the sea and everything. (Ali)

*Framing and narrating place*

Walking through the forest, getting to the top of the northern mountain and viewing the city, the apartment building and the harbor become a way of relating to the city, of making it 'mine'. The forest, the sea and the hills are central parts of how Ali, Hawa and Omar navigate and relate to Sundsvall, but also in the ways they narrate their home in Sundsvall, as told to relatives and friends 'back home' or in other countries. Ali says that when he phones his friends back in Jordan and Syria, he describes the 'true elements' of his new home, which here refers to the elements of nature, such as the landscape and weather. This reflection on nature as something 'real' is also made by Hawa, who says that she had never seen a forest in Saudi Arabia, and now, walking her way up the mountain connected the experience of being in the forest with being real. She states, 'Now I am living in the reality', which is a statement we connect to her now living outside of the refugee camps.

All the participants refer to the sea and *Norra Berget*, the northernmost of the two hills and nearest one to their apartment building, as places where they like to spend time and relax. Each participant has a story about the beauty of these places and talks about how much they like to be in the great outdoors. At the top of *Norra Berget*, Omar says:

> I stay here and I open my hands and my arms and breath and I look to the sea. In the summer it is wonderful. And you can see the sea and the bridge and you can see my place where I go to the [bench by the] sea and sit down.

All three participants talk about the feeling they get when coming up at the top of the mountain and viewing the city. The forest, the hill and the sea in Sundsvall are sights associated with the participants expectations of Sweden, what they imagined a Western or Swedish environment would be like, things that Hawa describes as things she had only seen 'in movies before'. She says the following:

> I have never been out around to see the nature. We didn't have those things. […] I have been here for a year, and I am slowly getting used to it, and I am kind of enjoying it. I like seeing the forest and going outside and exploring and everything. I can enjoy it.

In a sense, the participants' experiences of nature[2]—the hills, the forest, the sea and the view of the city—are related to their past experiences, becoming a way of characterising the town as 'something new'. In this way, the present, the past and their imaginings are connected in their place-making strategies. No site can be understood apart from its interconnections through time and space, and these interconnections can be studied in a single space (Feldman 2011). We argue that this practice is the result of places being mouldable, here the opposite from what would be static. The participants use the fact that places are in a constant state of being made and remade also by the people who only temporarily inhabit them, and they use this in home-making processes (for a comparison, see Butcher 2010).

---

2    The Swedish integration courses, in most cases, also emphasize the importance of nature to many Swedes. This means that they often contain excursions into nature etc, which was also the case for the participants of this study. In Sweden one has Outdoor Access Rights which means the right to walk, cycle, ride, ski and camp on any land with the exception of private gardens, near a dwelling house or land under cultivation.

*The practice of sitting on a bench*

While walking with the participants, all three highlighted the importance of being able to claim or inhabit space in the city. One such strategy showed the importance of public benches in the city, especially along one particular street. These are all benches that you may use without buying something and you may sit there for as long as you want. All the participants fill the benches with their own unique stories. Hawa, for example, describes one bench in the town centre as a place of relaxation, a place to sit and have a take-away coffee, while Omar describes one of the benches as a place for social activities. He and his friends use the bench as a place to enjoy time together. Sundsvall's public seating is a site where the participants enact space and their place-making strategies. The benches where the participants would sit and people-watch can be understood as their way of inserting themselves into the town picture. Hawa, who says she is planning for a life in Sundsvall, also expresses this, thinking that she needs to be 'a completely new person' and stating, 'I just said to myself, if you are going to live here, you are going to be like them'. Omar says that the bench is a 'special place' where he can meet friends and where they can 'find each other'—they meet up there and then go somewhere else.

The benches the participants photographed are mostly positioned in similar places. Yet each participant also refers to other benches in the town: they describe how they would sit down there to people-watch, but also how the benches are natural meeting places where they could practice their Swedish with others. Benches located in different places might be associated with different meanings and practices, as is evident in Omar's walk when he explains that he has different benches for different purposes. As he takes the researcher along his route, he showed different benches and the purposes he gives them: the benches in the city centre are social benches for meeting friends. The bench located at the seafront is not a social place but a "very quiet" place that he likes because it gives him "peace of mind". He usually visits this bench when he wants to think of his art or if he is "kind of upset", and it is a place where he can "think of his family". In this way, the benches become part of routinised everyday practices. In addition, these benches also become a place for connecting with memories of homes, both physical and social, and as such enabling place for a space where the past and future can be fluid (Kymäläinen and Nordström 2010).

Ali also links the experience of nature with watching people going about their lives, and he likes using the benches on the seafront and along the river-bank, where he can enjoy the quiet surroundings: "Yes, you can see more people sit down here. You can talk with them, and yes, you can meet other people. I like this place; sometimes I sit here" (Ali). Sitting on the benches in town, whether outdoors or in the library, can be seen as a strategy to actively inhabit a place (see Giritli Nygren and Schmauch 2012). The freedom to sit on a pub-lic bench for as long as one wants without having to retreat to a commercial space such as a coffee shop or a restaurant. It can also be viewed through a different lens, where public seating can be seen as a way to connect to their new surroundings; here, the practice of sitting on a bench could also be in-terpreted using Butcher's framing (2010) of home as an expression of self and evolving together with a place. To follow this line of reasoning (Butcher 2010), public benches can be a way of gaining personal, social and cultural places, hence avoiding feeling out of place. The social act and the bodily involvement of sitting on a bench inhabits the space and transforms the notion of the town. Of course, making your own space in a new town is about finding somewhere to live, but it is also about using one's agency to find and actively create places where one can "fit in".

*Home-making through place tak-*
*ing*

All three participants have the same "home where one lives" (Brah 1996): the apartment building. Even though none of them own their apartment, they all refer to their room as their "own space" and "home", a place where they can "feel free and be themselves". This echoes Schmauch and Giritli Nygren's finding (2012), which is prompted by bell hooks' concept of "homeplace" (1984), that this is because those who normally occupy the hegemonic position are absent: here Ali, Hawa and Omar are able to be "subjects" in their own right and not (only) be defined by their position as migrants. They described it as being within their own four walls; moreover, they could withdraw from the strange surroundings and be/interact/behave as the persons they used to be in, what they refer to as, the homes from where they come. The fact that their rooms are their own space is partly because it is in these rooms that they are in contact with family members they have left behind. Just as Ahmed (1999) describes, being at home is when the subject and space inhabit each other; indeed, our participants' rooms meld past and present together into a place where they live with places they came from (see Robertson et al. 2016).

For all the participants, to leave their rooms is a chance to explore and interact with the new town and its different social and spatial surroundings, not to mention to search for familiarities and characteristics from the past in their new material setting, much as the participants did in the study by Robertson et al. (2016). Thus, Ali describes one of the "Arab food shops" in town, owned by a Syrian, as one of the places that remind him of where he used to shop before he fled to Sweden. He talks about the similarities to the products he used to buy and the fact that the signs are in Arabic, which he says makes him "feel like you are back home". In this way, the participants carry their homes within themselves, seeking out places in their surroundings that would give them a sense of "being at home" (see Brah 1996). The "Arab shop" and the possible presence of other such places where new residents can stay in touch with old habits gives them a chance to maintain their ties to their past places while at the same time helping to generate new ones. In this way our study highlighting the important role that migrant businesses have as an important meeting place for developing new networks (see Çağlar & Glick Schiller 2018).

Another striking example is demonstrated by what the participants photographed and the way they talk about their special relationship to *Kulturmagasinet*, the free public library, which all three picked as one of their favourite spots in town, a part of their daily routine. They all refer to individual specific places at *Kulturmagasinet* as 'my place'—a particular table or a particular reading chair.

Much like Ahmed (1999) argues, here, the space that is most like home, the most comfortable and most familiar to the individual, is also the space in which the self is almost at home. Hawa shows this when she says that she leaves the library if "her place" is already taken—she would rather leave than sit somewhere else. The reason she gives is that the arrangement of the bookshelves makes her feel invisible. She often refers to being invisible and connects it with feeling safe: "Sweden is good; Sweden is safe. I am happy here. I have my own rights here. I can work. I can do whatever I want". Hawa associates feeling secure with being free—free to make decisions, free to act on her choice to leave the library instead of taking another seat. The participants insert themselves into the places in the library in various ways, but for two of them, *their place* in the library means a table with chairs and a quiet surrounding where they could learn Swedish. The library, with its many seating areas, is therefore described as a special place in town, one with which the participants feel connected in much the same way as they feel connected with their rooms in the accommodation. Earlier research (Lofland 1985) has shown how multiple forms of daily activities are based on shared affect, showing how places in the city turn casual informal meetings into ongoing and affective relationships (see also Pink 2012).

## Visualising and producing homeness

In this chapter, we have emphasised the ways in which Sundsvall's (perhaps temporal) residents create home while also showing how they actively inhabit spaces in a way that transforms the town and possibly themselves. The point of using the research techniques of walking, photographing and interviewing is to explore how new refugee residents join in producing urban space as a place and in understanding the home-making practices. Departing from the theoretical concept of home-making, the visual empirical material identify the situated life episodes that reveal how the participants engage in the places and how this engagement is a part of the inhabiting space. By their physical presence, they change the space, and this transforms the town, for they do not inhabit a place that is already constitute; rather, they have a hand in the very making of the town's space (see Ahmed 1999). By paying attention to the everyday practices and personal narratives, we can also see the rich and changing social meanings that places and everyday practices have. The home-making strategies in terms of everyday activities on the part of the participants—the routes they walk, the places they visit and even the benches they sit on—can be seen as embodied responses to place. The participants in the present study create their own social and spatial space through the action of their everyday activities. The participants' routes, the places narrated, are different but also connected: they show how home-making is related to former homes and new situations, relations and places. The process of settling is based on multiple new social relations, but also on maintenance of others. Indeed, the places are particular and specific but are connected by similar stories.

These processes enable them to connect with their surroundings, involving them in active home-making. Each of the participants has sites where they could build relations with their surroundings and where they believe they have a chance to integrate into their social environment. The methodology has enabled a better understating of the home-making strategies and how it relates to the institutional structure of the town and how home-making practices, situations, sites, institutions and so on are linked. The visual methodology captures the fact that the walks facilitate reflection on the details of the places, connecting them to a sense of past places and former homes and in this way encouraging active consideration of how strange environments can be made familiar (O'Neill and Hubbard 2010). As previous studies have shown, the participants in our study also show that refugees' home-making strategies include ways to integrate their past lives and places into their new settings (Risbeth and Powell 2013; Williamson 2016). The material shows that home-making strategies should be understood as effective, embodied responses to an appraisal of places that are like home—comfortable and familiar (see also Robertson et al. 2016). Returning to what was mentioned in the introduction about recent shifts in the Swedish refugee regime, only allowing temporary staying permits, it is important to illuminate the role of home-making strategies. This study shows how the participants used their own agency for home-making strategies, creating their own familiar routes across their new town, framing a place around them and inserting themselves into these new places to make a home in their new town. Turning back to the concepts of homeness (Ahmed 1999) and homeplace (hooks 1990), asking the informants to show us their town and their places can be understood as an exploration of their being-at-home spaces. These spaces are the ones most like home, most comfortable and familiar to the individual, where one finds the self as almost, but not quite, at home. In this sense, as we cited Avtar Brah previously: home is not necessarily connected to a physical place where you live or have lived, it can also be part of an imagination of a community or about origin from somewhere, as in diaspora contexts (Brah 1996, 192). Home is, as Hooks says, about making a homeplace in the meaning of having a safe site where you can be a subject.

## References

Ahmed, Sara. 1999. "Home and away: Narratives of migration and estrangement." *International Journal of Cultural Studies* 2, no. 3: 329–47.

Brah, Avtar. 1996. *Cartographies of Diaspora: Contesting Identities*. London: Routledge.

Butcher, Melissa. 2010. "From 'Fish out of water' to 'Fitting in': The challenge of re-placing home in a mobile world." *Population, Space & Place* 16: 23–36.

Cağlar, Ayşe, and Nina Glick Schiller. 2018. *Migrants and City-Making: Dispossession, Displacement, and Urban Regeneration*. Durham: Duke University Press

Castillo, Roberto. 2014. "Feeling at home in the 'Chocolate City': an exploration of place-making practices and structures of belonging amongst Africans in Guangzhou." *Inter-Asia Cultural Studies* 15, no. 2: 235–257.

Clark-Ibanez, Marisol. 2004. "Framing the social world with photo-elicitation interviews." *American Behavioural Scientist* 47, no. 12: 1507–27.

Easthope, Hazel. 2004. "A place called home." *Housing, Theory & Society* 21, no. 3: 128–38.

Evans, James, and Phil Jones. 2011. "The walking interview: Methodology, mobility and place." *Applied Geography* 31: 849–58.

Feldman, Gregory. 2011. "If ethnography is more than participant-observation, then relations are more than connections: The case for nonlocal ethnography in a world of apparatuses." *Anthropological Theory* 11: 375-95.

Fink, Janet. 2011. "Walking the neighbourhood, seeing the small details of community life: Reflections from a photography walking tour." *Critical Social Policy* 32, no. 1: 31–50.

Giritli Nygren, Katarina, and Ulrika Schmauch. 2012. "Picturing integrated places in segregated spaces: A participatory photo project conducted by migrant women." *Gender, Place & Culture* 19(5), 1-15.

Governmental Proposition 2015/16:174

Guillemin, Marilys, and Sarah Drew. 2010. "Questions of process in participant-generated visual methodologies." *Visual Studies* 25, no. 2: 175–88.

hooks, bell. 1984. *Feminist Theory: From Margin to Centre.* Boston: South End Press.

hooks, bell. 1990. *Yearning: Race, Gender and Culture Politics.* Toronto: Between the Lines Press.

Hudson, Christine, Lidén, Gustav, Sandberg, Linda, and Katarina Giritli Nygren. 2020. "Between central control and local autonomy – The changing role of Swedish municipalities in the implementation of integration policies." In *Local Integration of Migrants Policy. Palgrave Studies in Sub-National Governance,* edited by Jochen Fanzke, J. and José Ruano de la Fuente, 11 -34. Palgrave Mcmillian: London

Kusenbach, Margarethe. 2003. "Street phenomenology: The go-along as ethnographic research tool." *Ethnography* 4, no. 3: 455–85.

Kymäläinen, Päivi, and Paulina Nordström. 2010. "Temporary geographies of the city: The experienced spaces of asylum seekers in the city of Turku, Finland." *FENNIA* 188, no. 1: 76–89.

Lee, Jo, and Tim Ingold. 2006. "Fieldwork on foot: Perceiving, routing, socializing." In *Locating the Field: Space, Place and Context in Anthropology*, edited by Simon Coleman and Peter Collin, 68–86. Oxford: Berg.

Lofland, Lyn. H. 1985. *A World of Strangers: Order and Action in Urban Public Space*. New York: Waveland.

O'Neill, Maggie, and Phil Hubbard. 2010. "Walking, sensing, belonging: Ethno-mimesis as performative praxis." *Visual Studies* 25, no. 1: 46–58.

Pink, Sarah. 2007. *Doing Visual Ethnography: Images, Media and Representation in Research*, 2nd edn. London: SAGE.

Pink, Sarah. 2012. *Situating Everyday Life: Practices and Place*. London: SAGE.

Raffaetá, Roberta, and Cameron Duff. 2013. "Putting belonging into place: Place experience and sense of belonging among Ecuadorian migrants in an Italian Alpine region." *City & Society* 25, no. 3: 328–47.

Risbeth, Clara, and Mark Powell. 2013. "Place attachment and memory: Landscapes of belonging as experienced post-migration." *Journal of Landscape Research* 38, no. 2: 160–78.

Robertson, Zoë, Gifford, Sandra, Mcmichael, Celia and Ignacio Correa-Velez. 2016. "Through their eyes: Seeing experiences of settlement in photographs taken by refugee background youth in Melbourne, Australia." *Visual Studies* 36, no. 1: 34–49.

Schmauch, Ulrika, and Katarina Giritli Nygren. 2014. "The hidden boundaries of everyday place: Migrants, homeplace and the spatial practices of a small Swedish Town." *ACME, International e-journal for Critical Geographies* 13, no. 2: 372–93.

Williamson, Rebecca. 2016. "Everyday space, mobile subjects and place-based belonging in suburban Sydney." *Journal of Ethnic and Migration Studies* 42, no. 14: 2328–44.

# Contributors (in order of appearance)

**Heidrun Friese** Professor, Chemnitz University of Technology, Faculty of Philosophy, heidrun.friese@phil.tu-hemnitz.de, https://www.tu-chemnitz.de/phil/ifgk/ikk/professur/prof.html

**Alessandro Monsutti** Professor, Department of Anthropology and Sociology, Graduate Institute, Geneva, alessandro.monsutti@graduateinstitute.ch, graduateinstitute.ch/monsutti

**Leonardo Schiocchet** Social Anthropologist, Senior Researcher, Austrian Academy of Sciences' Insitute for Social Anthropology, Email: schiocchet@gmail.com

**Maria Six-Hohenbalken** Senior Researcher at the Institute for Social Anthropology (Austrian Academy of Sciences) maria.six-hohenbalken@oeaw.ac.at

**Seo Yeon Park** Social Anthropologist, IOM-Migration Research and Training Center, South Korea, Email: syparko5@gmail.com

**Sabine Bauer-Amin** Social Anthropologist, Associate Researcher at the Austrian Academy of Sciences' Institute for Social Anthropology, currently working for the International Rescue Committee Germany, Email: sabine.m.bauer@hotmail.de

**Denise Tan** Social Anthropologist, currently working for Amnesty International Austria, Email: denise.tan@mailbox.org

**Monika Mokre** Political Scientist, Institute of Culture Studies and Theatre History (Austrian Academy of Sciences), monika.mokre@oeaw.ac.at

**Mirian Alves de Souza**   Anthropology, Associate Professor of Department of Anthropology, University Federal Fluminense, Brazil, Email: mirianalves@id.uff.com, mirian.uff@gmail.com

**Katarina Giritli Nygren** Professor Sociology, Mid Sweden University, Katarina.giritli.nygren@miun.se

**Sara Nyhlén** Associate Professor Political Science, Mid Sweden University, sara.nyhlen@miun.se www.miun.se/saranyhlen

**Rozalie E. Böge** M.A. in Sociology, rozalieboege@gmail.com

GPSR Authorized Representative: Easy Access System Europe, Mustamäe tee
50, 10621 Tallinn, Estonia, gpsr.requests@easproject.com

9 7 8 3 8 3 7 6 5 8 0 2 6